Throwing Off the Cloak of Privilege

SOUTHERN DISSENT

UNIVERSITY PRESS OF FLORIDA / STATE UNIVERSITY SYSTEM

Florida A&M University, Tallahassee

Florida Atlantic University, Boca Raton

Florida Gulf Coast University, Ft. Myers

Florida International University, Miami

Florida State University, Tallahassee

University of Central Florida, Orlando

University of Florida, Gainesville

University of North Florida, Jacksonville

University of South Florida, Tampa

University of West Florida, Pensacola

Throwing Off the Cloak of Privilege

White Southern Women Activists
in the Civil Rights Era

EDITED BY GAIL S. MURRAY

FOREWORD BY STANLEY HARROLD AND RANDALL M. MILLER

UNIVERSITY PRESS OF FLORIDA

Gainesville · Tallahassee · Tampa · Boca Raton
Pensacola · Orlando · Miami · Jacksonville · Ft. Myers

Library of Congress Cataloging-in-Publication Data
Throwing off the cloak of privilege: white Southern women activists in the Civil Rights
Era / edited by Gail S. Murray; foreword by Stanley Harrold and Randall M. Miller.
p. cm.—(Southern dissent)
Includes bibliographical references (p.) and index.
ISBN 0-8130-2726-8 (cloth: alk. paper)
1. Women civil rights workers—Southern States—Biography. 2. Women
political activists—Southern States—Biography. 3. White women—Southern
States—Biography. 4. Southern States—Biography. 5. African Americans—Civil
rights—Southern States—History—20th century. 6. Civil rights movements—Southern
States—History—20th century. 7. Southern States—Race relations. 8. Women civil
rights workers—Southern States—History—20th century. 9. Women political
activists—Southern States—History—20th century. 10. White women—Southern
States—History—20th century. I. Murray, Gail Schmunk. II. Series.
E185.98.A1T49 2004
323'.092'309—dc22 [B]   2004042553

The University Press of Florida is the scholarly publishing agency for the State
University System of Florida, comprising Florida A&M University, Florida Atlantic
University, Florida Gulf Coast University, Florida International University, Florida
State University, University of Central Florida, University of Florida, University of
North Florida, University of South Florida, and University of West Florida.

University Press of Florida
15 Northwest 15th Street
Gainesville, FL 32611-2079
http://www.upf.com

To all the female civil rights activists
whose names have yet to appear in our written histories

Contents

Illustrations

Foreword

The civil rights movement was the greatest twentieth-century American grassroots reform movement. Although African Americans led the movement and were its major beneficiaries, its importance transcended race and ethnicity. It changed how all Americans perceived themselves and each other. Largely as the result of the national civil rights legislation it engendered, the movement changed how all Americans live. It influenced each American group's definition of liberty and equality, and it fostered appreciation for each group's history within an American narrative. The civil rights movement also inspired social justice activism among American Indians, college students, Hispanics, homosexuals, senior citizens, people with disabilities, and white (as well as black) women.

Understanding the many routes to activism is essential to comprehending the character of the civil rights revolution. It is therefore appropriate and important that Gail S. Murray has brought together in this volume eight original essays on white southern women who were active on behalf of black civil rights. These atypical white women contributed to the movement by working as journalists, propagandists, organizers, network builders, and advisors to young activists. No national script for activism dictated their interests and methods. Rather, various factors, including religion, leftist ideology, pragmatism, and self-interest, led them to join with African Americans in challenging the social and political assumptions of the Jim Crow South. Usually, local concerns drove them to protest, join biracial organizations, and press for equal access to public places, churches, and the ballot box. Their stories show the variety among, as well as the intensity of, their responses to racial injustice.

Neither the black freedom struggle nor the involvement of white women in it began with the civil rights movement. Black leaders first articulated a claim for equal rights at the time of the American Revolution. A few white women first actively supported that goal as participants in the antislavery movement, which reached its peak during the three decades prior to the Civil War. It is that movement which provides an excellent context for appreciating the

significance of the white southern woman described in this book. Those who
sought the abolition of slavery were similar to twentieth-century civil rights
activists in that they advocated freedom and equal rights for African Americans. White female abolitionists, like their civil rights counterparts, violated
racial taboos when they committed themselves to cooperation with black men
and women. Some white abolitionist women were part of the movement's leadership elite, but most of them, once again like their civil rights counterparts,
were "ordinary women." In 1998 historian Julie Roy Jeffrey described them as
part of a "great silent army of abolitionism" that carried out the day-to-day
work of reform. But nearly all white antislavery women, unlike the women
whose careers are analyzed in this book, labored not in the South but in the
North, where physical dangers and societal pressures were less severe. Before
the Civil War, almost all of the few southern white women who actively supported black freedom fled their section. And, when they reached the North,
they joined an antislavery movement led by, and largely shaped by, white men
and women.

In contrast, African Americans initiated, dominated, and provided most of
the support for the civil rights movement. At the local and state levels, black
men and women led in organizing against racial segregation and disfranchise-
ment. In order to support these black initiatives, white women had to concede
some of the racial privilege to which they had been accustomed. Some of them
affiliated with black organizations. Even those who worked in separate white
organizations dedicated to desegregation or voting rights were contributors to
an essentially black effort. Just as important, during the time period covered by
the essays in this volume, the civil rights movement was principally a southern
undertaking that faced fierce, sometimes violent, resistance from many of its
opponents. Therefore the white women of the South who opposed segregation and gave varying degrees of support to racial equality did so within a very
dangerous context. Unlike all but a few of their abolitionist predecessors, they
acted directly against powerful segregationist forces in their southern communities. Often they went against their own family's racial views. These factors
make these women all the more remarkable and make the essays in this collection all the more intriguing. By focusing on the backgrounds, perspectives,
achievements, and shortcomings of these southern dissenters, *Throwing Off
the Cloak of Privilege* expands our knowledge of the breadth and complexity of
the civil rights movement, biracial activism, and women's identities and interests.

Stanley Harrold and Randall M. Miller
Series Editors

Preface

The idea for this book began at the Fifth Conference on Southern Women's History, sponsored by the Southern Association for Women Historians, in June 2000. I joined with two friends to present a panel on "White Women in the Civil Rights Movement." The interest of the audience, the insightful comments of Joan Browning, and the encouragement of Meredith Morris-Babb, assistant editor-in-chief at the University Press of Florida, led me on a search for other scholars working on similar topics.

At the time, I was researching the Memphis Sanitation Strike and was acutely aware of the absence of women's voices in the history of that labor and civil rights struggle. What I knew of grassroots civil rights activity elsewhere suggested that African American women must have been intimately involved with that work stoppage and the public demonstrations that lasted six weeks and left three thousand families without a source of income. Following this conviction took me both backward and forward from 1968 to discover a whole network of black, white, and biracial organizations working on various kinds of racial justice issues. It also took me into the homes of fascinating, articulate average Memphians who had spent decades working for racial harmony, equity, and justice.

The essays collected here made their way to me through circuitous routes. I heard Catherine Fosl and Anne Braden present jointly at the Southern Association of Historians meeting and knew that I wanted Catherine to write for this volume. Activist and writer Joan Browning put me in touch with two researchers whose paths had crossed hers: Kathy Nasstrom and Edie Riehm, who both studied Georgia activists. I had met Marcia Synnott years ago and knew of her long interest in Alice Spearman Wright. Shannon Frystak and Laura Miller responded to an H-Net query about white civil rights activists. I learned about Cherisse Jones's dissertation topic from a mutual friend just in time to include her research here. Although I sought essays about North Carolina, Virginia, and Mississippi women, I found no historians able to finalize their work in time for this volume. I was disappointed, but I remain encour-

aged that the efforts of everyday southern women, both black and white, are
making their way into the historical record: more solid research is on the way.

The small explosion of works on African American and white civil rights
activists and their grassroots organizations is enlarging and revisioning the
standard narrative of the civil rights era. This field once had definite param-
eters: the *Brown* decision at one end and Dr. King's assassination at the other.
It once had good guys (federal law, the Supreme Court, and courageous black
leadership) and bad guys (White Citizens' Councils, racist policemen, and recalcitrant city governments). No more. Not only are most average southerners
left out of such a binary construction, but such polarizations provide no assistance in understanding why the goals of the movement have remained elusive.
As the actors in these essays struggle with the dark corners of racism in themselves and their communities, the reader can perhaps grasp more clearly how
elusive such transformations can be.

This anthology is certainly a communal effort. The editors of the Southern
Dissent series, Stan Harrold and Randall Miller, provided consistent encouragement, made suggestions about prospective authors, applied the red ink lib-
erally, and accomplished it all with a rare good humor. The Faculty Development Endowment and the dean of Rhodes College, Robert Llewellyn,
provided research funds for my work. Nancy Hunt and Tonya Mosley, administrative assistants to the Department of History, kept the paper trail visible and
the computer glitches to a minimum. I owe a great debt to the library staffs at
Rhodes College and the Mississippi Valley Special Collections, University of
Memphis. My writing colleagues have been unfailingly dependable and con-
scientious in sharing and comparing the wide range of women's activist experiences. The two outside readers provided positive encouragement as the book
neared completion. Many of us gathered at the Sixth Southern Conference on
Women's History at the University of Georgia in 2003 for lively conversations
about the growing scholarship on civil rights history. We discovered that even
after three years of working together, we are still friends.

Introduction

GAIL S. MURRAY

The men might as well hang their harps on a willow tree, as to try to settle the race problem in the South without the aid of the Southern white woman.
—Carrie Parks Johnson[1]

White women in the South have always been a little subversive. Perched on the pedestals where men placed them as long as they performed well in their half-person roles, they had a commanding view of the social landscape. It was not a pretty picture.
—Sara Alderman Murphy[2]

The Memphis Cares rally, a biracial gathering held in Crump Stadium in Memphis three days after the assassination of Dr. Martin Luther King Jr. For many white Memphians, this rally marked the beginning of their work with the Panel of American Women or the Concerned Women of Memphis and Shelby County. Courtesy of the Mississippi Valley Special Collections, McWherter Library, University of Memphis.

∞

A PERSISTENT MYTH of southern white womanhood in the twentieth century contends that the southern lady stands on a pedestal, the recipient of a long tradition of privilege and protection. Although reality may bear little resemblance to that proverbial pedestal, much of the support for male political power, racial segregation, and ingrained class mores has been premised on that myth. Sometimes women themselves co-opted the rhetoric of privilege to use to their advantage, as when they couched their arguments for suffrage in a discourse of white intellectual superiority over the recently enfranchised black man. The leisure time that allowed many southern women to pursue benevolent or reform activities, including suffrage and church work, was often made possible by the black women who managed their households, cooked their food, and tended their children. Assuredly, media images born in Little Rock and New Orleans of white mothers screaming invectives as African Americans sought to enroll in public schools confirm that many white women embraced a racial superiority ethic.

Yet, such depictions of white southern women disregard an extensive legacy of activists who assertively joined biracial organizations, worked on behalf of desegregation, advocated economic justice, and initiated efforts to educate their privileged white friends. Historical scholarship has profiled a small set of such "foremothers" who worked on behalf of fair treatment, economic and educational opportunities, and political rights for African Americans well before the traditional years of the civil rights movement. Jacquelyn Dowd Hall's *Revolt against Chivalry* (1979) brought the organizing work of Texan Jessie Daniel Ames and her Association of Southern Women for the Prevention of Lynching into the mainstream of southern history.[3] Ames's relentless efforts to involve southern white women, especially churchwomen, in monitoring southern justice and in publicizing incidents of vigilantism against people of color brought thousands of southern white women at least partially into the fold of racial activism. As the quotation that opens this essay illustrates, they saw improved race relations as a fertile field for women's work because it would benefit the harmony of community life.

Historian Susan Lynn makes the same point about the unique connection between female reform efforts and involvement in racial justice issues in the post–World War II period, although she considers southerners' activities only as they became part of national reform agendas. In tracing the link between suffrage activists at the beginning of the century and civil rights activism in the 1950s and 1960s, Lynn illustrates how progressive women's organizations developed many of their social action platforms around biracial efforts. Even when their style was "shaped in part by their class privileges," they "challeng[ed] the legitimacy of the system of racial segregation and discrimination [that persisted] in the United States."[4] Many white women saw racial justice as intimately connected to the creation and maintenance of humane, democratic communities.

Shortly after the black freedom struggle gained national attention through its direct action campaigns, journalist William Peters wrote that "[i]ncreasingly in the South, quietly and usually without fuss, white women—and more particularly white churchwomen—are lining up on the side of desegregation."[5] Prepared through years of study of race relations in missionary societies; practiced in shared worship, study, and benevolent projects through United Church Women and the Young Women's Christian Association; and dedicated to building a prejudice-free world for their children, many southern white women pushed forward racial justice reform.

This anthology seeks to extend our factual knowledge of southern white women in the civil rights movement and to illuminate the meaning of their activities in the light of feminist interpretation and contemporary social critique. It examines a variety of native-born white southern women, most of whom were married, middle-aged, and privileged. With the exception of Anne Braden and Frances Pauley, these women's life stories have not been fully documented, and only Braden wrote about her activist commitments. Most of these women are little known outside the oral tradition of their local communities.[6]

Some women brought years of experience in church groups or human welfare organizations to the civil rights movement; others became converts to racial justice only when local crises forced them to examine the hypocrisy and privilege in which they lived. Some demanded that their schools, churches, and women's clubs integrate; others formed new biracial, voluntary organizations to address white communities' fears and prejudice. Yet others directed community efforts to improve health care, educational opportunities, and housing for African Americans. Most came from urban settings, although both Dorothy Tilly of Atlanta and Alice Spearman of Columbia, South Carolina, traveled extensively in the rural areas of their respective states. These women, in their individual communities and sometimes through statewide organizations, worked for legislative change and enforcement of the civil rights laws and federal court orders. In many respects they recapitulated women's historic "social housekeeping" role. They concentrated their efforts on nurturing grassroots leadership, building networks of sympathetic volunteers across racial lines, and providing ways for genuine cross-racial friendships to develop. Their vision reached beyond the establishment of equal opportunity; they sought ways for individuals across race and class divides to genuinely appreciate and support one another. Who these women were, why they became committed to racial justice and equal opportunity, and how they organized to change southern society are the concerns of this anthology.

Although all the women profiled in this volume were considered leftist radicals in the southern communities in which they lived, in fact they "threw off the cloak of privilege" in varying degrees ranging along a continuum from radical to moderate.[7] Their self-perceptions ranged from that of a self-consciously independent reformer to a family-identified nurturer. They span three generations of southern women, from Atlantan Dorothy Tilly (1883–1970) to Memphian Jocelyn Wurzburg (b. 1940), and came from middle-class to elite families. They represent the upper South (Kentucky), the Southwest (Little Rock), the urban Delta (Memphis), the Deep South (Georgia and South Carolina), and the cosmopolitan (New Orleans). Finally, they came to different conclusions about the best way to engage southerners in social change.

Recent civil rights history has highlighted the many different voices and strategies that came together to produce "the movement." Racial difference is but one of the (imposed) categories that separated individual participants. To emphasize the contribution of "whites" might seem to detract from the centrality of African American agency throughout the fight for racial justice. As Catherine Fosl notes in her essay in this volume, "[a]n anthology such as this one, centering on white women, might seem at first glance to be problematic. As the political scientist Diane Fowlkes has pointed out, 'such a focus reinforces the racial privilege that white women enjoy, consciously or unconsciously.'" Yet, without the story of white response—in all its various guises—to black activism, the full story of the civil rights movement cannot be understood. A critical investigation of the white female activist experience remains necessary.

This collection begins with the figure of Dorothy Rogers Tilly (1883–1970), a principal link between the antilynching campaign of the 1930s and the direct action civil rights protests of the 1960s. It then follows southern white women's activism from the New Deal through the major legislation of 1964 and 1965 and into the early 1970s. In adopting such an extensive time frame for civil rights activity, this volume embraces the current trend of civil rights historiography, which has extended the temporal boundaries of the civil rights movement both forward and backward from the pivotal years. Early scholarship focused principally on the years of national activism, from the *Brown v. Board of Education* decision (1954) to the Voting Rights Act of 1965 or the assassination of Dr. Martin Luther King Jr. in 1968. Today, numerous historians argue that the issues that first gained sustained national attention with the *Brown* decision and the Montgomery bus boycott (1955–56) had their roots further back, in the lives and works of people like Ida B. Wells-Barnett, A. Philip Randolph, Howard W. Odum, Charles Houston, Myles Horton, and many others. Historian Robert J. Norrell contends that black community leaders nurtured protest organizations from the 1930s onward. With the fundamental shift in power from the states to the federal government during the Depression and World War II, the stage was set "for the national government to override the southern states' autonomy" and facilitate the civil rights victories of the 1954–65 era.[8] Patricia Sullivan's *Days of Hope: Race and Democracy in the New Deal Era* (1996) foregrounds African Americans' goals and protests during the Depression. Scholars Adam Fairclough and August Meier suggest that the civil rights movement is rooted in the even earlier "revolt" against Booker T. Washington and accommodationism by the Niagara Movement and the NAACP.[9] Indeed, the goals of the civil rights movement are implicit in Homer Plessy's 1896 challenge to segregation. Although civil rights history was first explored through the history of concrete legislative and judicial changes in the decade between 1954 and 1965, clearly, then, a comprehensive study of biracial organizing and the fight for racial justice must begin much earlier.[10]

Likewise, the King assassination in Memphis in 1968 does not mark the end of the civil rights movement. Although the national media directed attention more to the war in Vietnam and the subsequent downfall of the presidency of Lyndon B. Johnson than to civil rights activism after 1968, Black Power campaigns and biracial community efforts continued to mobilize volunteers, including many who argue that the freedom struggle the civil rights movement represents is an ongoing one. Particularly when scholars focus on a "redefinition of the concept of equality to mean equality of *results* rather than just equality of *opportunity*," in Professor Meier's words, the civil rights movement extends into the present.[11]

In profiling southern white women and the organizations and networks they utilized to work for racial justice, this collection has no intention of wresting the locus of civil rights activity away from the African Americans who envisioned, led, and lived "the movement." In fact, almost every white woman profiled in this collection identified African Americans who patiently tutored and enlarged her understanding of the daily indignities and disabilities racial discrimination perpetrated. As civil rights history has focused more and more on local campaigns to uncover both the intransigence of white southern communities and the courage of local blacks in claiming their freedoms, African American agency has emerged as central to the movement's success. In urban areas, however, biracial organizing became a vibrant strategy with potential both for black self-assertion and for educating whites and eradicating their prejudice. In these settings, white female activists often supported civil rights campaigns as extensions of the human welfare work already engaging them. Sometimes their efforts took place within all-white organizations such as Dorothy Tilly's Fellowship of the Concerned. Others grew out of vibrant interracial organizations like the Panels of American Women described in the essays on Little Rock, New Orleans, and Memphis. Most white activists readily acknowledged their indebtedness to mentors in the African American community. Kathryn Nasstrom's essay on Frances Pauley, for example, illustrates how Pauley's work with black community leaders and students in Georgia deepened her commitment to radical social change. Thus, to bring together a collection of research on southern white civil rights activists is less to rewrite the play than to enlarge the cast of characters. It is also to explore the multiple layers of white responses to the crumbling of white privilege.

Literature on Women and Civil Rights

Even within such an extended chronology of the civil rights era, scholarly attention to women as organizers, strategizers, and movement participants has been minimal. John Egerton's magisterial study of early southern civil rights activists, *Speak Now against the Day: The Generation before the Civil Rights Movement in the South* (1994), profiles only a few notable southern women like Anne Braden of Louisville, Virginia Foster Durr from Birmingham, and Lillian Smith of Georgia. Egerton overlooks most of the grassroots organizing of southern women, black and white, particularly as it was part of women's study programs in the Women's Missionary Society of the Methodist Church, the Young Women's Christian Association, or the United Council of Church Women. Likewise, David Chappell's *Inside Agitators* (1994) constructs a history of white opposition to racial discrimination from the 1880s through the Civil Rights Act of 1964 that largely ignores women's participation because it defines civil rights advocacy primarily in terms of political action.[12] Because men headed the national organizations, spoke with the media, and often worked with and through black clergy, traditional civil rights studies have not showcased women's contributions.

The first major scholarly work to address the strategic importance of women in the civil rights movement grew out of a conference at Georgia State University in 1988 that brought together scholars and former participants to examine the role of women in the civil rights movement. The program concentrated on African American activists, both local and national, as scholars profiled Fannie Lou Hamer, Ella Baker, Mary Fair Burks and JoAnn Gibson Robinson, Septima Clark, and Modjeska Simkins among others. Papers from this conference represent the first published collection of studies on female civil rights activists.[13] In the last decade, additional biographies of these and other remarkable black women activists have detailed how grassroots populations were motivated and supported through long, if not always successful, direct action campaigns led by women. Scholars have also examined African American women's work in nurturing, feeding, housing, comforting, and hiding other activists.[14]

Nevertheless, few full-length monographs on racial justice advocacy by or about southern white women exist. Anne Loveland and Rose Gladney have written extensively about the life, activism, and writing of Lillian Smith, the provocative mid-century author.[15] Sarah Patton Boyle, a prominent Virginian, has described her "racial conversion" and the patient but forthright black newspaper editor, T. J. Sellers, who helped bring it about. In her 1962 memoir she reveals much about the genteel paternalism that pervaded early efforts by whites to understand African Americans' demands for equality. Mississippian Florence Mars wrote a moving account of life in Neshoba County in 1964, the summer James Chaney, Andrew Goodman, and Michael Schwerner were murdered near Philadelphia, Mississippi. Sara Mitchell Parsons, whose integrationist stance on the Atlanta School Board brought considerable alienation from her suburban friends, recently published her autobiography, *From Southern Wrongs to Civil Rights: The Memoir of a White Civil Rights Activist* (2000).[16]

Oral historian Hollinger F. Barnard has compiled Alabaman Virginia Durr's autobiography from extensive oral interviews. Intimately schooled in southern ladyhood, Durr's commitment to African American rights moved from southern noblesse oblige to embrace the efforts of the Southern Conference on Human Welfare and the National Committee to Abolish the Poll Tax; her own efforts included personal lobbying of southerner congressmen. Likewise, scholar Kathryn Nasstrom interviewed Frances Pauley over a series of years and edited the interviews to present an autobiographical portrait along with Nasstrom's own commentary on Pauley's lifelong activism. Another contributor to this volume, Catherine Fosl, recently published a deeply researched biography of Anne Braden based on extensive oral interviews.[17]

Little other scholarship on white female civil rights activism exists, other than studies of those impassioned college students who went South (a few were native southerners) to defeat Jim Crow in the early sixties. They downplayed racial and gender difference in their activism, preferring to emphasize the emotional power of the "beloved community" as they saw it unfolding through biracial mobilization. In *Personal Politics: The Roots of Women's Liberation in the Civil Rights Movement and the New Left* (1980), historian Sara Evans attributes the awakening of her feminist consciousness to experiences in the civil rights struggle. Many of the white student activists who left the Student Nonviolent Coordinating Committee (SNCC) turned to activism on behalf of women's issues.[18] However, many participants have argued that women's participation in direct action campaigns differed little from that of men. In fact, Mary King and Casey Hayden, who wrote the original feminist protest letter in SNCC in 1965, maintain that gender discrimination did not hinder their fight for racial justice.[19]

Five of the essayists in the *Deep in Our Hearts* (2000) collection grew up in the South—Joan Browning, Sue Thrasher, Dorothy Burlage, Casey Hayden, and Connie Curry—and their essays represent personal and individualized interpretations of their movement experience, which often found them on the frontlines of strategy making and risk taking. These women wrote their memoirs after second-wave feminism brought gender discrimination to the forefront, and thus they consciously address gender issues in their memoirs. White southern college students dedicated to racial justice organized the Southern Student Organizing Committee (SSOC) in 1964 prior to the influx of northern college students into the South. The committee's female members "were especially prominent in community-organizing projects," including various War on Poverty initiatives.

For the most part, the experiences of college students differed greatly from those of the homemakers profiled in this collection. The women featured here had to negotiate the boundaries of southern gender and racial norms with additional baggage in hand: their marital responsibilities, social status, and domestic roles were already well established when they became involved in racial justice activities.[20] The white southern college students and the women profiled in this volume shared only their proclivity for community organizing and their abhorrence of racial injustice.

Unifying Themes in Southern White Female Activism

This anthology asks why some white women who grew up in the South in material comfort, imbibing both a biblical defense of segregation and established second-class status for African Americans, came to reject those southern mores and instead advocated desegregation and equal opportunity at the cost of friendships, status, economic security, and sometimes family support. Some similar experiences, characteristics, and decisions emerge in the essays that follow. All the women shared a basic optimism, perhaps ill founded, about the willingness of white southerners to change. They held deep commitments to equal justice and fair play, and many had had a moment of insight into the degradation of racial prejudice. Most of the women described an identification with mothering and social housekeeping that carried them across racial barriers. All depended on a network of like-minded women for sustenance and support. Some used their social privilege as entrée to potential colleagues or policy makers; others readily used gender conventions to their advantage when it was politically necessary.

Social movement theory has devoted considerable attention to when and how dispossessed people begin to take action on their own behalf, but it has had little to say about why outsiders—that is, those from the dominant group—become outraged at social and economic injustice and risk their own social and physical security to work for change.[21] Many social psychologists argue that altruism—voluntarily acting with the goal of benefiting another at some cost to oneself—is a part of human nature. Some argue that there is even an "altruistic personality" that can be identified regardless of ethnic and gender distinctions.[22] However, none of these approaches fully explains why some white women joined the civil rights struggle while the majority of their peers did not.

In his analysis of southern memoirs and autobiographies, Fred Hobson has found what he labels a "white southern racial conversion narrative" created by writers who struggled to understand the impact of racial conventions on their growing up. Hobson argues that the authors he studied "confess racial wrongdoing and are 'convicted' in varying degrees" so that they move "from racism to something approaching racial enlightenment." Although their language parallels religious conversion narratives common in Christian literature and most of them grew up in intensely religious homes, not all the authors described their racial conversion in explicitly religious terms. Some authors believed they had escaped a kind of "bondage" much like slavery and had made their way to "freedom" when they confronted their own racial prejudices.[23]

According to Hobson, Lillian Smith was the first white southerner to "tell the white South what it cannot tell itself." He argues that "[i]t is no accident that the two southern writers who first emerged in the 1940s as authors of racial conversion narratives were women ... [because] what was a liability—that is, a detachment from the centers of political, economic, and editorial power—was, in the area of social commentary and moral reflection, a distinct advantage."[24] Smith challenged southern racial mores in the novel *Strange Fruit* (1944) and especially in her introspective analysis of the South, *Killers of the Dream* (1949). She openly advocated desegregation and civil rights in her public appeal for immediate implementation of the *Brown* decision in *Now Is the Time* (1955), and she frequently expressed a strong racial critique in other essays and letters in national magazines. *Killers of the Dream* is more than "a book about her racial conversion; the writing process was part *of* the conversion, part of the shedding of old beliefs, the transformation."[25]

Virginia Foster Durr, a figure overlooked by Hobson, first had her racial prejudice challenged when she was assigned to eat with a black student at Wellesley College. Her "conversion" to racial justice came slowly, however, as she entered into Washington politics with her husband, Clifford, when he served in the Roosevelt administration. As she repeatedly observed competent African Americans being denied vocational and political opportunities, she confronted the lies of black inferiority and laziness that she had grown up with in Alabama and became active in the work of the Southern Conference on Human Welfare and in campaigns against the poll tax. On her return to Birmingham after World War II, Durr could no longer accept the white paternalism that had earlier seemed so normal. While never rejecting the privilege of class, she became a determined advocate for civil rights in Birmingham.[26]

Like Smith and Durr, many of the women profiled in this collection developed their commitment to racial justice out of the deep-seated childhood conviction that people with privilege had a responsibility to work to bring social advantages to others. In the early twentieth century, Dorothy Tilly, Alice Spearman, Frances Pauley, and Anne Braden all exemplified southern daughters whose Christian convictions of the brotherhood of all people combined with a sense of politeness toward, and responsibility for, people of color. As each gained experience with more radicalized friends, including African American activists, she was able to enlarge her Christian social vision, reject southern mores, utilize her gender role, and become a powerful voice for racial and economic justice. In the process, most of these women became pariahs in their church and social circles.

Dorothy Tilly was forty-seven years old and a longtime advocate of improved race relations when she first ate a meal alongside African American women at Paine College in Augusta, Georgia, in 1930. From that experience, Tilly's philosophy rather quickly evolved from "separate but equal" to advocacy of desegregation and personal challenges to Jim Crow practices. She then sought to use her vast network of southern female connections to convert all southern Christians to civil rights advocacy and legal compliance. Alice Spearman combined genteel paternalism with her liberal Baptist convictions and YWCA experience to become the longtime chair of the South Carolina Council on Human Relations. In that role she built grassroots organizations across the state through diplomacy, conciliation, and confrontation. Frances Pauley's entire life work was an unfolding, enlarging conversion to the needs of the dispossessed, whether they were African Americans, the poor, or the aged. Beginning with social justice work in the women's division of the Methodist church, she also gained organizing experience through the League of Women Voters. When she took over as head of the Georgia Council on Human Relations at age fifty-five, she had many years of interracial work behind her.

Like Virginia Durr, Anne Braden's racial awareness began in college when she first ate with an African American student. "It was," wrote Braden, "a turning point in my life. All the cramping walls of a lifetime seemed to have come tumbling down."[27] Her conversion continued as she worked as a reporter in Alabama and Kentucky, befriending labor and civil rights activists in Louisville. Braden not only rejected her southern upbringing (although, she emphasizes, never her family), she also created a new identity that drew sustenance from trying to reference values and decisions from an African American perspective. She wrote that she was driven to strike out against segregation "before any more children grew up absorbing the poison I had absorbed."[28] As Catherine Fosl relates in her essay in this volume, Braden refers to her transformation as "turning myself inside out." Since then Braden has been devoted to cultivating sensibilities outside the mainstream culture of white America in what she calls "the other America," a community of activists around the nation dedicated to enacting the ideals of social and racial justice in their daily lives.[29]

In the essays on Little Rock, Memphis, and New Orleans we shall see controversies surrounding school desegregation, hiring of African Americans in downtown businesses, and police brutality against civil rights advocates bring racial conversions to several women. In Memphis, some women became activists only after the assassination of Dr. Martin Luther King Jr. Initially believing that their city had "good race relations" because there had been no violence during desegregation, many came to face and understand their ignorance about African Americans' constant struggles. One referred to the Memphis Sanitation Workers' strike as a "Paul of Tarsus experience" that opened her eyes to the double oppression of race and class in her supposedly genteel city.[30] Often such insights came through conversations with African Americans at biracial meetings. As the title of this anthology suggests, these women sought to "throw off the cloak of privilege" insofar as that privilege conveyed an acceptance of and participation in racial discrimination.

Another characteristic shared by many of these activists is their belief that racial discrimination was defiling the world in which they lived and reared their children. They often couched their civil rights arguments in terms of their maternal identity. As Rhoda Lois Blumberg observes in her study of forty-one midwestern civil rights activists, "good mothering" in the 1950s and 1960s assumed participation in the PTA, cooperative nursery schools, and other child-centered activities. Most of the women Blumberg studied saw "racial justice as being connected to their roles as mothers. They did not see Civil Rights as someone else's cause."[31] In this volume, similar logic informed Dorothy Tilly's actions when she recruited white churchwomen to the Fellowship of the Concerned on the basis of building a more tolerant, peaceful world for their children. Memphis women who volunteered in inner-city public schools in the early 1960s did so not only for the sake of the children they served, but also for their own children, who would live out their lives in an integrated world. Their volunteer experiences sensitized them to the interconnectedness of race, limited job opportunity, and poverty.

As Laura Miller explains in her essay, many women joined the Women's Emergency Committee (WEC) in Little Rock only as concerned mothers dedicated to reopening the closed public high schools; desegregation was merely the by-product of achieving that goal. WEC leaders appealed for business and professional support to reopen the schools because strong public schools were necessary to recruit business and industry to Little Rock. When women in Little Rock, Memphis, and New Orleans formed local Panels of American Women, they aimed their messages at white audiences and spoke not on behalf of any organization or cause, but "simply as a housewife and a mother," emphasizing that more important than religious or ethnic/racial difference was the common experience of raising a family, volunteering in the community, and promoting peaceful neighborhoods. Inner-city children going without lunch prompted a Memphis activist to initiate a broad-based social service program staffed by volunteer women, mostly mothers, who went so far as to enroll their own (white) children in African American neighborhood kindergartens in order to qualify for federal funding that required an integrated constituency. These women came to identify with black women as *mothers* and worked with them to eliminate the kinds of discrimination that affected them as parents. Because this volume focuses on white activists, we do not hear the voices of African American mothers who may have found the idea of "common-ground through mothering" not only foreign but offensive, since their activism went on without benefit of paid child care or household help.

This anthology spans women's activism over three generations. Yet, every woman profiled relied heavily on an intergenerational network of female support. When genteel southern women discovered like-minded women through volunteer work at the YWCA, in their local church, or with the Urban League, they formed fast friendships and counted on each other to understand the commitments to, and the limits of, the challenges they might make to southern mores. Dorothy Tilly used multistate contacts developed through leadership roles with Methodist churchwomen and Church Women United to create the Fellowship of the Concerned. Alice Spearman called on lifelong friendships to advance the work of the South Carolina Council on Human Relations. Whether one follows Alice Spearman into polite Charleston society, Frances Pauley into rural Georgia, Anne Shafer into Memphis churches, or Rosa Keller from the country club to the schools of New Orleans, one finds a constant barrage of phone calls and letters, strategy sessions, and general membership meetings with a variety of female associates.

Southern white women could use the privileges granted by their color and gender when it suited their purposes. In Little Rock, Memphis, and New Orleans, male community leaders called on white female activists to mobilize support for school desegregation, antipoverty programs, and integration of public parks, knowing that the women had far more experience rallying citizens around human welfare issues than they did. Women in Little Rock deliberately picked their most attractive members to lobby in the halls of the state capitol. When male labor organizers in Memphis sought to avoid a second sanitation workers' strike in 1969, they took their case to a well-organized network of female activists, who helped turn public opinion toward a settlement.

These women discovered liabilities inherent in their activism as well. Most experienced harassment from segregationists, ranging from the truckload of sand dumped on Memphian Anne Shafer's lawn to the eggs and bottles thrown at New Orleans women who transported black children to newly desegregated schools. Those activists with children feared for their safety and worried about the time they spent away from their families attending meetings and strategy sessions. Frances Pauley and Anne Braden received multiple threats on their lives. Braden and her husband were indicted on charges of sedition in the 1950s for helping a black family buy a home in a white neighborhood in Louisville.

In addition to physical harassment, the subjects of these essays agonized over those friends and volunteer associates whom they could not sway toward racial tolerance. In South Carolina, some United Church Women groups refused to follow national programs developed to support desegregation. Members of the Fellowship of the Concerned saw Mississippi members stop attending annual meetings for fear of local repercussions. Alice Spearman alternately coddled and harried prominent South Carolina women who simply would not give up their commitment to "separate but equal." Activists who refused to belong to segregated clubs or attend whites-only functions gave up old friends.

Equally Important Differences

The women discussed in this volume not only span the twentieth century and represent diverse southern regions, they also vary greatly in the strategies they chose to engage race discrimination practices. On a spectrum from radical to moderate, Anne Braden's life represents the most radical disassociation from southern mores. As a young reporter in her twenties she came to identify with working-class people and cultivated friendships with socialists, Communists, labor organizers, and African American civil rights activists. She was jailed in 1951 for protesting the execution of Willis McGee in Mississippi, was later charged with sedition in Louisville, and served as a mentor to many of the students who flocked south to participate in voter registration campaigns. By contrast, Dorothy Tilly managed to remain a white-gloved southern lady who played to women's domestic and moral roles even as she urged acceptance of desegregation and equal opportunity for people of color. Generally, the Church Women United in South Carolina preferred to sponsor programs to "uplift" and educate African Americans rather than advocate a fully integrated society.

The political alienation experienced by the other subjects of this volume falls somewhere between the radicalism of Braden and the moderation of Tilly. Alice Spearman, of the South Carolina Council on Human Relations, became suspect among the cautious middle-class whites with whom the group worked, but remained moderate in her approach to direct action and confrontation. Her Georgia counterpart, Frances Pauley, could often be found on picket lines or harassing public officials. Sara Murphy of Little Rock and Jocelyn Wurzburg of Memphis challenged deep-seated white prejudice through presentations by their respective Panels of American Women, but they did so wearing white gloves and pearls.

Regional and demographic differences also contributed to the extent to which each woman felt she could flaunt the mores of her community by advocating political and social change. Rosa Keller in New Orleans and Frances Pauley in Atlanta could expect far more sympathetic support for desegregation and voting rights efforts than could the United Church Women in the towns of South Carolina. From whatever position and discomfort level, in whichever decade from the 1930s through the 1970s, in whatever region, these women saw themselves as exercising their rights as citizens and mothers to equalize justice and opportunity in America.

Although committed to working for civil rights, these female activists did not agree on the best methods for changing white racial attitudes. As far back as 1930, when Jessie Daniel Ames took up the banner of antilynching, activists disagreed over whether or not to create segregated organizations to fight for human rights. African American journalist Ida B. Wells-Barnett brought factual data to bear on the trumped-up charges that accompanied most lynchings and garnered the support of both the National Association of Colored Women and the NAACP. Yet, Ames purposely refused to join Wells-Barnett to create a biracial campaign. Instead, she created a whites-only organization. She employed a strategy designed to appeal to white women's sense of Christian brotherhood and justice without raising the specter of racial equality, thus winning support for her cause from thousands of white women who would have rejected membership in any interracial organization. By seeking out churchwomen in small towns and rural settings, she extended racial awareness more broadly than could more urban-based organizations like the YWCA.[32] Similar strategic decisions faced the white college students who left SNCC in the mid-sixties in order to concentrate their efforts on the intransigence of white communities, especially through the Southern Conference Educational Fund and the Southern Student Organizing Committee.[33]

The same is true of the women profiled in this volume. Dorothy Tilly elected to focus on changing the attitudes of white churchwomen through a segregated group she named the Fellowship of the Concerned, believing that women's changed attitudes would influence their children, husbands, and neighbors. Adolphine Fletcher Terry and Irene Samuel of the Women's Emergency Committee in Little Rock elected to avoid the "integrationist" and "interracial" labels that might attract reprisals from segregationists and organized within the white community alone, as did Rosa Keller and Gladys Cahn with Save Our Schools in New Orleans.

Alice Spearman and Frances Pauley dedicated much of their careers to leading biracial councils on human relations in their respective states. Both believed firmly that advocates of an integrated society had to model biracial cooperation and work in both African American and white communities. Many white activists sought "tutoring" from African American friends in order to root out paternalistic tendencies and radicalize their understanding of race-class dynamics as they committed themselves to biracial work. Anne Braden, newspaperwoman and co-director of the Southern Conference Educational Fund, vowed never to join any segregated or white-dominated organization and worked exclusively within black-led interracial groups. The Panels of American Women in Little Rock, Memphis, and New Orleans required multiethnic, biracial, and Protestant-Catholic-Jewish participation.

Change came much more slowly than any of these women had imagined it would. The fervor with which they had set out to convert city councilmen, school board members, neighbors, and even co-volunteers was quenched many times. As Sara Mitchell Parsons writes in her memoir, "I was also feeling frustrated. . . . Nothing I did appeared to make any difference. . . . I despaired of being able to change the attitudes of the majority of [white] Atlantans."[34] We know little about the southern white women who entered the civil rights struggle briefly and then left it to resume private lives, other volunteer causes, or professional careers.[35] The activists highlighted in this volume spent their adult lives, whether as paid professional organizers or volunteers, pursuing racial justice and equal opportunity.

Organization of the Book

This anthology is divided into two parts. The first section contains four essays, each about an individual activist, arranged in chronological order. Edith Riehm's study of Dorothy Tilly (b. 1883) brings into focus the dynamics that impelled a "quintessential southern lady" to devote seventy years to the cause of racial justice. Tilly's contributions to race relations bridged an older mode of conciliatory action within the white community and the black-led direct action campaigns of the 1950s and 1960s. As one of the few southern activists who never lived outside the South, Tilly treated African American goals for equality with a measure of noblesse oblige and was slower than younger activists to appreciate the multiple handicaps perpetuated by legal segregation. Her extensive travels throughout the South, first with the Methodist Women's Missionary Society and later with the Southern Region Council, and her experi-

ence in race relations distinguished her enough to make her one of two southerners chosen by President Harry S. Truman for his Committee on Civil
Rights. Convinced of the interlocking relationship between inferior education, limited job opportunity, and segregation, she worked tirelessly to convince other southerners, especially the white churchwomen in the Fellowship
of the Concerned, to embrace civil rights legislation.

Alice Norwood Spearman Wright (b. 1902) also cultivated churchwomen,
but more especially clubwomen, through her work with the South Carolina
Federation of Women's Clubs. She led the biracial South Carolina Council on
Human Relations during the turbulent 1960s, establishing local branches in
some of the most segregated territory outside Mississippi. Marcia Synnott's
essay captures in detail the extended network of female mentors and co-workers who supported Spearman's work over a span of fifty years and reveals the
finesse with which Spearman approached various constituencies as she built
her biracial councils. She maintained good relationships with many moderates
and refused to move faster than she believed her constituency would follow.
Though shunning overt protests, her subtle and genteel undermining of white
supremacy moved many South Carolinians into toleration and acceptance.

Frances Freeborn Pauley (b. 1905), executive director of the Georgia Council on Human Relations, was Spearman's contemporary. Author Kathryn
Nasstrom has chosen to examine how Pauley herself understood her activism
in terms of both her whiteness and her gender. Nasstrom is particularly interested in the way that autobiography and biography work together to reveal a
life. The dialectical interplay of Pauley's oral history and Nasstrom's analysis
as biographer provides an imaginative model for understanding women's activism. Pauley also provides an engaging model of a woman whose activism
persisted into retirement and whose efforts toward creating a just and peaceful
society extended over many decades.

Catherine Fosl explores the activism of arguably the most radical southern
white woman in the civil rights lexicon, Anne McCarty Braden (b. 1924),
whose career began immediately after World War II and continues today. Like
the women in the previous three essays, Braden has spent her life working for
racial justice organizations. However, she represents the second generation of
activists, born after the women's suffrage movement had reshaped women's
public role. Fosl explores the ways in which Braden rejected white privilege
and transgressed the south's racial boundaries to forge empowering relationships with African Americans. Using an interdisciplinary approach, Fosl explores Braden's understanding of how both whiteness and gender shaped her
role in the civil rights movement.

The second part of the anthology centers on women's organizations and informal networks in cities or regions. Cherisse Jones's essay details the role of United Church Women (UCW) in combating prejudice and discrimination in South Carolina, principally in Columbia. Established in 1941, the United Council of Church Women, as it was originally known, embraced integration as one of its founding principles, for interdenominationalism implied inter-racialism. The *Brown* decision in 1954 frightened many racial moderates, and the state UCW leadership barely affirmed support of school desegregation. Despite the pleas of some members, South Carolina UCW chapters did not put their energies into pursing civil rights legislation. Instead, they preferred to concentrate on maternalistic projects directed at improving educational and vocational opportunities for blacks. Jones's scholarship reveals how many Protestant white women sought to uphold Christian ideals without paying the price of social ostracism. Not until the 1960s brought national UCW programs to South Carolina did many African American and white women work to-gether on racial justice issues.

The remaining essays examine the activism of white women in three south-ern cities: Little Rock, New Orleans, and Memphis. Laura Miller's essay on the Little Rock Women's Emergency Committee to Open Our Schools reveals how a handful of women put together a powerful lobby that elected moderates to the school board, adopted a workable plan for desegregation, and built po-litical coalitions. However, they did so by engaging in the very strategy they sought to destroy—segregation. Miller's essay explores the reasons behind that decision, the political experience gained by WEC members, the subse-quent demise of the organization, and the emergence of the Panel of American Women.

Shannon Frystak's essay on New Orleans and Gail Murray's essay on Mem-phis examine the influences on prominent white women of their experiences in the YWCA, Urban League, and/or United Church Women as precursors of their civil rights activism in the 1960s. In both cities, the support of a network of like-minded women greatly helped individual women to persist through so-cial ostracism and harassment. Frystak's essay begins with an analysis of a net-work of privileged New Orleans women who created the Save Our Schools organization to facilitate peaceful public school desegregation after Louisi-ana's governor threatened to imitate Little Rock and close the New Orleans public schools. She examines the years of experience in other "liberal" causes that brought these women together and then traces their continuing activism with the biracial Community Relations Council. In profiling Rosa Freeman

Keller (b. 1911), Frystak not only shows the influence of a wealthy matron but also reveals the importance in New Orleans of a network of Jewish women.

Murray describes a biracial group formed in Memphis to test restaurant desegregation compliance and another group that facilitated free-lunch and enrichment programs in all-black schools. She argues that women's experiences in these biracial organizations positioned them for political action following the sanitation workers' strike of 1968. Murray examines the work of the Memphis Panel of American Women and shows its influence on a dramatic political confrontation between a conservative city council and women seeking equal opportunity for African Americans.

All of the essays in *Throwing Off the Cloak of Privilege* are published here for the first time. These female "inside agitators," to borrow David Chappell's term, must be reckoned with as the motives, strategies, and human costs of the civil rights struggle are recounted and analyzed. The authors of this collection hope their research will spur further investigation of the many unnamed women, black and white, whose talents, sacrifices, visions, and mistakes were part of the ongoing struggle for human dignity and voice in American life.

Notes

I wish to thank Jennifer Brady, Kathryn Nasstrom, Stanley Harrold, and Randall Miller for their insightful reading of the Introduction and chapter 8. Their pointed criticisms and gentle suggestions made both essays appreciably better.

1. As quoted in Jacquelyn Dowd Hall, *Revolt against Chivalry: Jessie Daniel Ames and the Women's Campaign against Lynching* (1979; reprint, New York: Columbia University Press, 1993), 89. Carrie Johnson was a leading Methodist laywoman at the turn of the twentieth century.

2. Sara Alderman Murphy, *Breaking the Silence: Little Rock's Women's Emergency Committee to Open Our Schools, 1958–1963*, edited by Patrick C. Murphy II (Fayetteville: University of Arkansas Press, 1997), xiii.

3. Hall, *Revolt against Chivalry*.

4. Susan Lynn, *Progressive Women in Conservative Times: Racial Justice, Peace and Feminism, 1945 to the 1960s* (New Brunswick: Rutgers University Press, 1992), 3, 9.

5. William Peters, *The Southern Temper* (1959), as quoted in Timothy Tyson, "Dynamite and 'The Silent South': A Story from the Second Reconstruction in South Carolina," in *Jumpin' Jim Crow*, ed. Jane Dailey, Glenda Gilmore, and Bryant Simon (Princeton: Princeton University Press, 2000), 284.

6. Kathryn L. Nasstrom, *Everybody's Grandmother and Nobody's Fool: Frances Freeborn Pauley and the Struggle for Social Justice* (Ithaca: Cornell University Press, 2000);

Catherine Fosl, *Subversive Southerner: Anne Braden and the Struggle for Racial Justice in the Cold War South* (New York: Palgrave Macmillan, 2002); Anne Braden, *The Wall Between* (1958; Knoxville: University of Tennessee Press, 1999).

7. For a provocative discussion of "radical" politics from both the left and the right, see Kathleen Blee, ed., *No Middle Ground: Women and Radical Protest* (New York: New York University Press, 1998), especially the Introduction.

8. Robert J. Norrell, *Reaping the Whirlwind: The Civil Rights Movement in Tuskegee* (New York: Random House, 1985). The quotation is from Norrell, "One Thing We Did Right: Reflections on the Movement," in *New Directions in Civil Rights Studies,* ed. Armstead L. Robinson and Patricia Sullivan (Charlottesville: University Press of Virginia, 1991), 67.

9. Patricia Sullivan, *Days of Hope: Race and Democracy in the New Deal Era* (Chapel Hill: University of North Carolina Press, 1996); Adam Fairclough, *Race and Democracy: The Civil Rights Struggle in Louisiana, 1915–1972* (Athens: University of Georgia Press, 1995); August Meier, "Epilogue: Toward a Synthesis of Civil Rights History," in Robinson and Sullivan, eds., *New Directions,* 211–24.

10. Further discussion of the "boundaries" of the civil rights movement can be found in Kathryn L. Nasstrom, "Beginnings and Endings: Life Stories and the Periodization of the Civil Rights Movement," *Journal of American History* 86 (June 1999): 700–711. See also Charles W. Eagles, "Toward New Histories of the Civil Rights Era," *Journal of Southern History* 66 (November 2000): 815–48; Patricia Sullivan, "Southern Reformers, the New Deal and the Movement's Foundation," in Robinson and Sullivan, eds., *New Directions,* 81–104; Belinda Robnett, *How Long? How Long? African American Women in the Struggle for Civil Rights* (New York: Oxford University Press, 1997); Steven F. Lawson, "Freedom Then, Freedom Now: The Historiography of the Civil Rights Movement," *American Historical Review* 96 (April 1991): 456–71; and Lawson, "Civil Rights and Black Liberation," in *A Companion to American Women's History,* ed. Nancy A. Hewitt (Oxford, England: Blackwell, 2002), 397–413.

11. Meier, "Epilogue," 223. See also the chapter "'In All Its Incarnations': White Antiracist Culture," in *A Promise and a Way of Life: White Antiracist Activism,* ed. Becky Thompson (Minneapolis: University of Minnesota, 2001), 325–63.

12. John Egerton, *Speak Now against the Day: The Generation before the Civil Rights Movement in the South* (New York: Knopf, 1994); David L. Chappell, *Inside Agitators: White Southerners in the Civil Rights Movement* (Baltimore: Johns Hopkins University Press, 1994).

13. Vicki L. Crawford, Jacqueline Anne Rouse, and Barbara Woods, eds., *Women in the Civil Rights Movement: Trailblazers and Torchbearers, 1941–1965* (Bloomington: Indiana University Press, 1990).

14. Cynthia Stokes Brown, ed., *Ready from Within: Septima Clark and the Civil Rights Movement* (Navarro, Calif.: Wild Trees Press, 1986); David Garrow, ed., *The Montgomery Bus Boycott and the Women Who Started It: The Memoir of JoAnn Gibson Robinson* (Knoxville: University of Tennessee Press, 1987); Charles Payne, *I've Got the*

Light of Freedom: The Organizing Tradition and the Mississippi Freedom Struggle (Berkley: University of California Press, 1995); Robnett, *How Long? How Long?*; Cynthia Griggs Fleming, *Soon We Will Not Cry: The Liberation of Ruby Doris Smith Robinson* (Lanham, Md.: Rowman and Littlefield, 1998); Joanne Grant, *Ella Baker: Freedom Bound* (New York: Wiley and Sons, 1998); Chana Kai Lee, *For Freedom's Sake: The Life of Fannie Lou Hamer* (Urbana: University of Illinois Press, 1999); Bettye Collier-Thomas and V. P. Franklin, *Sisters in the Struggle: African American Women in the Civil Rights–Black Power Movement* (New York: New York University Press, 2002). See also Deborah F. Atwater, guest editor, *Journal of Black Studies* 26.5 (May 1996), on African American women in the civil rights movement. Joanne Grant best elaborates the nurturer theme, as does Jenny Iron, "The Shaping of Activist Recruitment and Participation: A Study of Women in the Mississippi Civil Rights Movement," *Gender and Society* 12, special issue: Gender and Social Movements, part 1 (December 1998): 692–709.

15. Anne C. Loveland, *Lillian Smith: A Southerner Confronting the South* (Baton Rouge: Louisiana University Press, 1986); Margaret Rose Gladney, ed., *How Am I to Be Heard? Letters of Lillian Smith* (Chapel Hill: University of North Carolina Press, 1993.)

16. Florence Mars, *Witness in Philadelphia* (Baton Rouge: Louisiana State University Press, 1977); Sarah Patton Boyle, *The Desegregated Heart: A Virginian's Stand in Time of Transition* (New York: Morrow, 1962; reissued with Introduction and Letters, ed. Jennifer Ritterhouse, Charlottesville: University of Virginia Press, 2001); Sara Mitchell Parsons, *From Southern Wrongs to Civil Rights: The Memoir of a White Civil Rights Activist* (Tuscaloosa: University of Alabama Press, 2000).

17. Virginia Foster Durr, *Outside the Magic Circle: The Autobiography of Virgina Foster Durr,* edited by Hollinger F. Barnard (New York: Simon and Schuster, 1985); Nasstrom, *Everybody's Grandmother and Nobody's Fool*; Fosl, *Subversive Southerner.*

18. Sara Evans, *Personal Politics: The Roots of Women's Liberation in the Civil Rights Movement and the New Left* (New York: Vintage Books, 1980); see also Casey Hayden, "Fields of Blue," in *Deep in Our Hearts: Nine White Women in the Freedom Movement,* ed. Constance Curry et al. (Athens: University of Georgia Press, 2000), 361–67.

19. Mary King, *Freedom Song: A Personal Story of the 1960s Civil Rights Movement* (New York: Morrow, 1987); Hayden, "Fields of Blue," 361–67.

20. Christina Greene, "'We'll Take Our Stand': Race, Class, and Gender in the Southern Student Organizing Committee, 1964–1969," in *Hidden Histories of Women in the New South,* ed. Virginia Bernhard et al. (Columbia: University of Missouri Press, 1994), 191.

21. Rhoda Lois Blumberg, "White Mothers as Civil Rights Activists," in *Women and Social Protest,* ed. Guida West and Rhoda Lois Blumberg (New York: Oxford University Press, 1990), 167.

22. Jane Allyn Piliavin and Hong-Wen Charg, "Altruism: A Review of Recent Theory and Research," *Annual Review of Sociology* 16 (1990): 27–65; on the altruistic

personality, see C. Daniel Batson, *The Altruism Questions: Toward a Social-Psychological Answer* (Hillsdale, N.J.: Lawrence Erlbaum Associates, 1991), 177–201.

23. Fred Hobson, *But Now I See: The White Southern Racial Conversion Narrative* (Baton Rouge: Louisiana State University Press, 1999), 2, 5.

24. Ibid., 18. The other southern writer he profiles is Katherine Du Pre Lumpkin, whose critique of race prejudice was much more conciliatory than Smith's.

25. See Loveland, *Lillian Smith;* Gladney, *How Am I To Be Heard?* Quote from *Killers of the Dream* in Hobson, *Now I See,* 24–25.

26. Durr, *Outside the Magic Circle.*

27. Thompson, *A Promise and a Way of Life,* 56.

28. As quoted in Hobson, *Now I See,* 88.

29. Fosl, *Subversive Southerner,* Introduction; Thompson, *A Promise and a Way of Life,* 326.

30. Annabelle Whittemore, interview with Gail S. Murray, October 19, 1999, in possession of the interviewer.

31. Blumberg, "White Mothers," 166, 168.

32. For additional information on Wells-Barnett's campaign and the work of the National Association of Colored Women, see Linda O. McMurry, *To Keep the Waters Troubled: The Life of Ida B. Wells* (New York: Oxford University Press, 1998); Jacqueline Jones Royster, ed., *Southern Horrors and Other Writings: The Anti-Lynching Campaign of Ida B. Wells, 1892–1900* (Boston: Bedford Books, 1997); Ida B. Wells, *Crusade for Justice: The Autobiography of Ida B. Wells,* edited by Alfreda M. Duster (Chicago: University of Chicago Press, 1970); Floris Barnett Cash, *African American Women and Social Action: Clubwomen and Volunteerism from Jim Crow to the New Deal, 1896–1936* (New York: Greenwood Press, 2001). On Jessie Daniel Ames, see Hall, *Revolt against Chivalry.*

33. For examples of these women's experiences in SNCC, see Curry et al., eds., *Deep in Our Hearts*; King, *Freedom Song*; and Evans, *Personal Politics.* For a detailed study of the controversies in SNCC, see Clayborne Carson, *In Struggle: SNCC and the Black Awakening of the 1960s* (Cambridge: Harvard University Press, 1981). For the Southern Conference Educational Fund, see Irwin Kilbaner, *Conscience of a Troubled South* (Brooklyn, N.Y.: Carlson, 1989); and Linda Reed, *Simple Decency and Common Sense: The Southern Conference Movement, 1938–1963* (Bloomington: Indiana University Press, 1991).

34. Parsons, *Southern Wrongs,* 142.

35. For the example of South Carolinian Claudia Sanders, see Tyson, "Dynamite and 'The Silent South,'" 275–97.

chapter 1

Dorothy Tilly and
the Fellowship of the Concerned

EDITH HOLBROOK RIEHM

*I have had the opportunity since my return from Mammoth Cave to read every word of
"Gleanings from the Conference of the Fellowship of the Concerned." I have been greatly
impressed with the thorough preparation which must have been made for the conference
and its obvious good results. Nearly all of the discussions of integration in which young
people participate create the belief that the difficulties are not found with the young
people themselves but with their parents. In the average home in the mind of the child
the mother is the dominant figure. When most of them see things aright, our problem is
largely solved. Mrs. Tilly is working in the most strategic area in the South.[1]*

—Marion A. Wright, Executive Director, Southern Regional Council, 1955

Dorothy Tilly and the National Women's Committee for Civil Rights meeting with President
John F. Kennedy, July 1963. Kennedy urged the women to work locally to implement his civil
rights program. Tilly (the first woman on Kennedy's right) responded by organizing the 1963
Fellowship of the Concerned Annual Meeting around the theme "Let Freedom Ring." Cour-
tesy of the Dorothy Rogers Tilly Papers, Special Collections, Robert W. Woodruff Library,
Emory University.

IN 1949, Dorothy Tilly, the Southern Regional Council's director of women's work, set out to revitalize women's role in southern race relations. Following a pattern that characterized her life's work, she summoned prominent liberals—African American and white, religious and political leaders—to a Workshop of Southern Church Women.[2] Inspired by keynote speakers such as Eleanor Roosevelt, all of the participants pledged the following at the conference's conclusion:

> I AM concerned that our constitutional freedoms are not shared by all our people; my religion convinces me that they must be and gives me the courage to study, work, and lead others to the fulfillment of equal justice under the law. I will respond to calls from the Southern Regional Council to serve my faith and my community in the defense of justice.[3]

The conference's success, coupled with its participants' enthusiasm and commitment, inspired Dorothy Tilly to create an annual forum at which leaders of religious organizations for southern women could devise strategies aimed at improving southern race relations. Once back home, their mission would be to share their convictions with other southern women. Tilly named her creation the Fellowship of the Concerned (FOC), and by 1950 it had more than four thousand members.[4]

Under Tilly's guidance, this large biracial and interfaith network focused initially on examining inequities in southern courtrooms.[5] In 1953, however, she shifted the FOC's mission from that of a Christian duty to improve the lives of African Americans in the segregated South to the more forthright and radical goal of preparing white southern society for the inevitable end of segregation. Tilly directed FOC members to attack prejudice at its roots in white southern homes and induce women to teach tolerance to their children and husbands. Tilly believed that by raising more tolerant children, white women could have a far-reaching effect on reducing racial prejudice and could work toward establishing a society in which all citizens enjoyed equal opportunities. The FOC crusade exemplified the essence of women's work, laying the foundation for reform by setting examples that others could follow. Initially, at the local level, Tilly enlisted primarily white women for this crusade because they were experienced in effecting social reform under the protective and comfortable guise of domesticity.

Dorothy Tilly preached what she had long practiced. In 1955, when Marion Wright described Tilly's work as "strategic," Tilly was seventy-two years old. A social reformer since the 1910s, she had learned, through her own activism in women's reform organizations, the unique power women could wield to improve southern society. In creating the FOC in 1949, she segued her activism and influence into the nascent civil rights movement. Dorothy Tilly's work is important not only because it represents an often-overlooked link between women's early reform efforts and the modern civil rights movement, but also because it illustrates the continuum of white women's activism from 1910 through the late 1960s.

An accurate understanding of the FOC must begin with an exploration of Tilly's background and of the motivations, influences, and experiences that led her, an upper-middle-class, white southern woman, to not only embrace racial equality in the segregated South but also to become a public civil rights advocate. This essay contains four inextricably linked parts. The first explores Tilly's formative years, her inspiration, and her early efforts in traditional church work and women's reform. The second examines her evolution from race relations reformer to civil rights leader through activism in the Southern Regional Council (SRC) and the President's Committee on Civil Rights. The third describes how she orchestrated a well-established strategy and activist network on behalf of the FOC in the 1950s and 1960s. The fourth evaluates the FOC's strengths and limitations, and considers the extent to which Tilly and her churchwomen overcame obstacles in changing the conservative attitudes of white southerners during the critical years of the civil rights movement. My conclusion examines the relevance of Tilly's work in today's society, where racism still abides, if less visibly.

Motivations and Interracial Reform Work

Dorothy Tilly entered the reactionary world of southern Redemption in 1883, a time of receding rights for African Americans and expanding public roles for white women.[6] The segregated society in which she was reared shaped her racial attitudes, and she consequently grew up accepting the separate-but-equal paradigm. She was descended from Virginia gentry on both sides, and prior to the Civil War her maternal grandfather had owned a two-thousand-acre Georgia plantation.[7] Her father, Richard Wade Rogers, made his living as a Methodist minister. Together, he and his wife, Frances (Fannie), had eleven children, eight of whom survived infancy. Richard and Fannie raised their eight children in a religious yet nurturing middle-class household and sent all of them to college.[8] At a young age, Tilly's parents and grandmother instilled in her a responsibility to help the needy. She herself became a devout Methodist with a lifelong close relationship with the teachings of Christ. She continually drew strength from her faith and often quoted scripture.[9] At her parent's prompting, Dorothy undertook her first volunteerism at the age of twelve, presiding over the local Children's Missionary Society.[10]

During the late nineteenth and early twentieth centuries, southern female colleges geared their curricula toward promoting the public roles considered acceptable for women, and many white southern women attended college to become better prepared for their role in society. With her parents' encouragement, Dorothy earned her undergraduate degrees at Reinhardt and Wesleyan Colleges.[11]

Although she was certainly influenced by the South's white-supremacist ideology, her father's vocation ensured that young Dorothy learned early about the suffering and hardships many African Americans and poor whites faced. Later in her life, she recalled, "[T]hroughout my youth . . . I saw and heard the troubles of the community, both Negro and white, pour over the doorstep of the parsonage. . . . [R]egardless of color, people were people first."[12] These early experiences taught her to accept African Americans as people, though not as social equals.

When Dorothy met Milton Eben Tilly, she found a true soul mate who believed, as she did, in helping the less fortunate. They married in November 1903, and one year later Tilly gave birth to their only child, a son, Eben Fletcher Tilly. Her pregnancy was difficult, and Tilly's doctors advised her not to have more children. With any dreams she may have had about a large family dashed, Tilly devoted herself to her marriage and to raising her young son while her husband, a chemicals salesman, provided his family with a comfortable middle-class lifestyle.[13]

As she matured, Tilly projected the image of the quintessential "southern lady"—aristocratic, genteel, soft-spoken, well-dressed, Christian, and white. Tilly linked her public identity with that of her husband, and she so epitomized the respectable southern lady archetype that more than three decades after her death contemporaries still refer to her as "Mrs. Tilly."[14] She put this image to good use in her reform efforts by quietly challenging southern society from within the safe and gendered boundaries that circumscribed the life of a proper southern lady.

When Eben reached adolescence, his parents enrolled him in a military boarding school. With their son gone, Milton encouraged his wife to find a productive outlet, so she joined the Women's Missionary Society of the Meth-

odist Church (WMS) as a children's religion instructor. She also attended
Methodist conferences at Scarritt College for Christian Workers in Nashville
and Garrett Seminary in Chicago.[15] Her inability to have more children probably prompted Tilly to become active in children's issues, and in 1918 the
WMS appointed her to head its Children's Work for North Georgia program,
a position she held for thirteen years. In this role she traveled throughout her
territory collecting information about births and raising money for orphans.[16]

Tilly's charitable work with the WMS, deemed acceptable for women of
her class and station, nevertheless reintroduced her to white indigent families
and to the inequalities African Americans suffered, and suggested the politiciz-
ing potential of such knowledge. By 1913 the WMS had adopted a race relations program encouraging "churchwomen's groups to study and remedy
practical conditions for Negroes, including public schools, recreation facilities, jails and courts, housing and sanitation."[17] Tilly began children's book
groups where her white students read to African American children. Under
her guidance, her students also organized fund-raisers, collecting pennies to
buy a piano for a black school and donating flower seeds to the poor.[18]

By the late 1920s Tilly had become a role model for other WMS members.
She expanded this leadership role by teaching Christian Leadership School
seminars designed to promote improved race relations. Her students included
biracial women's Methodist groups at Lake Junaluska in North Carolina and
African American women at Paine College, the all-black women's school in
Augusta, Georgia.[19]

Tilly's tenure with the WMS introduced her to other white women who,
like her, were determined to foster better race relations. Tilly first met Thelma
Stevens in 1929 when Stevens was the WMS director of the Bethlehem Community Center for Negroes in Augusta, Georgia. In 1930, their paths crossed
again when the WMS sent Tilly to conduct a seminar at Paine. The much
younger Stevens held far more progressive views at the time than did Tilly.
When she invited Tilly to lunch in the Paine College cafeteria, Tilly hesitated,
explaining that she had never eaten "with Negro people." Stevens then asked,
"You don't mind, do you?" to which Tilly could only reply, "No, I don't
mind."[20] Thus Tilly, at age forty-seven, broke through an entrenched southern
social taboo by eating with African Americans in a socially equal setting.
Stevens later recalled that Tilly's interaction with African American conference attendees became "more collegial" because of this experience.[21] Nine
years later, Tilly traveled to a Lake Junaluska conference accompanied by two
white women and one black woman, Mrs. Harvey. The front gate attendant
stopped the car and redirected Mrs. Harvey to the rear entrance. Tilly gently

yet firmly insisted that all four women remain together, and finally the attendant acquiesced and allowed the car to pass.[22]

These episodes demonstrate the gradual transformation that led Tilly to repudiate segregation completely by 1939. More critically, they reveal not only the diverse roles white women reformers held simultaneously as colleagues, friends, mentors, and students, but also the nurturing community these women created. Within this network, women formed enduring friendships, encouraging each other to expand their racial views and instilling confidence in, and providing validation to, each other as they transgressed the color line.[23]

Tilly's mission work also led to a fruitful association with the Commission on Interracial Cooperation (CIC), which periodically enlisted WMS members in staging various protests.[24] Founded in 1919, the biracial CIC sought to improve race relations through education, investigation, and persuasion. A moderate organization true to its progressive roots, the CIC did not directly challenge segregation.[25] Tilly made valuable contacts through the CIC and formed friendships with Mary McLeod Bethune and Will Alexander among others. Her friendship with Bethune gave Tilly the additional insight she needed to move beyond working *for* African Americans to working *with* them.

When she joined the CIC in 1930 she met another female mentor, Jessie Daniel Ames, who had managed the CIC's Women's Division since 1929 and by 1930 was focused on stopping the wave of lynchings that was sweeping across the South. In 1931, Ames created the Association of Southern Women for the Prevention of Lynching (ASWPL), drawing "members from three interrelated societies, the CIC, ASWPL, and WMS."[26] Tilly expanded her activism by joining the ASWPL, developing organizational skills as Ames successfully forged a regional antilynching crusade. Tilly's first roles in the ASWPL were as secretary and field reporter. As the ASWPL grew in size and influence, she was appointed Georgia's state representative and traveled across the state meeting with rural folk and educating them on how to prevent lynching, and investigating the causes of the incidents that did occur.[27] ASWPL members developed local volunteer networks to head off lynching sentiment from within their own communities. These networks endured, and Tilly would later call on them in her SRC and FOC work.

The WMS, CIC, and ASWPL were not Tilly's sole supporters. She always credited her husband, Milton, who backed her financially, suggested ideas for reform opportunities, and bolstered her self-confidence. As a white businessman, he was not in a position to take a public stand himself. While society permitted white women to become involved in charity work for African Americans, it imposed implicit restrictions on white men. During the early years of the Depression, Milton would drive his wife through the Atlanta slums, and on one of these outings she asked him why he tormented her with these images of "poor, hungry, jobless people." Milton explained that he did it purposely, "because I thought if you saw the people hurting long enough, that you would hurt, too—and if you hurt bad enough, you'd do something about it! *I can't do it myself*, but I'll make it possible if money is needed for you to get involved. I'll back you! I'll take you when and where you need to go."[28] The Tillys' successful marriage lasted until Milton's death in 1961.

By the end of the 1930s, Dorothy Tilly had established herself within Methodist female organizations as an experienced and influential conference speaker and a mentor to other female Methodist activists.[29] The effective and extensive community formed through biracial women's religious reform organizations, coupled with her own religious devotion, nurturing childhood, and husband's untiring support, combined to imbue Tilly with the inspiration and motivation she needed to expand her role as a race relations leader.

From Regional Race Relations to National Civil Rights

The 1940s ushered in a more aggressive approach to southern race relations.[30] During this decade, Tilly expanded her activism and influence with the newly formed Southern Regional Council and achieved national recognition when she accepted a post on President Harry S. Truman's Committee on Civil Rights. By the decade's end, Dorothy Tilly had emerged as a trailblazer in the nascent civil rights movement.

When Jessie Daniel Ames dissolved the ASWPL in 1942, Tilly diversified her race relations activism. She organized leading southern churchwomen to boycott Ku Klux Klan member–owned businesses and worked for the passage of Georgia's first antilynching law. She and her network also lobbied the Georgia legislature to appropriate funds for an African American girls' training school. When Georgia's governor, Eugene Talmadge, vetoed the proposal, he unwittingly galvanized the churchwomen, who then obtained twenty-eight thousand signatures of registered voters who supported the school. Their petition ensured that the Georgia legislature would grant the necessary funds at its next session.[31] Tilly also joined the Women's Society of Christian Service and campaigned aggressively against the poll tax, traveling to eight southern states calling for its repeal. At these speaking engagements she approached her white audiences sympathetically as a fellow southerner, applauding the progress southerners had made in race relations and encouraging them to continue.[32] She was not always successful, but she extended her influence and earned a reputation as an "organizer of women."[33]

In 1943, Will Alexander, former CIC executive director and now director of the Farm Security Administration in Washington, D.C., appointed Tilly to run the Emergency Committee for Food Production (ECFP). While she was in Washington, Tilly met Eleanor Roosevelt, and the two women began a long friendship.[34]

When her ECFP post ended in 1944, Tilly returned to Atlanta and helped form the Southern Regional Council, successor to the defunct CIC. When Jessie Daniel Ames unexpectedly retired from the SRC, Tilly became its director of women's work.[35] In this role, she continued creating programs through which churchwomen could foster social change in the South. Her employment with the SRC was to last twenty-five years.

Although many Methodist women like Tilly had long been active in improving southern race relations, the Methodist church had avoided developing a formal policy to address racial inequities among its members. As late as 1956, the Women's Division of the Methodist church "petitioned the General Conference of the Methodist Church . . . requesting 'that the institutions of the church, local churches, colleges, universities, theological schools, hospitals, and homes carefully study their policies and practices as they relate to race, making certain that these policies and practices are Christian.'"[36] Tilly was often vexed by her own church's refusal to oppose segregation openly. She criticized and ridiculed church bishops and leaders, yet she never left the Methodist church.[37] Instead, she relied on the SRC to act when the church would not and considered the SRC its "more liberal and militant arm."[38] In return, Tilly was invaluable to the SRC, utilizing her extensive churchwomen's network to assist the SRC in exposing racial injustices. In 1946, the SRC sent her to investigate the lynching of four African Americans in Monroe, Georgia, and a race riot in Columbia, Tennessee.[39] Both incidents were highly publicized, attracting even President Truman's attention. Already considering reelection, Truman knew that he needed to address civil rights in order to attract the votes of northern blacks. In what could be deemed a blatant political move, he issued Executive Order 9808 on December 5, 1946, establishing a federal committee on civil rights.[40]

Truman delegated the task of membership selection for this committee to his assistant on civil rights, David K. Niles, who worked for several weeks soliciting members. Ultimately, the committee consisted of fifteen prominent liberals, including two African Americans and two women. Tilly, by now recognized as a race relations expert, was issued an invitation to join the President's Committee on Civil Rights (PCCR). She accepted the post, and for the next ten months she traveled by train roughly every two weeks to attend committee meetings. She brought to this committee three decades of southern race relations experience and an unquestionably thorough understanding of her native South's strengths and shortcomings. In return, the committee's findings illuminated for her the extent to which racism permeated not only the South but the United States as a whole.[41]

Tilly and Frank Porter Graham, her fellow southern committee member, disagreed with some of the PCCR's initial recommendations, which among other things threatened to cut the South's federal education funds unless the region immediately abolished segregation.[42] Although Tilly opposed segregation, she knew southern conservatives would vehemently defy federal intervention in this matter and might retaliate, thereby unraveling the progress she and other southern liberals had labored so long to achieve. To avoid this, Tilly advised the committee to proceed cautiously, imploring them not to single out the South. Racism was a nationwide epidemic, and she believed education to be part of the cure. "Now about my South and the report," she wrote to the committee,

> the report is too beligerant [sic]. It is rather vicious as it raises a "whip-hand" against the South. It does not express an understanding of the problems of the South, but even drags in sentences to point up at the sins of the section. I admit the accusations are just but we will have to use another method or else we undo the social progress the South has made in the last twenty-five years. . . .
>
> The question of one school system [not two that are segregated] makes the groups always "see red." As I said before, the South will stay ignorant before it will be forced to having non-segregated schools. I believe every Southern newspaper will attack the report editorially on this score.
>
> We cannot avoid facing the segregation—but make it with a different approach. The report sounds like we are mad at someone or some section of our nation. . . .
>
> After all, do we not want to strengthen the civil rights of our people? Isn't this the real purpose of our committee? As the report is, it will be rejected by the South and the South knows how to REBEL [sic].[43]

Nevertheless, after their initial dissent Tilly and Graham supported the PCCR's final report, "To Secure These Rights," which advocated segregation's immediate end. For Tilly, it was the most difficult yet most significant decision of her career. When she refocused her race relations activism onto the struggle for civil rights, she subjected herself to years of "verbal abuse and threats" from many white southerners who castigated her efforts, labeling her "a parasite" of the Methodist church, a socialist, and a Communist.[44] Tilly's leap thrust her across a divide where even her image as a southern lady afforded no protection from certain white supremacists. An unsigned letter Tilly received in 1948 threatened dire consequences to her actions:

> Your recommendations are naught, but by your actions you have precipi-
> tated and agitated more assault, more rape and more bloodshed than the
> South has ever seen. You have prepared more hangmen's nooses than have
> ever been prepared—or would have been prepared in the history of the
> whole Southland. . . . You are not worthy to live in the south [*sic*]. . . . You are
> ignorant of conditions in the South and the understanding of the colored
> race. You are agitating the Negro. Their feeble minds, and yours, cannot
> grasp the resulting chaos your recommendations will bring.[45]

Thus, Tilly had personally confronted segregation's roots: defiant and deep-seated white racist attitudes. Yet, even in the midst of the onslaught, Tilly refused to denigrate her enemies, relying on Christ's message to "love thy neighbor." She also pitied them, recognizing that their attitude was the result of ignorance and poverty.[46] These experiences reinforced her conviction that education and proper guidance were the only ways to remedy racist attitudes.

The Fellowship of the Concerned

While Dorothy Tilly repudiated segregation as morally unjust, she also recognized that her stance against it had developed gradually, and she therefore wondered whether the more conservative white southerners would ever accept desegregation. Guided by her faith, however, she believed optimistically in people's innate goodness and thought that by reaching good southerners she could guide others into this new way of thinking.[47] To execute this mission, she again turned to the southern churchwomen, whom she believed were best suited to help transform southern white racist attitudes, and in 1949 she created the Fellowship of the Concerned. "Whenever there has been a crisis in human relations in the South," she later said, "churchwomen have come together to face the issues and work out a program of action."[48]

Tilly structured the FOC informally. Its members paid no dues and elected no officers. Along with former ASWPL members, she recruited from the extensive southern churchwomen's network, including from such interconnected organizations as the United Church Women and the Women's Christian Mission Society.[49] Beginning in 1949, Tilly organized annual regional FOC meetings that served as two-day race relations conferences. She selected a conference theme and then used her widespread influence to engage prominent speakers—both black and white—to educate and inspire FOC members. For example, Ruby Hurley, a regional director for the National Association for the Advancement of Colored People (NAACP), carefully explained the NAACP's work in order to dispel negative myths about it. Other noteworthy speakers included Coretta Scott King and Grace Towns Hamilton. The many lessons FOC faculty taught proved fruitful. As early as 1950, some Georgia churchwomen attacked prejudice by helping to expunge antiblack racial stereotypes. They convinced two local newspapers to alter their news coverage of blacks by decreasing crime stories and increasing coverage of positive events in black communities.[50] In 1955, "one very large PTA" in Louisiana responded to the FOC's mission by scheduling "a program on Desegregation" that included Urban League participation. That same year, Florida churchwomen recommended the formation of local, biracial councils on human relations.[51]

Knowing that many white southerners perceived the FOC's work as controversial, Tilly enlisted prominent network members to identify qualified southern women as potential participants.[52] Reserving a portion of each annual conference for workshop planning, she also provided tools and distributed reading materials such as Lillian Smith's *Now Is the Time* and Tilly's own pamphlet, *Christian Conscience and the Supreme Court Decision.*[53] Armed with the knowledge gained from these conferences, attendees devised strategies and organized subsequent state-level meetings with their local FOC constituents. Tilly pushed conference information down to local FOC members through articles in the SRC's publication, *New South,* and by mailing them copies of the FOC conference highlights.[54]

During its tenure, three overriding issues commanded the FOC's attention: the "Know Your Courts as Your Schools" project in 1949 and the early 1950s; desegregation from 1953 to 1960; and support for the Civil Rights Act of 1964 between 1963 and 1965. Although FOC conferences were biracial, the "Know Your Courts as Your Schools" project called for a cadre of well-dressed, well-mannered, *white* southern churchwomen to sit silently in courtrooms observing trials where African Americans were defendants.[55] Tilly instigated this program because she believed that socially prominent women sitting in southern courtrooms would shame local authorities and juries to withstand pressure imposed "from other sources," thereby prompting them to deliver justice.[56] And the presence of the silent but vigilant churchwomen in southern courtrooms *did* make a difference. While Tilly recognized that justice was not always served, she discovered that the women's seemingly innocuous presence frequently awakened a community's social conscience, sometimes shaming them into preventing injustices. Therefore, she declared victoriously, "we may not always get justice . . . but we can get public opinion so stirred up that the same thing can't happen in that community again."[57]

Along with the courtroom visitation campaign, several southern churchwomen also assisted their black domestic workers in voter registration.[58] While this activity demonstrates a degree of maternalism toward blacks, it also proves that women were willing to defy Jim Crow laws. They not only helped blacks register to vote but also scrutinized voter registration forms, thus identifying municipalities that overtly disenfranchised their black citizens. Additionally, many women visited their local sheriffs to encourage them to hire African Americans as deputies.[59] Although there is no evidence that the visits increased the hiring of African Americans, they do illustrate the women's willingness to promote local change.

Superficially, churchwomen's visits to sheriffs may appear to have been merely social and perhaps futile calls, yet they are significant because they turned large numbers of white women into advocates for African American rights. From her own experiences, Tilly knew that many white southerners were ignorant of African Americans' abilities and rarely considered the hardships they suffered daily. Consequently, the women's visits had a potentially far-reaching impact on FOC members because they forced many white women to witness Jim Crow in practice, inducing them to move beyond a mere paternalistic concern to a more authentic empathy. Although this was not the FOC's ostensible purpose, it had always been part of Tilly's agenda. She recognized that in order for the FOC to be effective, its members had to face their own prejudice as well as acknowledge the harsh inequities of segregation. This was no minor task in the 1940s and 1950s; it meant overcoming a lifetime of racist socialization among people who seemingly had no motivation to change.

In 1953, Tilly shifted the FOC's focus to addressing desegregation. With the 1954 *Brown* decision pending, she tried to prepare her constituents for the crucial mission that lay ahead: "[T]he South is waiting for the Supreme Court decision on the segregated school question," she wrote. "Whatever way the decision is rendered . . . we'll have a difficult time. We as white church women must be the interpreters and shock absorbers."[60] Tilly now portrayed her cadre of white churchwomen as the South's essential social catalysts.

White southern conservatives did indeed react vehemently against the 1954 *Brown* decision. Consequently, at the FOC's 1954 annual conference and at a special meeting convened in February 1955, Tilly focused on teaching women how to prepare white communities for school desegregation. Drawing on accepted familial roles, she placed the responsibility for the success or failure of desegregation squarely on parents. She even wrote an SRC-sponsored pamphlet arguing that "these twelve million children—Negro and white—will be the victors or victims of change, in proportion to how well the parents and teachers prepare them for this new venture in brotherhood and neighborliness."[61] Because mothers were largely responsible for developing children's attitudes and most teachers were women, Tilly believed that the responsibility for changing society rested ultimately with women.

For the special desegregation meeting in 1955, Tilly solicited speakers such as Alabama native Noreen Tatum, who encouraged FOC members to embrace the possibility of an integrated society. Tatum asked attendees to imagine the dilemma faced by Negro mothers who must explain to their children why they could never sit on the front seat of a bus.[62] Tatum's example portrayed the imagined black woman as a mother—not a servant—thereby giving her an identity to which FOC women could relate. Tatum also wrote to FOC members in 1955 reminding them of their duty as Christian women in facing this task:

> The importance of our stand as Christian women to the Christian missionary enterprise cannot be overestimated. What we say, what we do will affect the spread and power of Christianity now and for years to come. Missionary women who have a large investment of life, prayer and money in world missions cannot afford to rest on their past achievements. We are caught in the stream of change—whether we like it or not.[63]

Her appeal denotes a pragmatic reason for supporting civil rights: with society in flux, women should help facilitate this inevitable change or face decreasing influence and perhaps a more violent society.

Some verbal reports presented during the special February meeting indicated that FOC members throughout the South were already initiating biracial meetings where African Americans and whites met to discuss common concerns. Other reports hinted at the resistance some FOC members encountered. For example, one Atlantan reported that the tenacity of the United Church Women was solely responsible for establishing their interracial meetings in her city because their minister forbade such activities.[64] On the other hand, some women could not shed the "separate-but-equal" paradigm, evidence that Tilly's message had not completely permeated FOC ranks. In the 1956 annual meeting, one resistant attendee asserted, "[W]e have no problem in our County, for I am Chairman of the School Board, and we have equalized the school buildings and the teacher's salaries." Attitudes such as this reinforced the difficult challenge Tilly and the FOC faced. But before she could respond, another attendee retorted that the FOC's purpose was to facilitate compliance with the *Brown* decision, not defiance against it.[65]

Many FOC members, prodded by Tilly, adopted an insistent approach favoring desegregation and planned to set examples in their communities for others to emulate. Throughout 1955 and early 1956, state-level meetings were held in Florida, Georgia, Alabama, Tennessee, Mississippi, Louisiana, South Carolina, and Texas. The tireless Tilly attended all but one of the meetings. At the most promising one, held in Montgomery, Rosa Parks and others vowed to "build bridges of understanding along racial lines." Encouraging reports continued to pour in from Montgomery FOC members, and Tilly learned that they were among the first white patrons to ride the buses after the boycott ended, thus openly displaying their support for desegregation.[66]

The annual FOC meetings armed members with ideas designed to help them convert others to accept desegregation. Tilly herself suggested that FOC members attend school board meetings to influence and pressure those in a position to hasten change.[67] She also scheduled speakers from desegregated southern school districts such as Louisville, Kentucky, who offered ideas on how FOC members could participate in, if not facilitate, their own community's desegregation efforts.[68]

Harkening back to her teaching days in the WMS, Tilly encouraged women to teach their children to accept desegregation. The next generation, she promised, "will be able to do many things we cannot do, if started off in the right direction." Specifically she urged members to "work on [your] husbands" to shift their viewpoints. If that failed, she encouraged women to "reach husbands through children" by teaching "children what is right," because husbands could learn indirectly from their children. Other speakers told women to "broaden social consciences in children" by exposing them to different views and introducing them to African American friends.[69] Tilly consistently designed the annual meetings to assert the moral superiority of Christian wives and mothers and their duty to effect change.

The third major FOC initiative involved gaining support for the pending Civil Rights Bill. In July 1963, President John F. Kennedy had personally summoned Tilly to the White House to join the National Women's Committee for Civil Rights.[70] Acknowledging women as the vanguard in social reform, Kennedy convened more than three hundred leaders of women's organizations and entrusted them to "influence public opinion" and thereby win support for

his civil rights agenda. Tilly organized the 1963 annual FOC conference in response to Kennedy's request. Once the 1964 Civil Rights Act passed, she positioned 1965's annual FOC meeting to address compliance with the new legislation.[71] Unlike the earlier "Know Your Courts" project, Tilly engaged local
members both white and black to monitor compliance. She distributed a
"Study of the City" questionnaire and instructed them to evaluate their community's compliance with the 1964 Civil Rights Act. Not surprisingly, the responses to the questionnaire varied. For example, in the Brunswick/St.
Simons, Georgia, area, many employers hired only token African Americans.
In Jackson, Mississippi, some churches promoted open resistance to the legislation, indicating that in those churches FOC efforts were ignored. However,
some hope emerged unexpectedly amid the disappointments; according to
one Georgia woman, most public facilities in Marietta had integrated even before the 1964 Civil Rights Act passed.[72]

After 1965, the FOC's initiatives became less thematically consistent as
Tilly tried to focus on current dynamic civil rights activities. The tenor of the
civil rights movement had changed dramatically since the 1960 student-led sit-
ins. The maternal and domestic themes that had characterized the 1950s FOC
no longer seemed effective or relevant. Tilly struggled to keep her organization
vital in the face of increasingly militant black and white activism.[73] Even within
the SRC, younger, more radical activists perceived Tilly and her FOC as maternalistic, obsolete, and unnecessarily utilizing scarce funds.[74] Yet she clung
resolutely to the belief that the FOC still played a vital role in changing racial
attitudes and therefore continued to hold annual meetings and attend state-
level workshops. In the late 1960s, many of those who attended the meetings
did so largely out of their devotion to and respect for Tilly.[75] By 1968, however,
Dorothy Tilly was eighty-five years old, seriously ill, and barely able to attend
the annual meeting. In 1969, her son, Eben, placed her in a nursing home
where she died in 1970.[76] After she entered the nursing home, the FOC died
suddenly and silently, proving not only that Dorothy Tilly was its driving force,
but also that in the light of more radical civil rights activism, it had outlived its
effectiveness.

A Qualified Success

When viewed from the perspective of the greater civil rights movement, the
FOC's activism may appear benign, naïve, and even patronizing. Admittedly,
FOC activists were not radical. Adopting the vision of their optimistic leader,
Dorothy Tilly, they worked from within local, often troubled institutions to

effect change slowly rather than force it. The FOC was in many ways successful, yet its story must be considered with an awareness and sensitivity to both
its limitations and its strengths.

The FOC's major challenges included recruiting members, working within
self-imposed boundaries, and overcoming the obstacles it encountered in a
dynamic civil rights movement. Its controversial objective—preparing white
southerners for desegregation in an openly hostile environment—rendered
FOC membership practically untenable for most whites, who were unwilling
to accept blacks as social equals. Even moderates risked ostracism if they
openly expressed their political views. Tilly thus had to recruit southern white
women who were willing to work for change without alienating others who
were not. She relied on her network to nominate the "right" women to attend
annual meetings and generate interest at the local level. FOC members agreed
in 1956 to narrow their focus to building "lines of communication among like-
minded people,"[77] because FOC efforts to reach the more conservative whites
had failed.

FOC membership across the South, estimated to be approximately four
thousand at its peak, was significantly lower than that of its predecessor, the
ASWPL, which at its zenith had approximately forty thousand members.[78]
Although all twelve southern states were represented in this number, Tilly admitted in 1950 that FOC membership was "not moving quite as fast, I think, as
any of us would wish."[79] The ASWPL's larger membership is understandable.
It had a narrow mission—to end lynching—while the FOC's purpose challenged the very bedrock of segregation on which white supremacy stood. In
the eyes of many of its members, the ASWPL's mission was simply a matter of
right versus wrong, and as southern Christian women they could easily defend
their stance against murder. The FOC's objectives were less straightforward
and much more threatening. Advocating desegregation and civil rights for African Americans implied accepting blacks as social equals, a much more com-
plicated and far less popular issue.

The elitist attitude exhibited by some FOC members, who viewed themselves as morally superior to other white southerners, might also have discouraged potential converts. Georgia activist Loretta Chappell, for example, dis-
dainfully described her "friends" who, although "nice" people and "good
church members," were nevertheless "so abysmally obtuse . . . in regard to the
real feelings of others."[80] Although these women's intentions were sincere and
their commitment was evident, their arrogance undoubtedly annoyed other
whites and thus negatively affected FOC membership and influence.

A more obvious recruiting deterrent was the danger inherent in civil rights activism. Following Tilly's PCCR service, the Ku Klux Klan threatened to bomb her Atlanta home. She also received harassing telephone calls (to disarm the perpetrators, she played a recording of the Lord's Prayer into the telephone).[81] In the minds of her attackers, she had crossed the line of acceptable behavior for a white southern lady and consequently deserved no protection. To save FOC members from a similar fate, Tilly discouraged publicity, knowing that it would attract danger, thwart recruitment, and detract from the organization's mission.[82] Her vision held that the FOC should work quietly; in doing so, it could make unimpeded progress.[83] Despite precautions against publicity, a Montgomery newspaper reporter showcased Alabama's state FOC meeting in a news article, identifying members and listing their vehicle license plate numbers. Many attendees subsequently received anonymous threatening telephone calls and hate mail.[84] The Montgomery FOC members reacted by temporarily ceasing FOC activities. Conditional commitment to civil rights activism also resonated in the words of Mississippi FOC member Anne Hunt Cunningham, who wrote Tilly in 1955 explaining why no Mississippians attended the annual FOC meeting:

> No, I feel positive now that for the present, we can not afford to have anyone travel through or hold meetings in the conference.... It's what goes on under cover [sic].... What we have won is won. But we can not afford to loose [sic] it by feeding the fires of anger in our midst. Life and property will be destroyed and I can't take that responsibility.[85]

Cunningham, like the Montgomery FOC members, demonstrated a tentative willingness to work for civil rights, reserving her right as a white woman to retreat from the cause when threatened. The pragmatic Tilly, who empathized, nevertheless reminded the Mississippi women of their duty: "I fully understand the difficulties you are facing," she responded, ". . . but I do hope it will be possible for United Church Women to be the interpreters of the Supreme Court decision, to the church women at least."[86]

Although troubled by the equivocations, Tilly and other SRC employees had to recognize these traits in some FOC members. In a 1956 grant application, SRC executive director George Mitchell conceded that FOC members' convictions varied: "some are timid, some are fluttery, some are halting in public appearance. But some are brave and deeply possessed of religion and purpose to make their religion bring consequences."[87] Most FOC members were housewives and mothers interested in improving society for their children's sake, not in creating and partaking in dangerous activities. Tilly knew that some FOC members would desert if pushed beyond their comfort level, but she accepted this limitation and deliberately—not naïvely—proceeded cautiously.

In the 1960s, with many civil rights activists demanding immediate social, political, and economic equality, organizations like the FOC had little room to practice gradualism and work on individual conversions. Tilly struggled unsuccessfully to plan proactive strategies and thus began reacting to civil rights issues, especially in the years 1961, 1962, and 1965–68, adjusting the FOC's focus almost annually. Surprisingly, FOC members did not address the discontinuity between annual themes until the 1968 conference, when they established follow-up agenda items for the 1969 meeting.[88] Ironically, this introspection came at what was to be the last annual conference.

While the FOC did have some limitations, when placed in the context of its time, its subtle victories were historically significant. Tilly designed the annual FOC meetings so they would have a far-reaching personal impact. During each two-day affair, white and black women met, ate, prayed, and learned together. Tilly's own development as an activist suggests just how important such individual cross-racial experiences could be in changing attitudes. For many members, the FOC conference was their first exposure to members of the other race as equals in a public, social setting. Black and white women attendees buzzed exuberantly between sessions, resembling "middle-aged school girls with their arms full of packets of material, earnestly conferring over their coffee about their panels or workshops."[89] The attendees drew inspiration for the daunting task awaiting them on their return home. One member's husband recalled the positive effect FOC meetings had on his wife: "Mary would go to Atlanta to the Fellowship once a year and be so restored that she was strengthened for another year at home. She came back another woman."[90]

Many participants roomed together, and after spending all day in their official capacity, they let down their guard at night, relating to each other not as members of different races but as southern mothers and wives facing similar concerns in the fight against racism. During one late-night gathering, a white woman shared the heartbreak she felt after her daughter was uninvited to a friend's birthday party because of her own FOC activities. Another admitted lying to her "segregationist" husband: "[I] didn't dare tell him where I was coming and didn't even give my telephone number, just said I was going to Atlanta to a church meeting."[91] African American women also shared their views and experiences; one poignantly described her difficulty in explaining to her northern granddaughter, who wanted desperately to try "colored" water, why she should not drink it.[92] FOC meetings fostered an environment where participants created a concerned community of mothers and wives who, across the color line, envisioned a brighter future for all citizens.

Lastly, the churchwomen's individual acts of dissent taken collectively demonstrate the FOC's efficacy and influence. Tilly's voluminous correspondence with FOC members reflects the triumphs and frustrations the women shared. Some of the FOC's most determined examples of dissent originated from one of the South's most troubled states, Mississippi. Examples include Jackson, Mississippi, members who, against obstacles, organized a biracial Prayer Fellowship in 1961. Mississippi member Ruth Beittel wrote Tilly to report her voter registration and school desegregation activities.[93] Furthermore, the FOC had been instrumental in forcing the resignation of the local United Church Women president after discovering her affiliation with the local White Citizens' Council.[94] FOC members in other states devised similar attacks on the white resistance by identifying those associated with White Citizens' Councils and then boycotting their businesses. At age seventy-six, Tilly drove around Georgia interviewing locals to determine the extent of the resistance to integration.[95]

FOC members continued challenging Jim Crow well into the 1960s. In 1965, for example, Atlantan Mary Williamson witnessed blatant discrimination at Atlanta's prestigious Piedmont Driving Club. She and her husband learned during a club event that a black guest had been refused admittance, and without hesitation they abruptly left the dinner.[96] When Williamson publicly repudiated discrimination, she epitomized Tilly's mission for the FOC—to set an example simply by doing the right thing. Perhaps the FOC's greatest and most enduring impact was that it made apathy toward Jim Crow practices much more difficult for whites, inducing women to change their attitudes and, at the grassroots level, encouraging others to do likewise.

FOC members consistently used unobtrusive tactics, leveraging their roles as wives and mothers and their perceived moral superiority as Christians to set an example. Dorothy Tilly believed this gendered approach to promoting more tolerance across the color line would accelerate social change in a nonthreatening manner. Through the efforts of FOC members, courts, families, and communities became more tolerant over time, acting more responsibly and slowly accepting desegregation. The influence of these housewives and mothers meant that Dorothy Tilly and the churchwomen, despite obstacles, significantly contributed to changing deep-seated biases held by many white southerners within less than a generation.

Conclusion

This study of Dorothy Tilly's career and the Fellowship of the Concerned adds to the growing civil rights movement's historiography, clearly demonstrating that privileged southern white women made significant contributions to the fight for racial equality. While these contributions may have varied in style and substance, they should not be underestimated. Southern white women reacted to racial inequality in the South in diverse ways. Their activism illuminates the relevance of individual women reformers such as Dorothy Tilly as well as the significance of women's religious organizations. These women, through their permanent liaisons and personal friendships, fostered an enduring good-old-girl community that successfully countered the provincial ideas held by many white southerners, thereby providing a continuum of increasing activism and influence in an extremely hostile environment.

Dorothy Tilly's example provides new insights into the vexing problems faced by those confronting racism today, when the ideas are less overt but equally pernicious. Historian Fred Hobson defines "racial conversion" as an experience by which "willing participants in a harsh, segregated society confess racial wrongdoings and are 'converted' in varying degrees, from racism to something approaching racial enlightenment."[97] His term applies mostly to a rare breed of southern liberals such as Lillian Smith. Most southern liberals who repudiated segregation did so gradually, more as a racial transition than a conversion. Dorothy Tilly was one such southerner who cultivated her increasingly liberal racial views over time through her own activist experiences and Christian faith, surrounding herself with people who encouraged one another to expand their racial attitudes.

Tilly recognized the inherently flawed assumption that laws would alter people's attitudes. She knew her South: federal legislation designed to enforce civil rights had historically been rejected and had infuriated many white southern conservatives. Her cautionary words to the PCCR foreshadowed the 1948 Dixiecrat defection and the massive white resistance that followed the two *Brown* decisions.[98] The fact that her predictions proved accurate only reinforced her commitment to a softer but nevertheless effective methodology of combating racism.

Dorothy Tilly's approach to civil rights—utilizing women to effect social change—was hardly innovative; women have long been regarded as the vanguards of social reform. However, when placed in historical context, Tilly's approach appears quite visionary. Her enlistment of southern mothers to raise more tolerant children addressed not only the present but also, and more important, the future. Clearly, her concept of teaching the next generation tolerance and acceptance resulted in a better society for all. Tilly's mission was straightforward and unwavering: as a privileged southern Christian woman, she had a duty to improve society, not with a clamor but quietly, leading by example so that others could embrace more tolerant attitudes toward African Americans. Her soft-pedaled approach, adopted by the unobtrusive FOC, succeeded in changing some conservative southern attitudes, promoting tolerance, and achieving lasting social change across the color line.

Notes

I would like to thank Margaret Holbrook, Catherine Hettrich, Nancy Carper, Karen Roegiers, Linda Hayes, and Chuck and Kathy Riehm, who offered assistance during my research trips. I am also grateful to the advisers, colleagues, and readers who reviewed various drafts of this essay: Michelle Brattain, Jacqueline Rouse, Cliff Kuhn, Christine Lutz, Anne Brophy, Robert Woodrum, Peter McDade, Patty Coury, Stanley Harrold, Randall M. Miller, Nancy Hewitt, and one anonymous reader. I must also thank Joan Browning, who, through a chance meeting at Emory University in February 2001, provided an introduction to Gail Murray. I owe a special debt of gratitude to Gail Murray and to my husband, Charles Riehm, who offered not only a great deal of patience but also unflagging support in helping me complete this project.

1. Letter from M. A. Wright to George S. Mitchell, August 24, 1955, Dorothy Tilly Papers, Robert W. Woodruff Library, Special Collections Department, Emory University, Atlanta, Georgia, box 2, folder 3 [hereinafter Tilly Papers, Emory University].

2. Notes from "Fellowship of the Concerned: Workshop of Southern Church Women, September 8–9, 1949, Atlanta"; Dorothy Tilly to Eleanor Roosevelt, September 14, 1949, Southern Regional Council Papers, Robert W. Woodruff Library, Atlanta University Center, Archives Department, reel 194 [hereinafter SRC Papers].

3. Pledge from "Fellowship of the Concerned: Workshop of Southern Church Women, September 8–9, 1949," SRC Papers, reel 194.

4. Arnold Shankman, "Dorothy Tilly and the Fellowship of the Concerned," in *From the Old South to the New: Essays on the Transitional South,* ed. Walter Fraser Jr. and Winfred B. Moore Jr. (Westport, Conn.: Greenwood Press, 1981), 244.

5. Notes from "Fellowship of the Concerned: Workshop of Southern Church Women, September 8–9, 1949," SRC Papers, reel 194.

6. Virginia Shadron, "Out of Our Homes: The Women's Rights Movement in the Methodist Episcopal Church, South: 1890–1918" (master's thesis, Emory University, 1976), 12–13.

7. Arnold Shankman, "Dorothy Tilly," in *Notable American Women: The Modern*

Period, a Biographical Dictionary, ed. Barbara Sicherman and Carol Hurd Green (Cambridge: Belknap Press of Harvard University Press, 1980), 690.

8. Shankman, "Dorothy Tilly and the Fellowship of the Concerned," 241; Dorothy Tilly, "Background," Tilly Papers, Emory University, box 1, folder 9.

9. Dorothy Tilly, *Why Are You Fearful?* Fellowship of the Concerned pamphlet, 1958, Dorothy Rogers Tilly Papers, Archives and Special Collections, Dacus Library, Winthrop University, box 1, folder 11 [hereinafter Tilly Papers, Winthrop University].

10. Ruth A. Collins, "We Are the Inheritors," in *Response: United Methodist Women,* July–August 1971, 30, Tilly Papers, Emory University, box 2, folder 4.

11. Shadron, "Out of Our Homes," 12–13. Shadron argues that prominent Methodist women sought higher education because it would provide the background necessary to fulfill their accepted public roles; Shankman, "Dorothy Tilly and the Fellowship of the Concerned," 241.

12. Collins, "We Are the Inheritors," 30.

13. Deborah Raemars, "Dorothy Tilly," in *Historic Georgia Mothers, 1776–1976,* comp. Janette Barber (Atlanta: Stern Printing, 1976), 65; Arnold Shankman, Biographical Checklist on Dorothy Tilly, 1978, Tilly Papers, Winthrop University, box 1, folder 2; Arnold Shankman, "Dorothy Tilly, Civil Rights, and the Methodist Church," *Methodist History* 18 (January 1980): 96.

14. Leslie Dunbar, telephone interview with the author, not transcribed, Norcross, Georgia, September 2001, in author's possession.

15. Shankman, "Dorothy Tilly, Civil Rights, and the Methodist Church," 96.

16. Ibid., 96–97.

17. Alice G. Knotts, *Fellowship of Love: Methodist Women Changing American Racial Attitudes, 1920–1968* (Nashville: Abingdon Press, 1996), 43.

18. Shankman, "Dorothy Tilly, Civil Rights, and the Methodist Church," 97.

19. Knotts, *Fellowship of Love,* 81, 261–63; Shankman, "Dorothy Tilly," *Notable American Women,* 691.

20. Knotts, *Fellowship of Love,* 261–62.

21. Ibid., 261–63; Thelma Stevens to Arnold Shankman, n.d., Tilly Papers, Winthrop University, box 1, folder 1.

22. Knotts, *Fellowship of Love,* 100.

23. Ibid., 261–64. Knotts describes a method utilized by some Methodist women reformers to encourage social transformation among those within their network.

24. Will Alexander to Carrie Johnson, May 2, 1922, Commission on Interracial Cooperation Papers, Robert W. Woodruff Library, Archives Department, Atlanta University Center, reel 1.

25. Dewey W. Grantham, *Southern Progressivism: The Reconciliation of Progress and Tradition* (Knoxville: University of Tennessee Press, 1983), 413.

26. Knotts, *Fellowship of Love,* 68.

27. Jacquelyn Dowd Hall, *Revolt against Chivalry: Jessie Daniel Ames and the Women's Campaign against Lynching* (New York: Columbia University Press, 1993),

217; Ames to Tilly, October 14, 1931, Association of Southern Women for the Prevention of Lynching Papers, Robert W. Woodruff Library, Archives Department, Atlanta University Center, reel 1.

28. Stevens to Shankman, Tilly Papers, Winthrop University, box 1, folder 1.

29. Kathryn L. Nasstrom, *Everybody's Grandmother and Nobody's Fool: Frances Freeborn Pauley and the Struggle for Social Justice* (Ithaca: Cornell University Press, 2000), 156–57. Nasstrom acknowledges that Tilly served as a mentor to Pauley during the Depression years.

30. Morton Sosna, *In Search of the Silent South* (New York: Columbia University Press, 1977), 18–19, 166–67. For more on the shift of American and southern liberalism, see Numan V. Bartley, *The New South, 1945–1980* (Baton Rouge: Louisiana State University Press, 1995).

31. Margaret Long, "Mrs. Dorothy Tilly: A Memoir," *New South* 25.2 (1970): 44.

32. Collins, "We Are the Inheritors," 31.

33. Nasstrom, *Everybody's Grandmother,* 149.

34. Shankman, "Dorothy Tilly, Civil Rights, and the Methodist Church," 101.

35. John Egerton, *Speak Now against the Day: The Generation before the Civil Rights Movement in the South* (New York: Knopf, 1994), 308–12.

36. Knotts, *Fellowship of Love,* 203, 211.

37. Tilly to Martha Bart, December 1, 1954, SRC Papers, reel 194.

38. Long, "Mrs. Dorothy Tilly," 46.

39. For more on the Columbia, Tennessee, incident, see, for example, Gail Williams O'Brien, *The Color of the Law: Race, Violence, and Justice in the Post World War II South* (Chapel Hill: University of North Carolina Press, 1999).

40. William C. Berman, *The Politics of Civil Rights in the Truman Administration* (Columbus: Ohio State University Press, 1970), 52.

41. Barton J. Bernstein, "The Ambiguous Legacy: The Truman Administration and Civil Rights," in *Politics and Policies of the Truman Administration,* ed. Barton J. Bernstein (Chicago: Quadrangle Books, 1970), 277–78; Berman, *The Politics of Civil Rights,* 55–56, 67–70.

42. Knotts, *Fellowship of Love,* 168.

43. Ibid., 169.

44. Franklin Acker, "Around the Town," *Independent,* November 11, 1947, Tilly Papers, Emory University, box 2, folder 5; Egerton, *Speak Now against the Day,* 563; Sarah Cunningham, "A Woman beyond Her Times," *Church Woman: An Interdenominational Magazine,* December 1966, 11, Tilly Papers, Emory University, box 2, folder 4; Helena Huntington Smith, "Mrs. Tilly's Crusade," *Collier's,* December 30, 1950, 67, Tilly Papers, Emory University, box 2, folder 4.

45. Anonymous letter to "The Two Southern Residents of the Civil Rights (?) Committee," mailed on February 8, 1948, Tilly Papers, Emory University, box 1, folder 4.

46. Long, "Mrs. Dorothy Tilly," 45.

47. Ibid., 44.

48. Tilly as quoted in Cunningham, "A Woman beyond Her Times," 7–8.

49. George S. Mitchell to Tilly, January 16, 1956, SRC Papers, reel 194.

50. Henry Lesesne, "The Southern Press and the Negro: Southern Regional Council Finds Discriminatory Treatment in News Disappearing," *New York Herald Tribune,* July 8, 1950.

51. Cunningham, "A Woman beyond Her Times," 9; Eliza Heard, "Who Remembers Willie," *New South* (July–August 1964): 3, Tilly Papers, Winthrop University, box 2, folder 4; Tilly to Ruby Hurley, October 24, 1956, SRC Papers, reel 194; "Justice Weighed in the Balance—Gleanings of Workshop—Fellowship of the Concerned, November 15–16, 1960," SRC Papers, reel 196; Tilly to Grace Towns Hamilton, October 26, 1956; and Tilly to Hurley, September 11, 1957, SRC Papers, reel 194; Tilly to Hurley, March 7, 1967; and Tilly to Mrs. Martin Luther King Jr., March 8, 1967, SRC Papers, reel 200; Mrs. Isabel Goldthwait to Tilly, July 18, 1955; and Dorothy C. Tomlin, "Floridians Meet to Discuss Better Relations," *St. Petersburg Times,* September 24, 1955, SRC Papers, reel 194.

52. George S. Mitchell to Lindsley F. Kimball, June 12, 1956, SRC Papers, reel 194.

53. Mrs. Candler Tatum to Tilly, March 1, 1955; and Mrs. C. F. Goldthwait to Tilly, February 27, 1955, SRC Papers, reel 194.

54. See, for example, Heard, "Who Remembers Willie"; "Gleanings from the Workshop of the Fellowship of the Concerned," SRC Papers, reel 194.

55. Smith, "Mrs. Tilly's Crusade," 67.

56. Tilly to Mrs. J. S. Van Winkle, May 31, 1950, SRC Papers, reel 194; Tilly, "Know Your Courts as Your Schools," *World Outlook,* 33, Tilly Papers, Emory University, box 1, folder 9.

57. Smith, "Mrs. Tilly's Crusade," 29.

58. Henry Lesesne, "The South Strikes at Inequality," *New York Herald Tribune,* April 15, 1950; Tilly to Reverend Francis J. Burkley, January 29, 1958, SRC Papers, reel 194.

59. "Report to the Board of Directors of the Southern Regional Council for the Period January 1 to October 1, 1952," Glenn Rainey Papers, Robert W. Woodruff Library, Special Collections Department, Emory University, box 19, folder 9.

60. Tilly to the Conference and District Secretaries of Christian Social Relations, July 31, 1953, SRC Papers, reel 194.

61. Susan McGrath Nelson, "Association of Southern Women for the Prevention of Lynching and the Fellowship of the Concerned and Racial Politics" (master's thesis, Emory University, 1982), 95.

62. Noreen Tatum, "What Shall I Do about Desegregation? Before You Decide, THINK ON THESE THINGS," February 1955 FOC meeting, SRC Papers, reel 194.

63. Noreen Tatum to Tilly, 1955, SRC Papers, reel 194.

64. Fellowship of the Concerned Opening Session Meeting Minutes, February 24, 1955, SRC Papers, reel 194 [hereinafter FOC meeting, minutes]; Nelson, "Association of Southern Women for the Prevention," 115.

65. Tilly to Esther Stamats, December 11, 1956, SRC Papers, reel 194.

66. "Report of Mrs. M. E. Tilly—1st quarter, 1956," Tilly Papers, Emory University, box 1, folder 1; Shankman, "Dorothy Tilly and the Fellowship of the Concerned," 245.

67. FOC meeting, minutes, February 1955, SRC Papers, reel 194.

68. Pearl C. Hummel to Tilly, October 23, 1956, SRC Papers, reel 194.

69. Nelson, "Association of Southern Women for the Prevention," 101–2.

70. "Church Leader Called for JFK's Conference," *Herald* (Sharon, Penn.), July 10, 1963, Tilly Papers, Emory University, box 2, folder 6.

71. Tilly, "You of the 1964 Workshop of the FOC," January 14, 1965, SRC Papers, reel 199.

72. Reports of the "Study of the Cities" questionnaire, September 29, 1965, SRC Papers, reel 199.

73. For more on the student sit-ins and the more radical responses of the civil rights movement in the 1960s, see Clayborne Carson, *In Struggle: SNCC and the Black Awakening of the 1960s* (Cambridge: Harvard University Press, 1981); or John Lewis and Michael D'Orso, *Walking with the Wind: A Memoir of the Movement* (San Diego: Harcourt Brace, 1999).

74. Shankman, "Dorothy Tilly and the Fellowship of the Concerned," 248; Long, "Mrs. Dorothy Tilly," 47.

75. Leslie Dunbar, telephone interview with the author, not transcribed, Norcross, Georgia, January 2000, in author's possession.

76. Shankman, "Dorothy Tilly and the Fellowship of the Concerned," 249.

77. Fellowship of the Concerned Workshop notes, 1956, SRC Papers, reel 194.

78. Shankman, "Dorothy Tilly and the Fellowship of the Concerned," 244.

79. Tilly to Mrs. J. S. Van Winkle, May 31, 1950, SRC Papers, reel 194.

80. Loretta Chappell to Tilly, February 25, 1964, SRC Papers, reel 199.

81. Shankman, "Dorothy Tilly," *Notable American Women*, 692; Long, "Mrs. Dorothy Tilly," 45.

82. F. W. Wolsey, "Georgia's Apprehensive Liberals," *Louisville Courier Journal*, February 19, 1967, 18, Leslie Dunbar Papers, Robert W. Woodruff Library, Special Collections Department, Emory University, box 2; Tilly to Laura B. McCray, April 27, 1959, SRC Papers, reel 194.

83. Mrs. C. R. (Elizabeth) Noble to Tilly, January 14, 1955; Tilly to Mrs. Laura B. McCray, April 27, 1959, SRC Papers, reel 194.

84. C. G. Gomillion to Tilly, January 13, 1959; Dr. Dow Kirkpatrick to Mr. M. G. Lowman, January 19, 1959; W. Wilson White to Tilly, received February 4, 1959; and Tilly to Kirkpatrick, February 3, 1959, SRC Papers, reel 194; Nelson, "Association of Southern Women for the Prevention," 114.

85. Anne Hunt Cunningham to Tilly, January 21, 1955, SRC Papers, reel 194.

86. Tilly to Mrs. C. R. Noble, March 24, 1955, SRC Papers, reel 194.

87. "Application for Funds," George S. Mitchell, Executive Director, SRC, 1955–56, SRC Papers, reel 194.

88. "Report of the Workshop of the Fellowship of the Concerned of the Southern Regional Council," October 23–24, 1968, SRC Papers, reel 200.

89. Heard, "Who Remembers Willie," 3.

90. Long, "Mrs. Dorothy Tilly," 50–51.

91. Heard, "Who Remembers Willie," 5.

92. Ibid., 4.

93. Mary Williamson to Tilly, January 29, 1965, SRC Papers, reel 199; Jane M. Schutt to Tilly, March 8, 1964; and Ruth Beittel to Tilly, February 25, 1964, SRC Papers, reel 199.

94. Tilly to Mrs. Stanley Wilson, April 18, 1958; and Tilly to Mrs. J. A. Burt, April 18, 1958, SRC Papers, reel 194.

95. Fellowship of the Concerned Workshop notes, 1956; Tilly to Dudley Ward, December 13, 1956, SRC Papers, reel 194.

96. Williamson to Tilly, January 29, 1965, SRC Papers, reel 199.

97. Fred Hobson, *But Now I See: The White Southern Racial Conversion Narrative* (Baton Rouge: Louisiana State University Press, 1999), 1–2.

98. For more on the Dixiecrats, see Kari Frederickson, *The Dixiecrat Revolt and the End of the Solid South: 1932–1968* (Chapel Hill: University of North Carolina Press, 2001); for more on the massive resistance movement, see Michael J. Klarman, "How *Brown* Changed Race Relations: The Backlash Thesis," *Journal of American History* 81 (June 1994): 81–116.

chapter 2

Crusaders and Clubwomen

Alice Norwood Spearman Wright and Her Women's Network

MARCIA G. SYNNOTT

Alice Norwood Spearman at Cheraw State Park, South Carolina, in 1963 arguing for the state to reopen the state parks, which it had closed rather than desegregate them. Courtesy of Kevin Mackey, *Cheraw Chronicle,* September 19, 1963.

IN MARCH 1963, Margaret McCulloch, a human and community relations consultant in Memphis, Tennessee, wrote Paul Rilling, the Southern Regional Council's director of field services, congratulating "all of you in the manner of the reception of [Harvey] Gantt's entry into Clemson" College two months earlier. Invited to speak at the November 1962 annual meeting, McCulloch in turn congratulated "both South Carolina & your affiliated S.C. Council on Human Relations on having such a fine worker as Mrs. Alice Spearman—she has such a rare combination of qualities of mind & training, of spirit & skills." These qualities served Spearman exceptionally well in building her network of white women activists.[1]

By January 1963, progress had indeed occurred in South Carolina's race relations: a historically white college had admitted its first African American student. Although most white South Carolinians remained reluctant to abandon segregation, a tiny minority of liberal whites advocated equal rights, the equal protection of the laws, and a decent livelihood for all. Among them was the dedicated and peripatetic Alice Buck Norwood Spearman (1902–1989). With her network of white women activists, Spearman served as an intergenerational bridge between nineteenth-century women reformers, such as the suffragists, and the student civil rights activists of the 1960s.[2]

Spearman's generation of activists, motivated by the belief that privileges and advantages brought responsibilities, did not reject their white identity, but they did push against its socially constructed limits. Women of this generation rarely risked serious injury or death for their activities, but by dissenting from traditional white racial attitudes they undermined conformity to the ideal of southern white womanhood. Often working sixteen to eighteen hours a day, Spearman and other white women activists willingly endured social ostracism for their causes.

Alice Spearman's life can best be illuminated by using the model of feminist biography, which foregrounds the interplay between gender and personal relationships and expands the meaning of women's public role. Noteworthy women rarely fit the mold of biographies typically written about famous men because their accomplishments often occurred in unexpected and sometimes unpublicized areas. In contrast to political leaders, who made public statements and sought to settle controversial issues by negotiating politically acceptable compromises, Spearman chose not to publicly assert leadership and acquiesced in the choice of a man as president of South Carolina Council on Human Relations (CHR). She led by networking, often behind the scenes, and by forging "a community of concern" with black and white people of goodwill. Spearman was "a visionary" with a strong "will to persevere," but administration was not "her forte," observed Rev. Fred M. Reese Jr., president of the South Carolina CHR in the 1960s. The methods she used to change stereotypical racial attitudes and prejudices included moral persuasion, education through workshops, personal consensus building, and grassroots recruitment techniques. To make an "invisible decision maker" like Alice Spearman part of the historical record is the challenge of a feminist biographer.[3]

Spearman felt that women could be most effective as reformers if they drew on their intuition and sensitivity to others while insisting on their legal equality with men. But equality did not mean trying "to compete, make money, become famous, exercise power," and be successful like men, Spearman said in 1973 when she received the Frank Porter Graham Civil Liberties Award in Chapel Hill, North Carolina. In her acceptance speech, "People on the March," she urged women to initiate political, economic, and social changes by using their "skill in human relations" and "qualities of persistence, patience and compassion." Although white males had "designed, directed and dominated" institutional structures in the United States, "*Blacks* and *Women*" were, Spearman emphasized, "in the vanguard of those pressing for change *now*."[4]

At every stage of her life, Spearman received significant support from others, women and men. Some were relatives; others were mentors, friends, and colleagues. Relationships with others helped define Spearman's sense of self and commitment to social justice. In turn, she learned to hone her skill in working through others to achieve her personal and professional goals. From her banker father, Samuel Wilkins Norwood, Spearman learned self-discipline and a work ethic. Her mother, Albertine Buck Norwood, nurtured her competitiveness and, indirectly, her feminism. The young Spearman was occasionally chastised for acting independently of parental instructions, yet she also learned from her childhood gender conditioning to use the demeanor of a southern lady, and on occasion to flirt, to get her way. Although there were tensions between the socially conservative parents and the young Spearman, they lived together on affectionate terms.[5]

Spearman developed her liberal views on race relations while attending Converse College in Spartanburg, South Carolina, where she became a student government leader and an activist in the Young Women's Christian Association (YWCA). A Baptist and a liberal on race relations, Spearman was drawn to the Student Division of YWCA, whose members felt relatively free to talk about racial prejudice and engage in social activism because the campus organization was funded by the YWCA's national board. Perhaps Spearman's most influential mentor in college was the somewhat older Lois MacDonald, the daughter of an Associated Reformed Presbyterian minister, who had earned a master's degree in comparative literature from Columbia University and served as YWCA branch secretary at the North Carolina College for Women in Greensboro. During the summer of 1922, when Spearman was a student-in-industry in the YWCA program in Atlanta, she and MacDonald worked at the Fulton Bag and Cotton Mill and shared a bedbug-infested room and indigestible food in a church home for girls. They learned firsthand about the hard lives of mill women, an experience Spearman never forgot. Later, MacDonald studied at the London School of Economics; earned her doctorate at New York University, where she subsequently taught economics; and published her dissertation on southern mill villages. MacDonald's "left-wing Socialist," if not communist, sympathies deepened the younger woman's concern for the economically and socially disadvantaged, a concern Spearman would demonstrate as a relief administrator in the 1930s.[6]

After graduating from Converse with a bachelor of arts degree in 1923, Spearman taught school in South Carolina. In 1926, she moved to New York City, where she earned a master's degree in religious education at Columbia Teachers' College and took courses at Union Theological Seminary. She also enrolled at the resident YWCA National Training School, taking courses on "The Women's Movement" and "Techniques for Working with Industrial Women." Well prepared for adult education work, Spearman then joined the Germantown YWCA in Philadelphia, Pennsylvania. In 1930, she began a three-year journey around the world and attended conferences in England, the Soviet Union, India, China, and Japan. Meeting cultured people of different races and teaching school in the Philippines and China helped Spearman develop a cosmopolitan outlook. By the time she returned home in 1932, her father had died after losing most of his assets in the Great Depression, although enough remained to take care of her mother.[7]

Family connections helped Spearman become the first South Carolina woman appointed to administer a county emergency relief program. During the 1934 United Textile Workers' strike, she set up relief programs in Horsecreek Valley, between Aiken, South Carolina, and Augusta, Georgia. Although she openly expressed sympathy for the strikers, she was not fired because of her family's prominence. Spearman was promoted to district relief supervisor and soon afterward became state supervisor of education for federal programs in adult and worker education. She won the confidence of workers and those on relief by adopting an egalitarian manner instead of the "maternalist" attitude of many Progressive era reformers, who maintained class distinctions. Spearman also served on the advisory committee of the Southern Summer School for Women Workers in Industry, which included such other liberal reformers as Will Alexander, director of the Commission on Interracial Cooperation (CIC) in Atlanta; Frank Porter Graham, president of the recently consolidated University of North Carolina; and her friend Lois MacDonald. In November 1936, she married Eugene H. Spearman and moved to his Newberry farm; their son, Eugene Jr., was born in 1937.[8]

As Spearman matured and began her career in human relations, she networked with many white and African American women who provided personal mentoring and emotional and moral support. While living in Newberry she joined the South Carolina CIC, and in 1943 she helped to organize its successor, the South Carolina Division of the Atlanta-based Southern Regional Council. For a time, she was the South Carolina Division's minimally paid executive secretary. But Spearman again needed full-time employment and moved to Columbia in 1951, where her son could attend better schools and her husband would be near the Veterans' Administration hospital (he died of lung cancer in 1962). On the strong recommendation of Eunice Temple Ford (Mrs. T. B.) Stackhouse, Spearman was hired as executive secretary of the South Carolina Federation of Women's Clubs and as associate editor of their publication, the *Clubwoman*. As part of her salary, Spearman and her family were provided a large upstairs apartment at the federation's headquarters, the home that Eunice Stackhouse's public-spirited banker husband, Thomas Bascom Stackhouse, had bequeathed to the organization.[9]

Stackhouse, called "the fairy godmother of the Federation," was "definitely a pioneer," acknowledged Spearman. A Baptist pastor's daughter and family friend, Stackhouse had earned a bachelor of arts degree with honors from Limestone College with tuition expenses paid for by Spearman's father. She later earned bachelor of philosophy and master of arts degrees from the University of Chicago. Stackhouse taught at Limestone College and served as dean of the faculty until her marriage in 1932. In 1942, because of her stature as an educator and a clubwoman, Governor Richard M. Jefferies appointed Stackhouse to be the first woman to serve on the South Carolina Probation, Pardon and Parole Board. Progressive on race relations, she organized a women's club for black women and believed that the racial problem was "fundamentally more a question of culture than . . . of color." In 1955, Stackhouse wrote a letter to the *Columbia (S.C.) State* in which she recalled sharing a table in the U.S. Justice Department's cafeteria with the black woman president of the New Jersey Parent-Teacher Association while both were attending Attorney General Thomas Clark's 1946 panel on preventing juvenile delinquency. It felt "no different," Stackhouse reported, than eating with a white woman, since they were "both professional women, interested in the same questions." Recognition of common interests also led Stackhouse to generously turn her dining room into a conference room for biracial meetings when the South Carolina Citizens Committee on Children and Youth was organized in 1947. Spearman respected Stackhouse for being "real progressive for a woman of her age" and benefited from the older woman's more centrist views on what could be accomplished in South Carolina. Stackhouse was also one of those who recommended Spearman for the position of full-time executive director of the South Carolina Council on Human Relations, the new name for the South Carolina Division of the SRC. Spearman held this position, partly funded through the Southern Regional Council, from October 1954 until September 1, 1967, years longer than any other SRC state council director.[10]

Spearman endeavored to develop programs that would attract white clubwomen and civic leaders to the South Carolina CHR by appealing to their interest in "new experiences" and their "strong sense of social responsibility." Her programs used some of the tactics—forums, workshops, and networking—of such older white women activists as Clelia (Mrs. C. P) McGowan of Charleston, former state chair of the South Carolina CIC; and Jessie Daniel Ames, founder of the Association of Southern Women for the Prevention of Lynching and CIC director of women's work and then of field work.[11]

Spearman also sought advice from an older group of women friends on the board of directors of the South Carolina CHR and tested her innovative ideas against their practical experience. In addition to Eunice Stackhouse, these advisers were Mary E. Frayser, Dr. Wil Lou Gray, Adele Johnston Minahan, and Rebecca C. Reid, all unmarried career women. Frayser had earned a bachelor of science degree from Columbia University and had held a series of teaching and state agency positions in Georgia, South Carolina, and Virginia. In 1926, she was appointed the home economist for Clemson and Winthrop Colleges and charged with coordinating their research. Frayser, who joined the Virginia suffrage movement in 1908, helped to establish the South Carolina Conference on the Status of Women in 1944, following her participation in the White House Conference on the Status of Women. Active in the South Carolina Federation of Women's Clubs and the South Carolina Federation of Business and Professional Women's Clubs, Frayser was elected president of the Council for the Common Good in 1950. Spearman agreed with Frayser on many issues, particularly on equal rights for women, but disagreed with her that voters should be qualified by education. Whereas Frayser viewed education as essential to citizenship and economic advancement, Spearman recognized that, given the inferiority of most of South Carolina's schools for blacks, "honesty" was an equally important qualification for voting.[12]

Dr. Wil Lou Gray became "the most influential woman in South Carolina," according to Marion Allen Wright, president of the Southern Regional Council from 1952 to 1958. Gray was also the only woman among thirty-four nominees for "South Carolina Man of the Half-Century." She had attended Laurensville Female College, graduated from Columbia College (South Carolina), and earned a master's degree in political science at Columbia University. From 1919 to 1946, Gray was supervisor of adult schools for the South Carolina Department of Education. In 1921, she founded a vacation boarding school to offer summer study for female textile mill workers. That project evolved into the year-round South Carolina Opportunity School for young working white adults after the state deeded to Gray 823 acres and the buildings at the decommissioned Columbia air base. Gray modeled her teaching methods after Booker T. Washington's emphasis on vocational training and "experiential learning." She also admired educator Mary McLeod Bethune, whom she invited to speak in 1938 at Washington Street Methodist Church in Columbia (some black visitors attended). After retiring as the Opportunity School's director, Gray accepted an appointment to the advisory board of Penn Community Services, Inc., on St. Helena Island. Gray envisioned Penn as "a real Mecca for our Negro leaders—a place where they can constantly go for information, fellowship, and inspiration." She suggested that Penn offer adult education courses in home service, practical nurse training, home improvements, and the individual and the community.[13] Although Spearman shared Gray's vision of Penn's importance to black advancement, she was critical of the more socially conservative Gray. Spearman commented that Gray "really sickens me" by acting as "such a martyr and such a sob-sister to these pitiful people . . . , but would never ruff anybody's feathers for anything under the sun." Of the women in Spearman's female network, Gray came the closest to personifying Progressive era maternalism toward those whom she endeavored to educate and socially uplift.[14]

To keep the South Carolina CHR financially solvent, Spearman called on its longtime board member and treasurer Adele Johnston "Minnie" Minahan, a Roman Catholic from Charleston. Minahan did "a good job digging up the membership fees," said Spearman. Moreover, as executive secretary of the South Carolina Conference on Social Work, Minahan "brought in speakers and created ripples in South Carolina that few organizations ever did." She was threatened by supporters of the White Citizens' Council because she permitted the South Carolina CHR to hold its fall 1956 annual meeting in affiliation with the biracial Social Workers' Conference. As a result, the council held an entirely separate fall annual meeting in 1957 and lost about half its usual audience. Spearman loved "old Miss Minahan" for being "a pioneer."[15]

Of this older group of women friends and advisers, Spearman turned most often to Rebecca Reid, the South Carolina CHR's secretary and later an honorary life member of its board. Spearman felt that Reid was a true kindred soul. After working her way through Converse College, Reid was appointed national student YWCA secretary. She then returned to Sumter to teach school, but was ousted, said Spearman, "because she was teaching all these brilliant young students Socialism." Despite being "pretty much persecuted there," Reid "was absolutely fearless." Attorney R. Beverley Herbert, president of the South Carolina CIC and later chairman of the South Carolina Division of the SRC, "said that he had never known a female St. Francis of Assisi until he knew Rebecca Reid."[16] Christian faith motivated Reid, a Congregationalist, as it motivated the Baptist Spearman, to include people of all races in an embrace of goodwill. Reid revealed her faith and personal feminism in a 1942 letter to John H. McCray, editor of the *Lighthouse and Informer,* an African American newspaper. In it she emphasized her belief that "we are like a large family and under God we are all one." Although many "white people want *all* the good things for the colored people," she noted, "the finest men refuse to lead—the worst element of men get in office—run the country—and run it to the dogs."[17]

Spearman admired the great courage that Reid had convincingly demonstrated in 1939 when she held her ground as two cars of hooded Klansmen drove into one of the two National Youth Administration (NYA) camps that she had set up in Lexington County, one for black girls in homemaking and the other for black boys in farming. After burning a large cross, the Klansmen posted placards proclaiming that "White supremacy must be maintained" and that it was "Time to Go to Work." Klansmen denounced whites in the NYA for "trying to put whites and blacks on social equality" and spending "tax money to feed, clothe and house hundreds of Negro youths in comfort and almost luxury" while "white women in Lexington county are picking cotton and working in textile mills to support themselves and their children." Reid, a strong supporter of President Franklin D. Roosevelt's New Deal, complained about the Klan's harassment to the NYA office in Washington, D.C., which decided to keep the camps open. Governor Burnet R. Maybank ordered an investigation of the Klan harassment, which then subsided.[18]

Committed to equal treatment for African Americans, Reid continued to encourage the South Carolina CHR to work toward improving their status until her death in September 1965 at age eighty-six. She urged opening all state parks to black residents, paying more money to black teachers, providing buses for black children, hiring black policemen, including blacks on juries, and opening hospitals to black physicians. Reid corresponded occasionally with Lillian Smith, asking for copies of her speeches on segregation's "conspiracy of silence." At a time when few white southerners could even be called racial moderates, the egalitarian Reid reinforced Spearman's racial liberalism.[19]

Spearman's energy and human relations skills as executive director won compliments from her network of women friends. In May 1958, Rebecca Reid attributed the growth in the South Carolina CHR's membership to Spearman's "ability to avoid antagonizing people, even those with whom you most drastically disagree." Spearman not only made many friends, she kept them. After dining with Eunice Stackhouse, Mary Frayser, and Wil Lou Gray, Reid reported that "it was agreed that you were holding down handsomely a most difficult job, and, *growing in the process.*" Indeed, said Reid, "Mrs. Stackhouse was especially sure that you had developed your skills in the demanding years." Reid complimented Spearman again in 1961 for "feeling your way with a pioneering spirit" in reaching a diverse audience.[20]

Each in her own way—Stackhouse, Frayser, Gray, Minahan, and Reid— contributed to the formative years of Alice Spearman's development as executive director of the South Carolina Council on Human Relations. With the exception of Reid, however, Spearman was more assertive than these older white women in cooperating with black women. Among those she cooperated with were South Carolina Federation of Colored Women's Clubs (SCFCWC) presidents Marion Birnie Wilkinson (widow of South Carolina State College president Dr. Robert Shaw Wilkinson) and Mamie E. Fields of Charleston, a South Carolina Council on Human Relations board member. Spearman also worked cooperatively in workshop projects of mutual concern with Marian Baxter Paul, state supervisor of Negro Home Demonstration Work, and Modjeska M. (Mrs. Andrew W.) Simkins, secretary of the South Carolina Conference of the National Association for the Advancement of Colored People. Both Paul and Wilkinson were active in the statewide biracial organization that began as the CIC, then became the South Carolina Division of the SRC, and eventually became the South Carolina Council on Human Relations.[21]

Spearman's struggle to recruit white clubwomen for the South Carolina CHR became increasingly difficult after the 1954 *Brown* v. *Board of Education of Topeka* decision and its 1955 implementation decree. In reaction to this landmark case, state leaders mounted a massive resistance campaign against those who favored compliance with desegregation. Segregationists spread fears that Communists were using integration—and intermarriage—to stir up trouble between the races. "They are afraid because they lack faith," observed James McBride Dabbs, Mayesville author, farmer, and Presbyterian church elder.[22]

Edith Mitchell Dabbs, James Dabbs's second wife, remained one of Spearman's few allies among white churchwomen. As president of the United Church Women (UCW), which included representatives from major Protestant denominations, Edith Dabbs held integrated annual meetings. Moreover, Dabbs expressed her convictions by writing an open letter to Governor James F. Byrnes after the 1954 Supreme Court decision, declaring "that enforced segregation had no place in any Christian activity and constituted a very real threat to our Democracy." By ensuring that all citizens were treated as "first class," Americans would give communism "a real death blow." After she stepped down, however, the UCW board, in abrogation of its constitution, convened with only its board members present, thereby "excluding most Negroes and greatly cutting the size and effectiveness of the group," according to Spearman. Because "they were afraid [she would] bring blacks," Spearman was no longer sent notices of their meetings. The UCW's "pussy-footing," she said, "was just pathetic."[23]

Spearman found that women in the YWCA, an organization that had meant so much to her as a young woman, were no more progressive than those in the UCW. Even the relatively moderate Columbia YWCA retreated in the repressive political climate, shutting its doors to nonmember biracial meetings. The YWCA rejected Spearman's suggestion, shortly after she became the South Carolina CHR's executive director, that women from various organizations be invited to discuss the *Brown* decision. In addition, the student YWCAs canceled their annual conference, which had been scheduled with Spearman's assistance at the Penn Center. "The YWCA in South Carolina," she observed, "got on the bandwagon when it was safe to get on the bandwagon." By the mid-1950s, Spearman concluded that few "people who are in favored positions" would risk losing "social prestige" by taking a controversial stand.[24]

Despite her disgust with their lack of courage, Spearman never broke her ties with prominent conservative white women, unlike southern activists Anne Braden and Frances Pauley, who are also profiled in this volume. The pragmatic Spearman realized that peaceful racial accommodation would partly depend on white women's acquiescence to desegregation, and she refused to give up on convincing them. Of all the white clubwomen and civic leaders that she cultivated, Spearman placed greatest importance on making an ally of Harriet

Porcher Stoney Simons, wife of Albert Simons, a Charleston architect, author, educator, and preservationist. Their correspondence during the 1950s and 1960s reveals how assiduously Spearman cultivated Harriet Simons, a pivotal white opinion maker, complimenting her "fine point of view, and clear thinking!" Simons had a genuine interest in interracial cooperation, saying that no work required "the moral support of like minded people more than does this biracial problem." She had been initiated into the work of the Commission on Interracial Cooperation by her mother, one of the organizers of the Charleston chapter, and chaired the steering committee that conducted a National Urban League survey in Charleston. In 1947, she organized and became the first president of the League of Women Voters of Charleston County, which during her tenure admitted black women to membership but did not include them at luncheons. As president of the South Carolina League of Women Voters from 1951 to 1955, Simons exerted statewide influence.[25]

By the mid-1950s Spearman found it almost impossible to reassure privileged white women such as Simons that the *Brown* decision would not threaten their racial and social hierarchies. Simons's breaking point occurred in November 1954 when SRC president Marion Wright praised Judge J. Waties Waring in an address at an NAACP testimonial dinner in Charleston. Judge Waring received a bronze plaque commemorating his 1951 dissent in the Clarendon County, South Carolina, public school case that subsequently "became the unanimous decision of the highest court of this nation in striking down color segregation in American secondary schools." Among those present at the dinner was attorney Thurgood Marshall, who had successfully argued the *Brown* case before the Supreme Court. At Wright's request, both Alice Spearman and Rebecca Reid attended the dinner. They had "stood manfully at your side in your civil rights struggle," said Wright, and "honored [this] occasion with their presence." Although Wright thought that "[e]verything went off quite well," Spearman later heard outraged reactions to Wright's speech from Harriet Simons and novelist Josephine Pinckney, a fellow Charlestonian.[26]

Both Simons and Pinckney wrote to Spearman expressing their opposition to Waring's judicial rulings. Feeling that African American pupils lagged far behind whites in their educational development and standards of behavior, the two women feared that public school desegregation would have negative social consequences for white pupils. Moreover, Simons and Pinckney were incensed that Waring had divorced his first wife of nearly thirty-two years, another Charlestonian, to marry a twice-divorced northerner. Spearman wrote George S. Mitchell, the SRC's executive director, in May 1956 that she had "temporarily given up working with Josephine Pinckney and Mrs. Albert

Simons, though I realize that they do wield considerable influence and that we shall eventually need them." For the next decade, Spearman wrote Simons periodically in an effort to encourage her to become involved in human relations activities, but the Charleston clubwoman continued to avoid taking a public stand on the desegregation issue.[27]

Conservative in the face of change, Simons declined to join the twelve "citizens of prominence" who contributed statements of "moderation and reason in the current controversy over segregation and desegregation" for *South Carolinians Speak: A Moderate Approach to Race Relations,* a booklet edited by five South Carolina ministers. The Reverend John Morris attributed her reluctance to family pressures and wrote to her that writing a piece would not "brand you as an out and out integrationist except with the most extreme fringe type of person who only desires a total white supremacy form of life." What was important, he said, was to freely discuss "an alternative" to "total segregation and disrespect for constituted law." The following year, Morris applauded Simons for giving copies of *South Carolinians Speak* to women in Columbia and sent her thirty more to distribute at her "discretion." The five ministers distributed about nine thousand free books to community and state leaders, but reactions from their parishioners eventually pressured them to leave, or consider leaving, South Carolina. In the hope that *South Carolinians Speak* would encourage thoughtful discussion of the desegregation issue by national political leaders, the South Carolina CHR authorized Alice Spearman to send copies to about two hundred U.S. senators and representatives.[28]

Many white South Carolinians were angered when President Dwight D. Eisenhower sent paratroopers to protect black students at Central High School in Little Rock, Arkansas, in September 1957. Both the Ku Klux Klan and the White Citizens' Councils became more active. "For the first time," Spearman noted in her fall quarterly report, "personal connections, relatives and friends, have visited the [Columbia] office of SCCHR to tell the executive director that she is to be ostracized and therefore is being advised to leave South Carolina." But Spearman refused to be intimidated, even after she was assaulted in her office by a young white man in 1957 or early 1958. After the attack, the man bolted down the stairway past Earl M. Middleton, an African American owner of an Orangeburg real estate business who served as first vice chairman of the council and on its board of directors. When Middleton entered the office, Spearman was lying on the floor with blood on her head and face. The police were called, but she apparently decided not to emphasize the attack lest family and friends pressure her to step down from the executive directorship. Her independence and self-reliance won the respect and admiration of many who knew her.[29]

Neither the stalwart Spearman nor the timid Harriet Simons expected that Klansmen would go so far as to dynamite the home of Mrs. Claudia Thomas Sanders, who contributed the essay "This I Believe" to *South Carolinians Speak.* Like Spearman and Simons, Sanders was a privileged white woman. A fifty-six-year-old Episcopal churchwoman, wife of a Gaffney physician, and mother of two children when she made her statement, Sanders had been educated at Ashley Hall in Charleston and Hollins College in Virginia. Though not a member of the South Carolina CHR, she was well known for her civic activities. Convinced by religious faith that progress in race relations was necessary, she suggested, in a moderate tone, that desegregation of public education begin in the first grade, since "[c]hildren are not born with prejudice." Sanders, like Spearman, evidently believed that religious faith should reach out horizontally to other people rather than being confined to a vertical relationship between a believer and God.[30]

A bomb planted by extremist whites exploded outside the Sanders home on the night of November 19, 1957, causing damage but no injuries. After the State Law Enforcement Division arrested five male textile workers for the bombing, the grand dragon of the South Carolina Independent Knights of the Ku Klux Klan stated at a rally, "We do not wish Mrs. James H. Sanders any harm." But he added: "If we could, we would send her back to Africa so she would be with her nigger friends!" By "a peculiar Jim Crow logic," notes historian Timothy B. Tyson, Sanders's support of gradual desegregation challenged "Ku Klux Klan justifications of racial terrorism" as a means of defending "white womanhood" from African American men's sexual desires.[31]

The Klan's violence and terrorism did not deter Spearman from showing her support for African Americans, though she realized that the South Carolina CHR had to maintain a defensive position during these years of massive resistance. She agreed to join the January 1, 1960, Emancipation Day pilgrimage to the Greenville Municipal Airport organized by state leaders of the NAACP and the Congress of Racial Equality to protest the airport's segregated waiting rooms. The previous October, the airport manager had told baseball star Jackie Robinson, who was visiting Greenville to address the annual meeting of the South Carolina State Conference of NAACP, to leave the whites-only waiting room. Organizers of the Emancipation Day pilgrimage invited Spearman to be a "platform guest on this Freedom Day Protest" and to help both in motivating the crowd and keeping it peaceful. When the South

Carolina CHR's executive committee unanimously decided that Spearman should not participate because negative press coverage would further discourage white membership, Spearman wrote the pilgrimage organizers telling them that she would be present but would not speak to the crowd. The demonstrations were orderly and dignified. Spearman noted that Governor Ernest F. Hollings's dispatch of highway patrolmen to protect the marchers was a first for any southern governor. A few days after the march, the Greenville Airport desegregated its waiting rooms.[32]

Spearman quickly recognized that the 1960 sit-in demonstrations by African American students that spread across the state from Rock Hill to Sumter, Charleston, Orangeburg, and Columbia "dramatically pointed up again the urgent need for leadership recruitment and training, and for developing meaningful communication among Negroes and white people." But when the South Carolina CHR's executive board discussed the sit-ins in an open meeting on March 6, 1960, the group divided on this issue along racial lines. The whites were cautious about supporting the sit-ins, which the blacks believed to be necessary. In a closed session, the executive board then drafted "a moderate, but helpful support statement" on the demonstrations that recognized that all citizens were entitled to equal rights and courteous treatment in public places. Despite the timidity of some of the white members, Spearman thought that on the whole, "the Council rose to the situation admirably" and acted constructively behind the scenes.[33]

The mounting number of civil rights demonstrations made whites like Harriet Simons uneasy. In March 1960, Simons admitted to Spearman that she was "probably becoming a bit timorous" and was "rapidly developing a split personality on the subject of integration." Simons feared its social consequences but recognized "that we have made bitter mistakes, that we have lost so much good will that I question how we are going to accomplish what most of us want, a decent honest relationship between the races which makes pushing and aggressiveness unnecessary and legal and economic rights secure." Simons enclosed a small check to support the SRC's "activities and courage," but, still upset by Marion Wright's speech honoring Judge Waring, she would not rejoin the organization.[34]

Spearman replied to Simons that the time was ripe for the appointment of community-based biracial committees and applauded President Eisenhower's support for their establishment. Spearman was disappointed that Governor Hollings had publicly stated "that the Negroes of South Carolina do not trust such a committee, nor do the whites." In her view, "Governor Hollings made a great mistake to have reacted so negatively to President Eisenhower's suggestion." Indeed, said Spearman, Eisenhower's "popularity will have influenced the thinking of many as yet silent South Carolinians."[35] Still hoping to convert the hesitant Simons, Spearman asked her to help the South Carolina CHR renew old memberships and recruit new members. Simons replied that she knew few prospects; nor would she volunteer to call together "a small, carefully screened group of concerned white leaders," even though African Americans were launching a challenge to the city's segregated system. Simons had come to believe that the public schools must remain open, though she remained opposed to their complete integration. But neither she, nor Wil Lou Gray, nor the seven white male "status leaders" whom Spearman contacted thought they should seek a conference with Governor Hollings, or make a public statement, or urge biracial committees openly to endorse the *Brown* decision.[36]

Hospitalized in the summer of 1962, Harriet Simons apologized to Spearman for having "to admit what a weak sister I have become, physically that is," and downplayed the current relevance of her opinions. The *News and Courier* belatedly reported on the black boycott of Charleston's King Street merchants that had begun in March. Publicity for the NAACP-led demonstrations for equal treatment had resulted, Simons wrote, in "greater employment of the Negroes." In addition, the integration of the Charleston County Library was "handled . . . with consummate skill and tact and a minimum of publicity." Spearman, who visited Charleston several times to cultivate white opinion makers during the boycott, wrote wives of politically influential men, emphasizing the need to marshal "as many of the constructive forces and resources in Charleston as possible, in order to help stabilize the potentially inflammatory situation." The rebirth of a biracial group could help during "the impending crisis."[37]

Spearman wrote Simons again in March 1963, again raising the question of a human relations council in Charleston and flattering Simons by saying: "My, what a help you can be with all of this!" She enclosed a copy of the council's most recent issue of *Progress,* which emphasized "the image created by South Carolina by its intelligent action in admitting Harvey Gantt to Clemson with dignity and honor." Spearman tried to reassure Simons about the pending Charleston public schools desegregation case by expressing the "hope that we may work quietly to lay effective foundations for what can be a peaceful transition" involving "possibly only a few Negroes."[38]

Spearman also cultivated Rowena (Mrs. Thomas) Tobias, whom Paul Rilling described as a "fort[y]ish, vivacious, energetic, balanced, optimistic" woman who was "Jewish, old Charleston, [and] well placed." Tobias, who owned a public relations and advertising business, had belonged to a small interracial committee founded in the fall of 1961 that had "disbanded" after failing to persuade the Charleston Merchants Association to negotiate with African Americans.[39] The resulting boycott by African Americans lasted until late September 1963. When about 120 businesses committed themselves to a six-point desegregation program, the African American boycott leaders announced an end to street marching and selective-buying campaigns that targeted certain merchants. Almost immediately, white toughs threw a Molotov cocktail into the doorway of Club Jamaica, a black social club; that incident was followed the next evening by a bombing of the Canaan Baptist Church, causing some property damage. To prevent interracial violence, Mayor J. Palmer Gaillard urged the formation of an unofficial biracial committee of Charleston's business and professional leaders. Among its fourteen members were Rowena Tobias; Albert Simons, Harriet Simons's husband; and naval shipyard mechanic Christopher Gantt, father of Harvey B. Gantt. The committee assisted the black marchers in reaching an agreement with most of the King Street merchants, who accepted the Charleston movement's demands. As conditions of this agreement, African Americans were to have equal employment opportunities and equal pay; courtesy titles would be used in addressing black customers; customer services, restrooms, and water fountains would be desegregated; black customers would be able to try on clothing and hats; and service would henceforth be on a first-come, first-served basis.[40] Spearman complimented Tobias for making "an unique and valuable contribution" to improving Charleston's race relations and recruited her for the South Carolina CHR's board of directors.[41]

Ultimately, both Rowena Tobias and Harriet Simons were involved in the organization of the biracial Charleston Council on Human Relations in 1965. Despite Simons's health problems and reluctance to take a leadership position in interracial work after 1954, she agreed to serve as chairwoman pro tem of an initial meeting. Tobias joined with South Carolina CHR directors to issue a call for a general meeting to elect officers and an executive committee and to adopt bylaws. The group was affiliated with the South Carolina CHR as it developed "a strong local council."[42]

South Carolina Council on Human Relations

The successes of the South Carolina CHR during the years of civil rights agitation resulted from a team effort. Two staff members in the Columbia office loyally assisted Spearman: Elizabeth Cowan (Mrs. Theodore J.) Ledeen, adviser

and program director of the South Carolina Student Council on Human Rela-
tions; and Charlotte A. (Mrs. Harry H.) Hickman, part-time state membership
director and office worker. Throughout most of the 1960s, Ledeen, nicknamed
Libby, often functioned as a "junior partner" to Spearman. The daughter of a
Baptist minister, Ledeen had earned a bachelor of science degree in home eco-
nomics from the Woman's College of the University of North Carolina in
Greensboro and a master of arts degree in religious education from Hartford
Theological Seminary in Connecticut.[43]

Mentored by Ledeen and Spearman, the South Carolina Student Council
was the first student council to be organized by a state human relations council
in response to sit-ins by African American students. During an eighteen-
month pilot project, which lasted from December 1960 to June 1962 and drew
on the lessons of the earlier Student Intercollegiate Group in Columbia, the
South Carolina Student Council brought together some 280 men and women
students from twenty colleges and universities—seven black and thirteen
white—who participated in one or more of its programs, conferences, or workshops. At day-long workshops in Columbia and weekend conferences at the
Penn Center, students discussed such issues as "the role of the student in the
changing South with a special consideration of problems in higher education;
economic growth and development; political life; citizenship; [and] religious
life and the churches." The South Carolina Student Council began to break
through the state's "conspiracy of silence" by supporting sit-ins and by con-
tributing to the smooth desegregation of Clemson College and the University
of South Carolina in January and September 1963, respectively.[44]

Charlotte Hickman, who quietly promoted the goals of the South Carolina
CHR, was a feisty "birthright Unitarian" from Baltimore who had moved with
her husband and son to Columbia in 1939. A member of the NAACP for more
than four decades, she proudly acknowledged "that for many years she was the
only white member in South Carolina." Hickman also belonged to the Columbia Women's Club and was a charter member of both the Columbia League of
Women Voters and the Columbia Unitarian Fellowship. An organizer of the
"unique and controversial" Columbia Book Forum, Hickman wanted to bring
in Lillian Smith, whose novel *Strange Fruit* (1944) dealt with miscegenation,
but had to cancel the meeting after Governor Olin D. Johnston telephoned to
say that if she brought "this woman here," he guaranteed that she would "have
no where to speak."[45]

But Hickman would not be silenced. While riding a city bus, for example
(Hickman did not drive a car), she reprimanded the driver for disparaging
black passengers. As Spearman recalled the story with a twinkle in her eyes,

the "very stylish and blond" Hickman spoke out: "I beg your pardon. Didn't you know that I have Negro blood? What you are saying is very offensive to me." As "a lifelong crusader for women's suffrage, religious freedom and civil rights," Hickman was, said Spearman, "very, very liberal, a darling person. She gave me a lot of support." The South Carolina CHR voted Hickman an honorary life membership on its board for her ten years of service. She died of cancer in 1964 at age seventy-six.[46]

During a ten-day trial desegregation plan at eight downtown Columbia chain stores in August 1962, Ledeen and Hickman, along with the South Carolina Student Council and the Columbia Council on Human Relations, encouraged black and white members to sit individually or together at lunch counters to make desegregation acceptable to the public. The police were unobtrusive. Functioning primarily as observers, Hickman and Ledeen developed "a mutually helpful relationship" with merchants. Councilman Hyman Rubin Sr. recalled Hickman as "a Unitarian lady, very progressive," who daily went to each store's lunch counter to buy a cup of coffee, though most whites were boycotting. When "[o]ne merchant threatened to withdraw," noted Spearman, "Hickman, more than anyone else, is believed to have been responsible for securing enough customers for his store to have changed his mind." Avoiding political stands in order to keep their organization's tax-exempt status, council staff members quietly involved themselves individually in "direct action."[47]

Supported by Mayor Lester L. Bates, who worked through the city council and an anonymous committee of eighty-five white leaders and a smaller all-black committee, Columbia desegregated its hotels, motels, and movie theaters smoothly, despite picketing by the National Association for the Preservation of White People. In 1963, the Downtowner Motor Inn became the first Columbia motel to desegregate, and the South Carolina CHR held its first integrated banquet there that November.[48] Council members called for reopening the state parks—twenty-two for whites and six for blacks—closed by the State Forestry Commission on September 8, 1963, to avoid a federal court desegregation order. At a hearing in Cheraw, site of the state's first park, Spearman spoke briefly but effectively in favor of the parks' reopening, which occurred on a restricted basis in the summer of 1964, with full desegregation the following year.[49]

After seven years of hard work, Spearman was being paid the same salary in 1961 as she had been receiving since 1954, which was "less than practically every other director of any Council in the entire Southern region." Writing confidentially to the Reverend Fred M. Reese Jr., then president of the South Carolina CHR, Charlotte Hickman asked that Spearman be given a one-thousand-dollar-a-year raise and, because hers was "a double job," a full-time co-director. Hickman felt that if the South Carolina CHR "should ever lose her," it "would fall to pieces" because she was "irreplaceable." She also believed a salary increase would boost Spearman's low spirits. However, the raise evidently did not materialize, perhaps because of the unspoken assumption that a woman, even one with a dying husband, did not need the same salary as a male head of the family.[50]

Although she never received the financial compensation she deserved, Spearman was richly rewarded by the tributes of friends and allies, as well as an honorary life membership on the board, when she retired as executive director in 1967. James M. Dabbs, who had formerly chaired the South Carolina Division and served as president of the SRC, eloquently described Spearman's self-assurance and courage, which were derived in part from her family's social prominence. Spearman "had the knack of getting into, and out of, dangerous situations," Dabbs said, although her friends "sometimes wondered if she even knew they were dangerous." In her eagerness "to know people and learn their opinions" she could be very direct. Yet her "charm more than compensated for the unsouthern directness of the questions." Spearman recalled "everything you told her and all the people she met. If there were many Alice Spearmans, computers wouldn't have a chance." Dabbs concluded his tribute to Spearman by saying, "May all of us prove worthy of this fine woman's great accomplishments."[51]

Conclusion

Although Alice Norwood Spearman Wright's civil rights activities were supported by two husbands, first Eugene Spearman and then Marion Wright, whom she married in 1970, she relied throughout her career on a network of strong women. Spearman incorporated into her own views the advice of an intergenerational band of privileged white women educators and civic leaders who encouraged her to grow and pioneer in the development of new programs and networks of inclusion. Although their activist paths were diverse in terms of time and location, these women shared in varying degrees a spirit of dissent from the South's race, class, and gender mores. The more conservative women in her network—Eunice Stackhouse, Mary Frayser, Wil Lou Gray, Adele Minahan, and Harriet Simons—were motivated by a Progressive era "maternalism" that sought to educate and uplift African Americans, if not to integrate fully with them. Spearman understood their more conservative viewpoint and never gave up trying to convert them to a more inclusive vision. Philosophically, she aligned herself more with those women who were fully committed to racial equality and who sought to build a biracial "community of concern" among African Americans and whites—Lois MacDonald, Rebecca Reid, Edith Dabbs, Rowena Tobias, Elizabeth Ledeen, and Charlotte Hickman. Although the impact of Alice Norwood Spearman Wright and her network of clubwomen and crusaders cannot easily be quantified, their human relations activities helped South Carolina survive the years of massive white resistance and black protests without the violence that marred the history of other Deep South states.[52]

Notes

I would like to thank the following repositories for allowing me to use their manuscripts and/or oral histories: the South Caroliniana Library, Columbia; the Southern Historical Collection, Library of the University of North Carolina at Chapel Hill; the South Carolina Historical Society, Charleston; and Archives and Special Collections, Dacus Library, Winthrop University, Rock Hill, South Carolina.

1. Margaret McCulloch to Paul Rilling, March 23, 1963, Southern Regional Council [hereinafter SRC] microfilm (Harvard University Library), reel 147, IV:440:1605–6.

2. Susan Lynn, *Progressive Women in Conservative Times: Racial Justice, Peace, and Feminism, 1945 to the 1960s* (New Brunswick: Rutgers University Press, 1992), 2.

3. Sara Alpern, Joyce Antler, Elisabeth Israels Perry, and Ingrid Winther Scobie, eds., *The Challenge of Feminist Biography: Writing the Lives of Modern American Women* (Urbana: University of Illinois Press, 1992), 6, 8, 1–15; Josephine Donovan, *Feminist Theory: The Intellectual Traditions of American Feminism*, new exp. ed. (New York: Continuum, 1992), 31–32, 59–63; Reverend Fred M. Reese Jr., interview by Marcia G. Synnott, December 13, 1994, Columbia, South Carolina, tape recording and notes in author's possession. For the concept of an "invisible decision maker," see Lois Lovelace Duke [now Lois Duke-Whitaker], ed., *Women in Politics: Outsiders or Insiders? A Collection of Readings* (Englewood Cliffs, N.J.: Prentice-Hall, 1993), 269, 267–78.

4. Alice Norwood Spearman Wright, speech delivered in Chapel Hill, North Carolina, October 20, 1973, Biographical Information File, 2002 addition to the Alice Norwood Spearman Wright Personal Papers, South Caroliniana Library, Columbia [hereinafter SCL], emphasis in the original.

5. Lynn, *Progressive Women in Conservative Times,* 31; biographical sketch of and interview of Alice Spearman Wright, by Jacquelyn [Dowd] Hall, February 28, 1976, Linville Falls, North Carolina, for the Southern Oral History Program Collection [hereinafter SOHPC], Manuscripts Department, Southern Historical Collection [hereinafter SHC], Wilson Library, University of North Carolina at Chapel Hill [hereinafter UNC-CH], G-65-1 4007-G, pp. 7–10, 12–16, 20–23, 28–31, 35–39, 44–45; Alice Spearman Wright, interview by Ann Y. Evans, Rock Hill, South Carolina, July 3, 1981, in

Women Leaders in South Carolina: An Oral History, ed. Ronald J. Chepesiuk, Ann Y. Evans, and Dr. Thomas S. Morgan (Rock Hill, South Carolina: Winthrop College [now Winthrop University] Archives and Special Collections), 42, 43.

6. Alice Spearman Wright, interview by Hall, February 28, 1976, 43, 48, 53–60, 63–69, 73–74; Alice Spearman Wright, interview by Evans, July 3, 1981, in *Women Leaders in South Carolina,* 43–46, 50–51; Lois MacDonald, interview by Mary Frederickson, August 25, 1977, Stockton, New Jersey, for the SOHPC, G-036 4007-G, 1–8, 16–17, 21–26, 29–37, 40–45; Lois MacDonald, interview by Marion Roydhouse, June 24, 1975, Stockton, New Jersey, for the SOHPC, G-035 4007-G, 47–51, 64–69; Marion W. Roydhouse, "Bridging Chasms: Community and the Southern YWCA," in *Visible Women: New Essays on American Activism,* ed. Nancy A. Hewitt and Suzanne Lebsock (Urbana: University of Illinois Press, 1993), 281–84, nn. 26 and 37, 270–95; Lynn, *Progressive Women in Conservative Times,* 23–24, 28–32, 45, 65–66. MacDonald did not mention Spearman in these Southern Oral History Program interviews. Also see Lois Mac-Donald, *Southern Mill Hills: A Study of Social and Economic Forces in Certain Textile Mill Villages* (New York: A. L. Hillman, 1928).

7. Spearman's mother died in 1958. Alice Spearman Wright, interview by Hall, February 28, 1976, 77–78; Alice Spearman Wright, interview by Hall, August 8, 1976, for the SOHPC, G-65-2 4007-G, 5–26. See Spearman's curriculum vitae, SCCHR, box 9, file 277.

8. Alice Spearman Wright, interview by Hall, August 8, 1976, 26–27, 26–40; Alice Spearman Wright, interview by Marcia G. Synnott, July 10 and 11, 1983, Linville Falls, North Carolina, tape recording in author's possession; Dewey W. Grantham, *Southern Progressivism: The Reconciliation of Progress and Tradition* (Knoxville: University of Tennessee Press, 1983), 208, 200–217. Sarah Wilkerson-Freeman, "The Creation of a Subversive Feminist Dominion: Interracialist Social Workers and the Georgia New Deal," *Journal of Women's History* 13.4 (2002): 132–54.

9. Eugene H. Spearman Jr., interview by Marcia G. Synnott, September 26, 1990, SCL, tape recording in author's possession; Alice Spearman Wright, interview by Synnott, July 10 and 11, 1983; Files of the South Carolina Federation of Women's Clubs, Alice Norwood Spearman Wright Personal Papers, clipping from the *Columbia (S.C.) State,* "Mr. Stackhouse Dies at Age of 82 at Hospital" [in 1939], Commission on Inter-racial Cooperation microfilm, VII:192:1413. The couple, having no children, adopted Eunice Stackhouse's niece, Jacqueline Roper Stackhouse.

10. Alice Norwood Spearman, "Women's Federation Pays Tribute to Mrs. Stack-house," letter to the editor of the *State,* May 5, 1959, clipping in SCCHR, box 39, file Administration; Alice Spearman Wright, interview by Synnott, July 11, 1983; Alice N. Spearman, Report, September 1955, SRC microfilm, IV:425:1403; Alice N. Spearman, Quarterly Report of the South Carolina Council on Human Relations, SCCHR, box 9, no. 279, October–December 1957; "Mrs. Stackhouse Suggests Fields for Racial Coop-eration," *Columbia State,* August 23, 1955, SCCHR, box 1. Stackhouse died at the Methodist Home in Orangeburg on February 2, 1980. Gadsden Shand to J. M. Dabbs,

September 8, 1952; and Eunice Ford Stackhouse to Dabbs, December 3, 1952, SCCHR, box 1, file 1952–1953; Alice N. Spearman to Dick Foster, April 13, 1954, SCCHR, box Spearman Persl & Planning Notes.

11. Alice N. Spearman to Mary Frayser, November 19, 1947, SCCHR, box 1; Alice Spearman Wright, interview by Hall, August 8, 1976, 49–51, 53–54.

12. Alice N. Spearman to Mary Frayser, November 19, 1947; and Mary E. Frayser to Mrs. Archie Shiffley, December 18, 1947, SCCHR, box 1; "Early Feminist Influence Reflected in Documents," *Greenville (S.C.) News,* March 16, 1977. See Mary E. Frayser to Mrs. Eugene Spearman, May 28, 1948, folder 358, Interracial Cooperation Papers related to South Carolina Division of Southern Regional Council; and Alice N. Spearman to Mary Frayser, [May] 27, [1948], folder 359, Interracial Cooperation Papers, in box 38, Mary E. Frayser Papers, Archives and Special Collections, Dacus Library, Winthrop University, Rock Hill, South Carolina.

13. Marion A. Wright to Paul W. Brown Jr., April 30, 1958, Marion A. Wright Papers, SHC, UNC-CH, series 2, Penn School, box 11, file 220. Wright maintained the friendships that he had made as chairman of both the South Carolina CIC and the South Carolina Division of the SRC after he retired as an attorney in Conway, South Carolina, in 1947 and moved to "Topknot," his home in Linville Falls, North Carolina. Mary Mac Ogden Motley, "The Making of a Southern Progressive, South Carolina's Wil Lou Gray 1883–1920" (master's thesis, University of North Carolina at Wilmington, 1997), has Gray's vita and the proclamation by Governor Richard W. Riley; see pp. iv, 6–10, 16–21, 28–45, 52–64, 67–68, 80–85. The July 20, 1953, *Newsweek* featured Gray's career. Awarded an honorary LL.D. in 1947 by Wofford College, Dr. Gray was inducted into the South Carolina Hall of Fame in 1974. The General Assembly commissioned the painting of her portrait for the State House. On the occasion of her one hundredth birthday, Governor Richard W. Riley proclaimed August 29, 1983, "Wil Lou Gray Day," based on her dedication to eradicating illiteracy and her advocacy for the elderly. Gray died in 1984.

14. Motley, "The Making of a Southern Progressive," i–ii, 60, 90, 88–101, 102, 108–14; Marion A. Wright to Paul W. Brown Jr., April 30, 1958, file 220, April 1958; Wil Lou Gray to Marion A. Wright, June 26, 1958; and Gray to Courtney Siceloff, June 26, 1958, file 222, Marion A. Wright Papers, series 2, Penn School, box 11; Marion Allen Wright Oral History [undated but prior to 1962], 21–23, Marion Allen Wright Collection, SCL, file Interviews, 1976–1978 and n.d.; Alice Spearman Wright, interview by Hall, August 8, 1976, 51; and Alice N. Spearman to Wil Lou Gray, December 29, 1961, SCCHR, box 2. Penn Community Services, Inc., near Beaufort, South Carolina, which began as a relief center and school for African Americans in 1862, became the Penn Normal, Industrial and Agricultural School from 1904 to 1948. Beginning in 1955, Penn Community Services, Inc., accepted biracial conference groups (*Penn News,* St. Helena Island, Frogmore, spring 1962, SRC microfilm, reel 42, I:1430:1433–34, 0052–55. For criticism of the term *maternalism,* see Wilkerson-Freeman, "The Creation of a Subversive Feminist Dominion."

15. Alice Spearman Wright, interview by Hall, August 8, 1976, 57; Alice N. Spearman, Quarterly Report, January–March 1958; and Quarterly Report, April–June 1958, SCCHR, box 9, file 279.

16. [Alice N. Spearman] to Rebecca Reid, December 4, 1961, SCCHR, box 2; Alice Spearman Wright, interview by Hall, August 8, 1976, 48, 49, 46–47.

17. Rebecca C. Reid to John H. McCray, handwritten, December 6, 1942, John H. McCray Papers, SCL.

18. Kate T. Davis to Jessie D. Ames, September 26, 1939; clipping from the *Columbia State,* editorial, "'Night Riders' in the Piedmont," September 26, 1939, 6; and "Governor Begins Probe of Hooded Bands' Visits," *State,* September 29, 1939, Commission on Interracial Cooperation microfilm (Harvard University Library), VII:192:1343–44, CIC VII:194:2075, 2091.

19. J[ames] McB[ride] D[abbs], "In Memoriam: Rebecca Reid," SCCHR, box 3, file November 16–30, 1965. In his eulogy at the council's annual meeting, Dabbs described Reid as "compassionate" but "a tough idealist, bending but never breaking, always resilient." Rebecca Reid to Alice Spearman and Mr. [James McBride] Dabbs, October 5, 1947; Dabbs to Spearman, October 12, 1947; and Lillian Smith to Rebecca Reid, October 19, 1957, SCCHR, box 1; Anne C. Loveland, *Lillian Smith: A Southerner Confronting the South. A Biography* (Baton Rouge: Louisiana State University Press, 1986), 50–60. Smith (quoted in ibid., 58) declined an invitation to join the SRC's board of directors for the reasons cited in her letter "Addressed to White Liberals," published in the September 18, 1944, *New Republic*: "We simply cannot turn away and refuse to look at what segregation is doing to the personality and character of every child, every grown up, white and colored, in the South today. Segregation is spiritual lynching."

20. RR [Rebecca Reid] memorandum to [Alice Spearman], May 2, 1958, SCCHR, box 2. [Rebecca Reid] to Alice [Spearman], [October 1961], SCCHR, box Spearman Persl & Planning Notes.

21. [Alice N. Spearman] to Mrs. [Marion B.] Wilkinson, February 7, 1947, SCCHR, box 1; Carmen Harris, "A Ray of Hope for Liberation: Marian B. Paul and the Radicalization of Home Demonstration Work in South Carolina, 1930–1959" (paper presented at the meeting of the American Studies Association, Nashville, Tennessee, October 30, 1994); see also Joan Marie Johnson, "'Drill into Us . . . the Rebel Tradition': The Contest over Southern Identity in Black and White Women's Clubs, South Carolina 1898–1930," *Journal of Southern History* 64 (2000): 525–62.

22. James M. Dabbs, "News of Religion," speech reported by James W. Crooker, "Segregationists Lacking in Faith Elder Charges," *Greenville News,* March 5, 1956, typescript, in SCCHR, box 1.

23. Alice N. Spearman, Quarterly Report, January–March, 1958, SCCHR, box 9, file 279; Alice N. Spearman to Paul Rilling, January 20, 1960, SRC microfilm edition, reel 147, IV:431:0647–48; Edith M. Dabbs to Governor James F. Byrnes, May 19, 1954, SRC microfilm, reel 196, VIII:59:1088; Mrs. James M. Dabbs quoted in Howard H. Quint, *Profile in Black and White: A Frank Portrait of South Carolina* (Washington, D.C.:

Public Affairs Press, 1958), 170; see also *Columbia Record,* May 24, 1954, A12; Alice Spearman Wright, interview by Hall, August 8, 1976, 45. Additional information on South Carolina United Church Women can be found in Cherisse R. Jones, "How Shall I Sing the Lord's Song?" in this volume.

24. Alice Spearman Wright, interview by Hall, August 8, 1976, 46, 43–44; Alice N. Spearman, Quarterly Report, January–March, 1958, SCCHR, box 9, 279; Alice N. Spearman to Paul Rilling, January 20, 1960, SRC microfilm edition, reel 147, IV:431:0647–48.

25. Harriet P. Simons to Alice N. Spearman, February 18, 1948; [Alice N. Spearman] to Mrs. [Albert] Simons, April 10, 1948; Mrs. Eugene H. Spearman to Mrs. Albert Simons, January 10, 1955, and February 3, 1955, SCCHR, box 1; Alice Spearman Wright, interview by Synnott, July 10, 1983; Alice Spearman Wright, interview by Hall, August 8, 1976, 54; Harriet P. Simons to Mary Frayser, April 9, 1947, Mary E. Frayser Papers, box 38, file 356 Interracial Cooperation Papers; Mrs. Albert Simons, comments, Minutes, August 18, 1954, League of Women Voters, Meeting of Presidents of Southern States Held in Atlanta, Georgia, July 27–28, 1954, Albert Simons Papers, 26-75-16, South Carolina Historical Society [hereinafter SCHS], Charleston; Mary L. Bryan, *Proud Heritage: A History of the League of Women Voters of South Carolina 1920–1976* ([Columbia, S.C.:] League of Women Voters of South Carolina, [1977]), 21–27, 29–42. Mamie E. Fields, a president of the SCFCWC, was a member of the League of Women Voters of Charleston County and later became a member of the South Carolina CHR's board of directors.

26. Tinsley E. Yarbrough, *A Passion for Justice: J. Waties Waring and Civil Rights* (New York: Oxford University Press, 1987), 127–212; presentation address of Marion A. Wright during a testimonial dinner given by the South Carolina Conference of the National Association for the Advancement of Colored People for the Honorable J. Waties Waring, former federal judge in the Eastern District of South Carolina, Charleston, November 6, 1954, released by Mrs. Andrew W. Simkins, Secretary South Carolina Conference of NAACP, file 26-76-2, in Albert Simons Papers, box 26–76, SCHS; program, "A Testimonial Dinner and Presentation of Bronze Plaque Commemorating the Historic Contribution of the Honorable J. Waties Waring . . . ," November 6, 1954, file on Correspondence: Waring, J. Waties, Papers of Arthur J. Clement Jr., SCL; M. A. Wright to J. M. Dabbs, November 30, 1954, file 61; and M. A. Wright to James M. Hinton and to A. J. Clement, December 7, 1954, file 63, Marion A. Wright Papers, SHC, UNC-CH, series I, SRC, box 3. Unable to attend, James M. Dabbs later praised the address.

27. Harriet Simons did not hold the extreme views of such newspaper editors as Thomas R. Waring of the *Charleston News and Courier,* who stereotyped African Americans as less clean, less healthy, and less intelligent and more prone to criminal and promiscuous behavior than whites (Papers of Thomas R. Waring, SCHS). Harriet P. Simons to the South Carolina Council on Human Relations (Mrs. Alice Spearman), February 7, 1955; Mrs. Eugene H. Spearman to Mrs. Albert Simons, March 10, 1955; and Harriet P. Simons to Mrs. Eugene H. Spearman, April 3, 1955, SCCHR, box 1; Alice

N. Spearman, South Carolina CHR, Report, March 1955, SRC microfilm, IV:425:1373; and Alice N. Spearman to George Mitchell, May 8, 1956, SRC microfilm, IV:431:1340; Alice N. Spearman to George Mitchell, May 20, 1955; Harriet P. Simons to Spearman, June 25, 1955; Josephine Pinckney to Alice N. Spearman, August 30, 1955; and Alice N. Spearman to Mrs. Albert Simons, November 17, 1955, SCCHR, box 1.

28. *South Carolinians Speak: A Moderate Approach to Race Relations,* comp. Revs. Ralph E. Cousins, Joseph R. Horn III, Larry A. Jackson, John S. Lyles, and John B. Morris (Dillon, S.C., 1957), iv, v, vi; Rev. John B. Morris to Harriet Simons, June 12, 1957; Rev. John B. Morris to Harriet Simons, January 31, 1958, Albert Simons Papers, box 26–76, file 26-76-4; Harriet Simons's correspondence with Concerned South Carolinians, SCHS; Rev. John B. Morris, Final Report on South Carolinians Speak, July 12, 1958; *Southern School News* 4 (January 1958): 12. Alice N. Spearman, Quarterly Report, April–June 1958, SCCHR, box 9, file 279. Lyles had to leave his church in Marion because of gubernatorial pressure against his participation in *South Carolinians Speak*; Morris entered a graduate program at Emory University in the fall of 1958; and Jackson left the state to become a minister in Santiago, Chile.

29. Alice N. Spearman, Quarterly Report, October–December 1957, SCCHR, box 9, file 279; Earl Middleton and Joy Barnes, conversation with Marcia G. Synnott, April 8, 2000, at The Citadel, Charleston, South Carolina; Earl Middleton, conversation with Synnott, April 27, 2000, SCL.

30. Quint, *Profile in Black and White,* 172–73; Mrs. Claudia Thomas Sanders, "This I Believe," *South Carolinians Speak,* 72, 69–73.

31. "Race Violence, Amity Mix in S.C. during Month," *Southern School News* 4.7 (1958): 12; *Columbia State,* January 4, 1958, B1; *Record,* January 13, 1958, 2; Timothy B. Tyson, "Dynamite and 'The Silent South': A Story from the Second Reconstruction in South Carolina," in *Jumpin' Jim Crow: Southern Politics from Civil War to Civil Rights,* ed. Jane Dailey, Glenda Elizabeth Gilmore, and Bryant Simon (Princeton: Princeton University Press, 2000), 290, 284, 276, 282–84, 289–91, 275–77. After one of the men who had signed a confession died in an accident, the jury did not convict the other Klansmen and the case was then closed (ibid., 290).

32. Memorandum to Mr. [Henry L.] Moon from Herbert Hill, Re: Press Release Item, October 21, 1959; Gloster B. Current to Robert L. Carter, memorandum, October 28, 1959, NAACP, Group III C Branch Files, C-143, 1956–65, Geographical File, South Carolina State Conference 1958–59, NAACP Papers, Library of Congress; Alice N. Spearman, Quarterly Reports, June 1959–August 1959 and December 1959–February 1960, SCCHR, box 9, file 279; Alice Spearman Wright, interview by Synnott, July 10, 1983; Alice Spearman Wright, interview by Hall, August 8, 1976, 80–82.

33. Alice N. Spearman, Quarterly Report, December 1959–February 1960, SCCHR, box 9, file 279; and Quarterly Reports, June 1960–August 1960 and September 1960–November 1960, SCCHR, box 9, file 280; Executive Board of the South Carolina Council on Human Relations (open meeting), Minutes [Rebecca Reid, secretary], March 6, 1960, SCCHR, box 8, file Board of Directors, 1956–1961, file 243; Paul Rilling,

Anniston, Alabama, telephone interview by Marcia G. Synnott, September 7, 1997; Paul Rilling, interoffice memo to Harold Fleming [SRC's executive director] and to Paul Anthony [administrative assistant], Report on visit to South Carolina, Sunday and Monday, March 6 and 7 [1960], March 10, 1960, SRC microfilm, reel 146, IV:417:0436–38; "Human Relations Council Defends Sit-in Students," typescript of article in *Columbia State,* March 7, 1960, SCCHR, box 2.

34. Harriet P. Simons to Alice Spearman, March 12, 1960, SCCHR, box 2; Martin J. Oppenheimer, *The Sit-in Movement of 1960,* preface by David J. Garrow (Brooklyn, N.Y.: Carlson, 1989), 42–43.

35. Alice N. Spearman to the President [Dwight D. Eisenhower], March 22, 1960; Alice N. Spearman to Mrs. Albert Simons, March 22, 1960, SCCHR, box 2.

36. Alice N. Spearman to Mrs. Albert Simons, February 19, 1961; Mrs. Albert Simons to Alice N. Spearman, March 25, 1961; "We, the undersigned, are concerned about the future of public education in South Carolina," probably drafted by L. P. Hollis with some editorial changes by James M. Dabbs [March 1961]; and Preliminary Report on Contacts and Recommendations [March 8, 1961], SCCHR, box 2; Alice N. Spearman, Quarterly Report, March 1961–May 1961, SCCHR, box 9, file 280. Interestingly enough, by 1961 the conservative *Charleston News and Courier* supported keeping the public schools open.

37. Harriet P. (Mrs. Albert) Simons to Alice N. Spearman, August 15, 1962; Alice N. Spearman to Mrs. Gedney Howe, July 24, 1962, SCCHR, box 3.

38. Alice N. Spearman to Mrs. Albert Simons, March 6 and 13, 1963, SCCHR, box 3.

39. Spencer Lavan to Alice N. Spearman, March 7, 1963; and Paul Rilling, Field Report on Charleston, S.C., Visit of May 14–16, 1962, dated May 17, 1962, SCCHR, box 3; Alice N. Spearman, Elizabeth C. Ledeen, and L. S. James, South Carolina CHR Quarterly Report, March–May 1963, SCCHR, box 9, file 281.

40. WIS-TV News, August 2, 1963, *Today in Carolina,* 7:25 A.M. and 8:25 A.M.; WIS-TV News, August 3, 1963, 11:05 P.M., transcripts, courtesy of Joe Wieder, Ways and Means Corporation, 1231 Lincoln Street, Columbia, SC (WIS-TV film footage has been donated to the University of South Carolina); Maxie Myron Cox, "1963—the Year of Decision: Desegregation in South Carolina" (Ph.D. diss., University of South Carolina, 1996), "1963—the Year of Decision: A Chronology," ix–xxvi, 418–19, 392–421, 346–466; "Volunteer Biracial Group for Charleston Is Formed," September 26, 1963, clipping in SCCHR, box 41 Topical, Civil Disorders: Charleston: 1963.

41. Alice N. Spearman to Charles Dixon, October 11, 1963; and John Youngblut, Report on Charleston, July 23–24, 1963, SCCHR, box 3; South Carolina CHR's 1964 Board of Directors, SCCHR, box 8, file 245; Alice N. Spearman, Elizabeth C. Ledeen, and L. S. James, Quarterly Report, March–May 1963, SCCHR, box 9, file 281.

42. Report of Project Director [George A. Bowdler], December 1964–February 1965, SCCHR, box 9, file 290; South Carolina CHR's 1965 Board of Directors, SCCHR, box 8, file 246; Mrs. Thomas J. Tobias, Father Henry L. Grant, and Members,

Board of Directors, South Carolina CHR, March 22, 1965, SCCHR, box 10, file Local Chapters: Charleston; Alice N. Spearman to Mrs. Thomas J. Tobias, June 16, 1965, SCCHR, box 3.

43. See Elizabeth Ledeen's curriculum vitae in SCCHR, box 9, Staff, file 277. After she retired in the spring of 1969, Ledeen's successor as director of information (Ledeen's last title) described her as "a woman of exceptional sensitivities" who served as "the quiet, hard-working 'junior partner' in the Columbia office who kept the Council in touch with, aware of, and involved with a vast array of concerns because she had encyclopedic concerns" (Leonard S. Buxton, Staff Report of the Director of Information [1969]; and Report of the Director of Information for June and July 1969, SCCHR, box 9, file 289). The South Carolina CHR paid Ledeen, but often just half-time; it eventually was able to give Hickman a small salary.

44. Alice N. Spearman, Quarterly Report, December 1959–February 1960, file 279; Alice N. Spearman, Quarterly Reports, September 1960–November 1960 and December 1960–February 1961, file 280, SCCHR, box 9; Summary of Student Program, South Carolina Council on Human Relations, Eighteen-month Pilot Project, December 1960–June 1962; South Carolina Council on Human Relations to the Field Foundation, Inc., Grant Requests [1962], SCCHR, box 3; [Elizabeth C. Ledeen], "The Situation in the Colleges in South Carolina" [c. fall of 1960]; "The Purpose of the Student Program of the South Carolina Council on Human Relations" [c. December 1960]; and "Student Program of the S.C. Council on Human Relations, January 9, 1961"; and file Student Council 1962, SCCHR, box 10, Student Council, 1960–1969 and n.d.; Paul Lofton, "Calm and Exemplary: Desegregation in Columbia, South Carolina," in Southern Businessmen and Desegregation, ed. Elizabeth Jacoway and David R. Colburn (Baton Rouge: Louisiana State University Press, 1982), 72, 70–81.

45. Charlotte A. Hickman, SCCHR, box 9, file 277; Alice Spearman Wright, interview by Synnott, July 10, 1983; Alice N. Spearman (executive director), Elizabeth C. Ledeen (program director), Gil Rowland (project director), and Charlotte A. Hickman (director of membership—finance), Quarterly Report, September 1962–November 1962, SCCHR, box 9, file 281.

46. Alice Spearman Wright, interview by Synnott, July 10, 1983; Alice Spearman Wright, interview by Hall, August 8, 1976, 101; Alice N. Spearman, Quarterly Report, September 1962–November 1962, SCCHR, box 9, 281; Charlotte A. Hickman, SCCHR, box 9, file 277.

47. Alice N. Spearman to Paul Rilling, August 22, 1962, SRC microfilm edition, reel 147, series IV: 431:0838; S. L. Gentry to Thomas R. Waring, September 17, 1962, 23-393-5 Citizens' Councils 1960–1963; and memorandum on the State Association of Citizens' Councils, Inc., February 19 [1959], 23-393-4 Citizens' Councils 1958–1960, T. R. Waring Jr. Papers, SCHS; Senator Hyman Rubin Sr., interview by grandson Hyman Rubin III, July 14, 1991, Columbia, South Carolina, with notes by Marcia G. Synnott; John Hammond Moore, Columbia and Richland County: A South Carolina Community, 1740–1990 (Columbia: University of South Carolina Press, 1993), 424; Alice N.

Spearman (executive director), Elizabeth C. Ledeen (program director), Gil Rowland (project director), Freddie Williams (student interne), Charlotte A. Hickman (director of membership—finance), Quarterly Reports, March 1962–May 1962 and June–August 1962, SCCHR, box 9, file 280; Alice N. Spearman et al., Quarterly Report, September 1962–November 1962, SCCHR, box 9, file 281.

48. Lofton, "Calm and Exemplary: Desegregation in Columbia, South Carolina," 72, 77–79, 70–81; Cox, "1963—the Year of Decision," "1963—the Year of Decision: A Chronology," ix–xxvi, 352–91, 346–466; Alice N. Spearman, Quarterly Report, September, October, November 1963, SCCHR, box 9, file 281.

49. Cox, "1963—the Year of Decision," 283–321, 273–95, 259–345; "Cheraw Park Hearing," with photograph of Alice Spearman by Kelvin Mackey, *Cheraw Chronicle,* September 19, 1963, 1. I thank Mr. Mackey for permission to reproduce his photograph in this essay.

50. Charlotte W. (Mrs. H. H.) Hickman to Rev. Fred M. Reese Jr., with copies to Paul Rilling and Paul Anthony, November 12, 1961, SRC microfilm edition, reel 146, IV:420:0741–42.

51. Alice N. Spearman, South Carolina CHR, Report of Executive Director, March–May, June–August, September 1967, SCCHR, box 9, file 281, and in SRC microfilm edition, reel 156, IV:782:1004; James M. Dabbs, tribute to Alice Spearman, *SCCHR Review,* December 1967, SRC microfilm edition, reel 156, IV:781:0890, 0888–91; Rev. Fred M. Reese Jr., interview by Synnott, December 13, 1994. To show their gratitude, the council presented Spearman with an orchid corsage and a three-piece luggage set. A group "of her closest friends" gave her a check for four hundred dollars "to make her first trip a more carefree one."

52. Karen Sacks, "Gender and Grassroots Leadership" (paper, University of California at Los Angeles, n.d.), cited by Charles Payne, "Men Led, but Women Organized: Movement Participation of Women in the Mississippi Delta," in *Women in the Civil Rights Movement: Trailblazers and Torchbearers, 1941–1965,* ed. Vicki Crawford, Jacqueline Anne Rouse, and Barbara Woods (Brooklyn, N.Y.: Carlson, 1990), 8–9. See also Wilkerson-Freeman's "The Creation of a Subversive Feminist Dominion."

chapter 3

Frances Freeborn Pauley

Using Autobiography and Biography to Interpret
a White Woman's Activist Identity

KATHRYN L. NASSTROM

Frances Freeborn Pauley (center) at a banquet of the Atlanta branch of the Urban League, 1961. Courtesy of Frances Freeborn Pauley Papers, Special Collections, Robert W. Woodruff Library, Emory University.

ON A JULY NIGHT IN 1965, Frances Freeborn Pauley, executive director of the Georgia Council on Human Relations, got a call from the Student Nonviolent Coordinating Committee (SNCC) in Baker County, Georgia, asking for her assistance after several civil rights workers had been beaten while attempting to register to vote. Pauley hurried across the state and arrived in time to take in a mass meeting. She later described the scene:

> I got there, and they had everything blacked out at that church so nobody could see in, and it was hot as Hades in that church. . . . Charles Sherrod had a towel around his neck that was bloody, and he kept dabbing places that were still bleeding, where he'd been beat up. He made a speech on why you were a bigger man if you didn't fight back. It was the most wonderful speech on nonviolence I ever heard in all my life. I'd just give anything in the whole wide world if I had a recording of it. A couple of men in the audience argued with him about it, saying, "I don't think we should take it. We should fight back." Quite an argument about nonviolence.
>
> In the meantime, one kid keeled over and fainted. I just thought it was from the heat. People took him out, and I thought as soon as he got outdoors in the air he'd come to. Well, the meeting was shortly over, and they said, "So-and-so is unconscious. Would you take him to the hospital?" So they put him in the car, it was late at night. I started out, and I was scared to go fast, because I was scared a cop might come out of the bushes somewhere. Yet I was scared not to go fast; I was wondering if he was dying. . . .
>
> The hospital wouldn't take him. They said there wasn't any doctor on duty. And I said, "Oh, but you're going to take him, and we'll get a doctor."
> . . .
>
> I called the black doctor, and he said he'd come. We waited and he didn't come. They had brought the boy into the emergency room, and he was still unconscious. So I called again and begged him to come. He didn't want to, but finally he came. He gave the SNCC worker a shot that brought him around to consciousness. . . .
>
> That was an awful night. I lived a long time that night.[1]

The narrator of this story, Frances Freeborn Pauley, is a white woman who was sixty years old on that hot summer night in southwest Georgia. As the story suggests, she was unusually involved in the civil rights movement. Few of her race, still fewer of her gender, and even fewer of her generation participated in mass meetings at African American churches, observed debates among blacks about the practice of nonviolence, or attended to injured civil rights workers. This essay examines how an older, white woman came to be so deeply involved in the civil rights movement, using the tools of autobiographical and biographical analysis to explore her activist identity.

I approach questions of Pauley's motivation, identity, and activism from a period of collaborative work with her that now stretches over more than a decade. I first met Frances Pauley in August 1991 when I interviewed her for a study of women's involvement in the civil rights movement in Atlanta. Four years later, I reintroduced myself and suggested that we work together on a book about her life. That work came to fruition in 2000 when we published *Everybody's Grandmother and Nobody's Fool: Frances Freeborn Pauley and the Struggle for Social Justice,* a book that blends autobiography and biography. It contains Pauley's life story, which I recorded through oral history and edited for publication, along with my interpretive essay on the significance of her life's work.[2] The present essay continues my engagement with Pauley's life story, seeking to merge the insights of autobiography and biography as it probes the relationship of text and context, self and society. In particular, I examine one of the salient differences in the interpretations that Pauley and I hold of her life: the extent to which we emphasize gender. In this day and age, it is nearly impossible not to comment on Pauley as a woman, but it is equally important to note that she most often does not. Nor does she comment to any great extent on the larger context of women's changing political participation of which she was a part. Attending to Pauley as a woman was the intellectual ground on which I undertook this project, however, and consequently, gender is central to my analysis of her identity and activism.

In the discussion of autobiography and biography that follows, I seek both to understand and present Pauley's identity as she did and to comment on that self-understanding from the vantage point of a feminist biographical practice. Biographers often face an unenviable task, especially if they write about subjects who have created an extensive autobiographical record, as Pauley has, of reconciling conflicting interpretations or overruling the autobiographer's interpretation. Here I argue that the richer interpretive possibilities lie in constructing a layering of interpretations generated by the self and others.

A sketch of Pauley's career will serve to introduce her and place her civil rights activism in the context of a lifetime of struggle for social justice. Frances Freeborn Pauley, born in 1905, grew up in the segregated South and devoted her life to the battle against discrimination and prejudice in that region. The human misery brought on by the Great Depression served as her impetus for activism. Married to William C. Pauley at the start of the Depression and occupied with raising two young daughters, Pauley noted first the suffering of families and children. She organized a small group of like-minded Methodist churchwomen to offer medical services to the indigent in DeKalb County, Georgia; DeKalb Clinic, the result of their efforts, served all ages and both races. The Great Depression was an important lesson for Pauley of the nearly equal suffering of the poor, regardless of color. As malnourished children made their way to the clinic, the need to provide proper meals became obvious and urgent. At the same time, the federal government provided the means for meeting that need, and a hot lunch program was soon introduced into the DeKalb County schools. Tucked among the New Deal's vast array of relief initiatives sat a surplus commodities distribution program of the Works Progress Administration (WPA). The WPA supplied the food and the staff to prepare the meals while Pauley spearheaded efforts to raise private funds to build the necessary kitchen facilities in each school. Within weeks, children were receiving hot meals in each of the county's schools.

The activism of the Depression years involved, of necessity, responding to the economic crisis. Following World War II, Pauley adopted a more proactive approach. Pauley remembers the postwar period as "a very fascinating time in Georgia politics" (43). The war that pulled the country out of the Depression changed the South, as it changed the nation, profoundly. One of the most evident changes was the intensified struggle for civil rights among African Americans. Pauley followed this turn as she came to believe that the "only issue of importance in the state for the near future would be desegregation" (50). Like many politically minded white women, she found in the League of Women Voters a vehicle for her interests in desegregation and the broader issues of democratic citizenship raised by the civil rights movement. Through the league in the early 1950s, Pauley organized opposition to the county unit system, Georgia's notoriously antidemocratic means of apportioning votes, which weighed the votes of the state's rural population more heavily than the votes of its urban citizens. Who got to vote and how those votes were counted was also a racial issue because most of the state's politically active African Americans resided in urban areas. Her success in this campaign, which prevented the institutionalization of the county unit system in the state constitution, earned her the grudging admiration of then Governor Herman Talmadge, a proponent of the county unit system, who groused: "I could have won that thing, if it hadn't been for that god-damned Frances Pauley" (45).

League work also launched Pauley's long-standing interest in public education and eventually took her into the controversy over school desegregation, the lightning rod for much of the early opposition to civil rights advances. In the 1940s, she campaigned, along with her colleagues in the league, to increase appropriations for teacher salaries, school construction to alleviate overcrowding, and educational instruction. The league took some pride in having helped bring about the Minimum Foundation Program for Education, a state law passed in 1949 that established a basic level of funding for all Georgia schools. In 1954, as president of the Georgia League of Women Voters, Pauley organized opposition to Georgia's proposed private school amendment, which authorized the state to divert public funds to private schools in the event of a court order to integrate. The amendment passed despite this effort, and Georgia went into the desegregation era with a legislature and a citizenry that appeared ready to resist federal law, if necessary, to preserve Jim Crow. Nonetheless, Pauley and the women of league persevered, believing that southern communities harbored latent support for desegregation that could be cultivated. In the late 1950s and early 1960s, Pauley helped to organize a group of white moderates in Georgia, who called themselves HOPE (an acronym for Help Our Public Education), to rally support for desegregation among white Georgians. In 1961, their efforts bore some fruit: Georgia's peaceful, if token, transition to desegregation, which took place in the Atlanta public schools in the fall of 1961, was due in part to HOPE's skillful public education campaign for, as the organization termed it, "children's rights to an education." HOPE's achievement was to turn a race issue into a public education issue and thereby defuse some of the emotional charge of the opposition to integration. Less public battles over democracy and desegregation marked these same years. Pauley frequently mentions, with pride, that it was during her tenure with the Georgia League of Women Voters that the league opened its membership to nonwhite women.

"It seemed to be a grassroots movement that was coming up all over the United States, and particularly all over the South," is how Pauley characterizes the civil rights movement of the 1960s (66). Her own response was to throw herself into full-time organizing for the movement. Pauley's tenure as executive director of the Georgia Council on Human Relations (1961–67), the state arm of the Southern Regional Council, provided her with an organizational base for movement activity. When she took over the council, Pauley set about establishing local interracial groups across the state and implementing a program of desegregation activity. At the height of her organizing, she had contacts in all of Georgia's 159 counties.[3] In many towns, Pauley found herself planning the first interracial meetings that any of her participants had attended, and finding a place to meet was often as difficult as locating willing recruits. Before the Civil Rights Act of 1964 was passed, such meetings were illegal, and Pauley was asking her fellow citizens to break the law. Beneath the legal and organizational obstacles lay the human dimension. "We were all trying to make sense out of this thing called racism and prejudice," she recalls (69). Pauley believed in the rule of law and supported the judicial activism of the courts as a means of changing behavior, but she worked on the more intangible terrain of intellect and emotion.

Pauley summarizes her role as being a "bridge," a term that captures the intermediary nature of her role in the movement (70). She was the bridge between blacks and whites in local councils, and she was also a bridge between black activists and white officialdom in many small towns. Pauley's strength as an organizer lay in searching out the possible in a time when many southerners, black as well as white, believed change was impossible. A skillful organizer, Pauley enabled the participation of others, helping them make decisions and take action. Her objectives were clear—"every one was a plan for action"—but she let others, with some judicious prodding, determine how they would reach their specific goals (71). Effective organizers work at the juncture of the leader and the led, blurring the distinction between the two as they develop leadership in others. In this regard, Pauley shares much with a number of African American women, most notably Ella Baker and Septima Clark, who similarly left their mark on the movement through their effective leadership as organizers.[4]

"It was a lot of fun, because you had some power behind you," Pauley says of her work as a civil rights specialist for the U.S. Department of Health, Education, and Welfare (106). From 1968 to 1973, the federal government employed Pauley to monitor and enforce school desegregation in the South. As coordinator for the state of Mississippi, Pauley deployed federal authority to persuade recalcitrant school districts to comply with federal regulations and was successful in a number of districts. Where voluntary measures were unsuccessful, she brought districts to administrative hearings and won cases to force desegregation. Advancing age and frustration over Richard Nixon's retreat from civil rights caused Pauley to leave the federal government after five years as a public servant, and she returned to her "old volunteer habits" (117).

In 1975, at the age of sixty-nine, Pauley founded the Georgia Poverty Rights Organization (GPRO), whose efforts with and on behalf of the poor she coordinated for more than a decade. Believing that the poor were "the ones that hadn't had a chance to have their voices heard," Pauley worked to educate the public and the Georgia legislature on the origins and nature of poverty and move them to more humane action (118). The most basic task of the GPRO was to preserve the gains of the 1960s, specifically the welfare stipends to which many poor Georgians, especially African Americans, had only recently gained access. The GPRO labored to convince the legislature to increase payments to keep pace with inflation and protested changes in eligibility requirements that removed many needy Georgians from the welfare rolls. This was a decidedly uphill battle, with more defeats than victories. However, Atlanta legislator Jim Martin summed up the impact of the GPRO's efforts: "Because Frances made us try, Georgia moved from the bottom of the states to close to the middle in the level of Aid to Families with Dependent Children benefits."[5] Moreover, the GPRO worked to establish the right of the poor to participate in the political system that determined their fate. Toward that goal, Pauley and her colleagues organized poverty rights chapters in numerous cities and towns, provided education on the intricacies of Georgia politics, and facilitated lobbying activities, including an annual Poor People's Day at the capitol.

In the late 1980s, the pace of activism slowed for Pauley, but even as she moved into retirement she continued to work on issues of long-standing interest, such as poverty and welfare rights; in addition, she took up new challenges, including homelessness, gay rights, and AIDS activism. Only the onset of macular degeneration in the mid-1990s ended her activist career. Frances Pauley died on February 16, 2003, at the age of ninety-seven, bringing to a close an activist life that spanned much of the twentieth century.

Autobiography, Text, Self

An autobiography, after all, is but an extended reply to one of the simplest and profoundest of questions: who are you and how did you come to be that way?
—Albert E. Stone[6]

Racially based movements have as their most fundamental task the creation of new identities, new racial meanings, new collective subjectivity.
—Michael Omi and Howard Winant[7]

Within an activist career that encompassed several decades and social movements, Frances Pauley's involvement in the civil rights movement of the 1960s represents a definable phase, both because of the intensity and drama of those years and because of the personal transformation she experienced. Her stories of the 1960s are among the most vivid in her autobiographical repertoire, and she delights in telling them. Through them she provides an extended answer to the question of how she came to be so deeply involved in the civil rights movement and what it meant to her.

In describing her civil rights activity, Pauley charts a three-stage evolution: an initial decision to support desegregation, a period of reeducation about race, and a course of action that took her further and further into the movement. She recalls a clear turning point that launched her into the movement: "I had made a resolve within myself in 1954 [the year of the U.S. Supreme Court's *Brown* decision outlawing racial segregation in public education] that I was not going to belong to, give my efforts to, give my money to, or support in any way anything that was segregated. That's what I believed, and I decided that I'd better live up to it" (50).

To meet this personal commitment, Pauley began by addressing her own ignorance: "I also realized how little I knew. I had been on the board of the Atlanta Urban League. I had been on different committees with blacks in different health organizations. But I hadn't really known black people . . . I didn't really know the problems" (51). She set out on a program of interracial self-education, taking advantage of the resources of nearby Atlanta University, a complex of prestigious black colleges and universities. "It didn't take long to make friends," she recalls. "If you're white in a black group, you stand out" (51). Pauley joined the integrated Women's International League for Peace and Freedom, whose Atlanta chapter was predominantly black; she began attending a weekly lecture series, known as the Hungry Club, at Atlanta's black YMCA; and she organized interracial political discussion groups through the American Fund for Political Education. She also put herself under the tutelage of Sadie Mays, an African American social reformer and the wife of Benjamin Mays, president of Morehouse College, who was willing to "correct a white person": "That was wonderful to have a friend like that because it meant well for my education. She never minced words" (51).

When she moved into the directorship of the Georgia Council on Human Relations in 1961, Pauley gained an organizational home for applying these lessons and working toward her goal of an integrated society. As Pauley describes her council years, she narrates two types of activities: the assistance she provided to black leaders and her own efforts to establish local interracial councils and plan a program of desegregation activity. As she traveled the state for the Georgia council, she offered her services to local civil rights initiatives. This brought her into contact with national and regional civil rights leaders, such as W. W. Law in Savannah and Martin Luther King Jr. during the extended campaign in Albany. In addition, she brought other blacks and whites into the movement through her own organizing efforts.

The bulk of Pauley's stories regarding the 1960s detail the prosaic but fundamental work of organizing. The following story of council activity in Rome, Georgia, is typical:

I remember going into Rome, and I visited with the white people, I visited with the black people. I got some leadership. By the time I got enough leadership on both sides, both black and white, we'd have a meeting. I remember the first meeting there was in the Episcopal church, and at this meeting, I started out by saying, "What is it that bothers you the most about segregation?"

One guy says, "The signs in the washateria—'white only.'" I remember this because the meeting was tense; they weren't used to having interracial meetings.

So here a white lady speaks up. She hadn't lived in Rome long, and she spoke up, "Oh, I thought that meant white clothes."

Well, of course, everybody laughed. So we decided we would desegregate the laundromat. Wherever the local group wanted to start, that's of course where we would start. (71)

The cumulative weight of Pauley's many stories describing the movement and her activities in cities and towns across the state constitute the heart of her answer to the question of how she became so integrated into the civil rights movement: it was the process of doing over and over the work of social change. She became so involved by the dint of persistent action.

In the civil rights movement Pauley experienced a social movement that sought to create what sociologists Michael Omi and Howard Winant call "new racial meanings" encompassing personal identities, social practices, and institutional structures.[8] Most participants, white as well as black, were transformed by their involvement in the movement, and certainly this was the case for those who, like Pauley, gave so much to it. Pauley's autobiography bears only traces of the turmoil that accompanied her years in the movement, but her private writings from the 1960s register a profound transition and change in her activist identity. In a letter to her children, Pauley wrote of the difficulty of reorienting the basis for her activism: "I have always tried to be of service. . . . But I am sensitive about this. . . . Because the Negroes have shown me how awful paternalism is—so I hesitate to say—or think—that I want to be of service. . . . But anyway I still do" (50). The 1960s were a turbulent period for Pauley because the moorings that had sustained her activism over the 1930s, 1940s, and 1950s, rooted in white, liberal organizations, no longer held firm. Her commitment to desegregation required not only learning new lessons from new friends but also significantly reconstructing her identity as an activist. Pauley struggled to find her role as a white person in a black-initiated and-led movement. "Can't you help *with*—and not *for*?" she wondered. "I would like to work shoulder to shoulder" (50). Even as Pauley threw herself into the movement and increasingly took her cues from African Americans, she experienced guilt and shame over white privilege: "I know I am in a superior position because I am white. But that makes me feel inferior. I know I have hated my white skin many times. I could go—and maybe help work—if only I weren't white" (50). Ultimately she turned her insecurity into a deepened sense of responsibility to the goals of the civil rights movement and her part in bringing them about.

The activist self that Pauley presents in her autobiography is defined largely in racial terms and is constructed through political activity. When she identifies herself in her stories, Pauley most often uses a racial descriptor: she is "white," a "white person." Other ways that Pauley might describe herself—according to her gender, class, or age, for example—figure in the text of her autobiography much less frequently. When Pauley calls attention to other aspects of her identity, she does so largely in terms of their instrumentality for her racial activism. In a twist on the phenomenon of interracial passing, for example, Pauley tried, and sometimes succeeded, to pass for a "southern lady." In describing her efforts to collect information from white residents of Newton, a small town in southwest Georgia, during a civil rights march in 1965, she explains, "I would chat with people, all of them just as friendly as they could be. I very easily passed for a very nice white southern lady" (95). She deployed the behavior expected of a woman of her race, region, and generation to her political advantage; in this case she donned the mantle of the "southern lady" in order to gauge the response of whites in Newton to civil rights protest.

At times Pauley's autobiography suggests that she deemphasized her gender even when others called attention to it. Describing her feelings when negotiations over a desegregation agreement between black leaders and white officials failed in Albany, Georgia, in 1962, Pauley recalls:

> I cried. I don't often cry, but I was so disappointed. I hadn't had any sleep and I was just fatigued. The weather was terrible, cold and raining, and I was chilled to the bone. Wyatt T. Walker looked at me and said, "My God, it's the first time I ever saw a white woman cry. I didn't know they could." I was the only white person in there, and I just wanted to bury my white skin. (86)

To be white in this setting meant to be singled out as different from the African Americans in the room with whom Pauley was aligned politically. Her participation in the movement had involved overcoming her whiteness, and she was uncomfortable, perhaps even ashamed, at this reminder of her race. Moreover, while Walker called attention to Pauley's white womanhood, she chose to represent herself without gender, as a "white person." Matters of race, not gender, concerned Pauley.

Pauley's tendency to emphasize her race in her autobiography is all the more striking because she most often does so in the context of difficult and anguished times. The Albany negotiation is one such instance; another, more individual and personal, concerns her friendship with Marion King, a member of the influential King family of Albany:

> When I was working in Albany, I knew Marion King. She was pregnant and had gone to take some food to her husband [Slater King] in jail. He had been jailed in the civil rights movement. The police beat her up and she lost her baby. She was in bed at home, and I went to see her. I was so angry, I was so furious with the police, I thought I just couldn't stand it, to sit by her bed and she had lost her baby that they had wanted so much, and her husband was in jail. She began to talk to me and told me that I simply must not hate, and that I must not be angry, that I wasn't hurting anybody but myself. I'll never forget that. That's what I say is real compassion. Here I was white and it was a white cop who beat her up. (54)

This story is worth explicating in some detail because it contains several shifts in emotion and perspective. At the beginning of the story, Pauley expresses great empathy for Marion King, and the repeated references to "baby" and "husband" suggest that Pauley viewed King as a woman and a mother. Yet with the reference to Pauley's anger, the focus of the story shifts from Marion King's plight to Pauley's, and King is the one doing the comforting, even instructing Pauley in the proper response to the situation. A deeply personal story begins to shift toward a moral and political lesson. Then, in a more abrupt transition, Pauley and the "white cop" take center stage. Moving through a set of complex emotions (empathy, anger, guilt), Pauley ends by feeling her whiteness and thereby a certain guilt by association and responsibility for the situation. The shared whiteness of Pauley and the police officer, the only thing they have in common, becomes the centerpiece and the end of Pauley's interpretation of this story.

In her autobiography Pauley deploys a "metalanguage of race" as she takes multiple identities and complex social relations and overlays a racial interpretation that glosses over other identities and important differences.[9] She seems to have experienced what novelist Doris Lessing described in a different context as "the thinning of language against the density of our experience."[10] But Pauley's stories themselves brim with details, scenes, and characters that resist elision; she offers much more at the level of narrative than she does at the level of analysis. There is rich material in her autobiography for her biographer.

Biography, Subtext, Context

If all life activity is defined as one kind of performance and the way the subject has viewed his or her life as another, the biographer must work with both matrices of performative identities. . . . The performative self is often the external self, and describing it may be the easiest phase in writing the biography. While biography draws on material about that self, good biography also attempts to unearth the hidden, more interior self.
—Linda Wagner-Martin[11]

No matter how feminist biographers sort out the complexities of any one individual woman's response [to the gender expectations of her time], they accept as a given that gender will always, in some way, be central to an understanding of a woman's life, even if that woman is not particularly conscious of that centrality or even denies it.
—Sara Alpern et al.[12]

Biography offers other interpretive tools for understanding Frances Pauley's civil rights activism and for making gender, class, and age more central to an interpretation of her life story than she does. Subtexts within Pauley's autobiography suggest that the years when she crafted a new racial identity were a time of major life transition, both personal and professional, that touched as well on gender, class, and age identity. Attending to these aspects of her identity allows us to see that she transgressed gender norms as well as racial norms in her activism, and helps us understand both the extent of her racial activism and its limits. Moreover, we gain insight into why Pauley delivered an autobiography with race as its central motif.[13]

When Pauley narrates the beginning of her tenure as executive director of the Georgia Council on Human Relations, she notes three dimensions to this transition: she undertook full-time work for the first time ("My kids were gone and I wanted something more to do"), she became a professional rather than a volunteer ("The Georgia council job was the first time I ever got paid for working"), and she began organizing a wider constituency ("I hadn't worked with black and white, men and women") (67). In all these ways, Pauley's new position involved a significant expansion of her career, undertaken at the age of fifty-five, but only the third dimension (the ramifications of interracial organizing) became the heart of her own analysis of her life story for these years. The first two, however, offer clues to a more personal interpretation, encouraging an analysis of self and family, motivation and rewards, costs and consequences.

When Pauley comments on her motivation for joining the civil rights movement, she emphasizes the principled nature of her decision and her desire to be of service to others. She does not speak, at least not directly and at length, of personal motivation. Yet her autobiography contains a subtext suggesting that the transition to full-time work was something she did for herself as much as in service to the movement. In one of the few statements in which Pauley comments directly on her own desires, she says of this time simply, "I really did want a job" (67). But if we read the descriptions of her activities as executive director of the Georgia council with an eye toward their personal meaning, it becomes clear that she crafted her new job to suit her interests and goals. Pauley received some institutional and financial support from the Southern Regional Council, but she raised the funds—and thus had control over their use—for the majority of the organization's activities. She set her own schedule, determined the council's agenda, and generally structured her work so as to meet her goals for interracial activism. Overall, she brought a more activist orientation to the position than the Southern Regional Council encouraged, for which she was often criticized. When she left the council in 1967, the president of the board of directors noted, "'Frances Pauley' has been the way we defined the spirit and work of the Georgia Council."[14]

If the program of the council bore the stamp of Pauley's personality and commitments, her more dramatic stories, such as the tale of the injured SNCC worker that opens this essay, provide a different sort of answer to the question of motivation. These stories suggest not the logic of principled decision and action, but rather her emotional connection to the movement. In assisting that SNCC worker, Pauley faced the terror of what appeared to be a life-or-death situation. Her desire to work "shoulder to shoulder" meant accepting responsibility and its consequences. In other stories she narrates how she overcame fear for her personal safety, developed the resilience to accept being shunned by some of her white friends after she became involved in the movement, and came to take immense pride and pleasure in her work. At times, these experiences strain the bounds of language, as when she struggles to describe the mass meetings of the early 1960s in Albany:

> That singing was so tremendous that now I get quite emotional sometimes
> when I even hear some of the songs. I don't think that there's any way of ever
> reading or seeing on television or ever getting a real feeling of what some of
> those mass meetings were like, and some of that singing was like. Sometimes

when I hear those songs again, they're almost hollow in comparison with the
way they were when those audiences sang them. It was something about that,
the movement and the feeling of the movement, that was just so compelling.
I suppose that's the reason that you always stick with it and keep on trying to
do something about it. (85)

These are the emotions that undergirded Pauley's perseverance, and they
point to the explanatory power of storytelling. Stories explain by evoking a
time, a place, and a personality that together make us understand why individuals came to take the actions they did, and why those experiences mattered
then—and continue to matter over a lifetime. They explain by answering the
descriptive question "how" rather than the analytical question "why." Pauley's
entry into the civil rights movement was, then, undertaken with several motives
and passions, personal and political, although the more personal and individual remain at the level of subtext, embedded as much in the form as in the
content of her storytelling.

Other factors intrinsic to the context in which Pauley worked compounded
her own relative silence on these personal matters. As an older white woman in
the civil rights movement, Pauley lacked any model for a transition to full-time
work in the movement, much less models for articulating its gender and age
import.[15] What she did have at her disposal (indeed, what surrounded and
consumed her) was a powerful racial narrative of the movement's multilayered
significance: the new sense of self and black consciousness it offered African
Americans; the goals of self-respect, liberation, and freedom, encompassing
the personal, racial, and social; and the hope of transforming U.S. society.
Pauley, who took her cues from blacks in the movement, also shaped the text of
her autobiography accordingly.

If Pauley had few models for a gendered interpretation of herself in the
movement, we likewise have few conceptual tools for undertaking one. Pauley
was in her fifties and sixties during the years of her involvement in the movement, a time—for women of her generation—typically viewed as years of de-
cline, with the task of bearing and raising children completed. There may be
ample evidence to suggest otherwise in the life stories of women, but biographers generally pay relatively little attention to the activities of later life and to
understanding the more general effects of aging on their subjects. In a recent
study of creativity in older writers, Anne M. Wyatt-Brown suggests that many
undertake in later life "a new beginning, a bold attempt to re-create their identities for the remainder of their lives."[16] Pauley lived such a "bold attempt": she
transgressed gender and age norms, as well as racial ones, in joining the move-

ment. Her refashioned identity was not solely racial; it was also that of an older woman undertaking significant and uncommon challenges. She lived out in vivid detail what she says only in passing: "I really did want something more to do" (67).

Viewing Pauley's activism of the 1960s in the context of her earlier work further explains the salience of race over gender in her autobiography. Her new position with the Georgia council involved a significant expansion of the constituency for her work. It included, in roughly equal measures, women and men, blacks and whites; previously, she had worked on racial matters largely with other whites and from within women's organizations. As Pauley narrates the challenges and drama of her civil rights work, the significance of her political past, which laid the groundwork for the developments of the 1960s, is obscured. Yet it remains a significant subtext in her autobiography, and drawing out its meaning makes it possible to appreciate that her racially defined political identity of the 1960s supplanted an older, more gendered identity rooted in a white, female, middle-class world of voluntarism.

Prior to joining the civil rights movement, Pauley worked for more than twenty years in the women's division of the Methodist church and in the League of Women Voters. Her autobiography indicates a complex relationship with this previous history; Pauley is at once critical of it and indebted to it. By 1960, she had come to associate her earlier activism with an approach that was "so damn cautious" and undertaken by "nice ladies with hats and gloves" (57, 66). Nonetheless, she characterizes the women who ran the League of Women Voters in the 1940s and 1950s as "very sophisticated leadership" and the league itself as a "one of the greatest training grounds" for women in politics (37). Not the least of the lessons from her league years was the resolve to overcome the "ridicule" of male legislators who resisted women "meddling in their business" (38). These years also provided her with a network of contacts around the state on which she drew for her council programs. From her involvement with church-based women's reform organizations, Pauley gained a level of comfort working with African American social reformers that set the stage for the biracial organizing of the 1960s. When Pauley took up the new challenges of the 1960s, she drew on a wealth of experience, and her self-confidence and maturity helped ensure that she would be taken seriously. The new racially defined self that she narrates for the 1960s, whose challenge was to learn to contribute to a black-led movement, could emerge because she had already confronted and surmounted many of the difficulties associated with her gender. The irony is that her training in the church and the league was so successful—in that she learned to be comfortable and competent in the white, male

world of legislative politics and the mixed-sex world of African American reform—that her gender identity disappears from her own frame for her story.
Her new racial identity emerges in a context in which gender no longer presents a particular problem for her political activism. The transition was, nonetheless, gendered, despite Pauley's own ensuing silence regarding it.

When Pauley undertook biracial organizing in the 1960s, she was, of course,
entering a social movement with its own constellation of gender relations—and
silences about those relations. Notably absent from her autobiography is a
sense of the gender dynamics within the movement she joined. Understanding
this silence requires probing past and present perceptions of the matter.
Among the most striking aspects of recent discussions among movement participants is the uniformity with which they indicate that present understand-
ings of gender, informed as they are by sophisticated theorizing, cannot be imposed on the past. Neither, many have argued, can the gender roles that
prevailed in the wider U.S. society of the time be applied to a movement that
was a world onto itself.[17] As Casey Hayden, one of the most active of the young
white women in SNCC put it, "You kind of got a new self created. A lot of the
old self-definitions fell away; they weren't appropriate anymore. You really
stopped thinking of yourself in terms of the limitations of sex or class or race.
. . . To be an organizer was very asexual—we were a community of organizers."[18] Even those who sought to call attention to gender differences in the
movement, such as Hayden and Mary King, who coauthored two position papers on women in the movement, nonetheless maintain that gender was not a
divisive issue.[19]

Pauley herself came to ponder these issues only in the early 1990s. Asked to
give a speech on women in the movement at the University of Georgia in 1991,
Pauley noted, "I never remember thinking of what sex they were. I was too
busy thinking about how I, a white woman, could fit into the work." (And here,
in the context of a symposium on women in the movement, it is notable that
she identifies herself by both her race and her gender.) Upon reflection, however, she continued:

> Since receiving your invitation, I have been thinking of the part that women
> did play. There couldn't have been a Movement without the women, but
> likewise we sure couldn't have done it alone. . . . I do have a feeling that King,
> as well as others of the Great Civil Rights Leaders, had little regard for the
> leadership qualities of women. Women still were wanted and needed to do
> the tedious but necessary chores in the various local offices of the groups
> making up the Movement: the Improvement Associations, the N.A.A.C.P.,

S.C.L.C., or C.O.R.E. and others, where the males jealously sought leadership.[20]

This retrospective assessment of sexism within the movement contrasts with the text of Pauley's autobiography, in which she describes women and men participating in the full range of movement activities. On occasion she observed a preponderance of women, as in a picket line in Baker County made up "mostly of women and a couple of kids" (95). In this regard, Pauley's autobiography squares with other interpretations of gender in the movement. Participants and scholars alike maintain that the movement, especially on the local level and within the organizational structure of SNCC (both of which were central to Pauley's experiences), although not without its stereotypical notions of gender roles, was quite egalitarian.[21] On the issue of leadership, the subject Pauley took as her theme for her speech in 1991, her autobiography does describe men more often taking leadership roles, but her rich memories of the leadership of Ella Baker and Septima Clark, as well as numerous local women in communities across Georgia, suggest that even on the leadership level she perceived, at the time, a relatively gender-equal movement. The civil rights movement was certainly more egalitarian than any movement she had encountered previously, and little that Pauley experienced in the 1960s caused her to see gender relations otherwise. Finally, and perhaps most significantly, her autobiography presents no evidence that she was ever told that her gender precluded any activities. Only decades later would Pauley come to consider the gender dynamics of the movement, and then only after the racial framing of her story was intact.

Pauley's entry into the movement had implications for her family life as well, and familial relations offer further clues to the gendered nature of her transition to full-time activism. An examination of family life suggests that despite all Pauley did to transgress southern societal norms with her activism, in other ways a secure and even traditional gender identity was important to her. Only after her daughters had left home did Pauley undertake a job that involved a fair amount of travel. Yet her husband, who was twelve years her senior, and her elderly father remained at home under her care: "The household was my entire responsibility. That was women's work. I'm still surprised when I see men cook and wash dishes and babysit. I would have felt funny to have Bill waiting on Papa. Papa wasn't his responsibility. Housework wasn't man's work" (32). Pauley took pride in her ability to manage a household, a responsibility she had accepted at an early age when her mother became quite ill. Her routine responsibilities at home may even have interjected a welcomed degree of normality into her often chaotic activist work. The letters Pauley wrote to her children during the 1960s intertwine news of her organizing activity with updates from the home front: "Must be off to the kitchen—I'm doing extra cooking for a change"; "Papa loused up my Saturday shopping but he enjoyed it"; "I must get to my mending. What happens to my clothes is a miracle. They disintegrate."[22] These remarks read as a domestic counterbalance to political turmoil.

Furthermore, Pauley managed the combined responsibilities of home and activism in large part because of the encouragement she received from her husband, of whom she says, "I was very lucky with my husband, because he thought that people ought to do what they wanted to do. He was proud of the things that I did. . . . He was always interested in what I was doing and always supportive, or I couldn't have done it" (88). There is little in the historical record of her activism to suggest otherwise. Bill occasionally traveled with Pauley on council work and at one point offered his assistance rebuilding several black churches that had been destroyed in white-supremacist attacks.

The overall structure of Pauley's storytelling, however, indicates that she understood family life and political activism as largely separate realms. While Pauley speaks with ease and affection about her family, she does not make them central to the story of her activism. Rather, they play supporting roles. Her story of traveling to Albany to join SNCC in a time of crisis is a case in point: "Bill and I were over in Brunswick, vacationing with our kids and grandchildren at the beach, at St. Simons, and I got a call from SNCC, this was Albany SNCC, asking me to come over. . . . So Bill and I raced over there, drove from Brunswick over to Albany, getting there at about two o'clock in the morning" (85). From this point, Pauley narrates a dramatic mass meeting, including SNCC's decision to invite Martin Luther King to Albany, for which the family vacation in Brunswick serves only as prelude.[23] Bill and the rest of the family disappear as characters in the story and its significance.

Nonetheless, family relations form a telling subtext in her autobiography, indicating that she managed them with some care. Pauley admits that she took pains to keep some parts of her activism hidden, particularly its dangers. Following her arrest for aiding civil rights workers in Albany, she asked for assistance from a reporter on the scene, saying, "Please call Southern Regional Council and tell them to get me a lawyer and a good one, fast. And for goodness sake, don't tell Bill or Papa" (87). When the household received crank phone calls, Pauley expressed relief that her father found the entire matter amusing rather than threatening.

While Pauley enjoyed the benefits of a supportive home life, her movement activities held the potential for tension in the household, which she avoided as much as possible. Moreover, an undercurrent in her autobiography suggests that Pauley's freedom to pursue her interests hinged on her *own* need to find the situation acceptable. "Papa and Bill were always very cooperative," she says. "For instance, they liked to go out and eat together. They enjoyed each other's company. I never felt that I was leaving them where they couldn't fend for themselves. It was really good that Papa was there, because they had each other."[24] In this passage, statements about others shade into statements about self, suggesting that whatever the benefit to Bill and Papa might have been, Pauley herself needed to believe that her activism did not bring hardship on her family. Since she took as her responsibility the well-being of the household and even others' happiness, the situation would have been untenable had the family not adapted so readily to her choices.

Pauley managed the demands of a full-time job and the care of a household in part because she relied on the assistance of domestic workers. During the years that Pauley was with the Georgia council, an African American woman named Bobby, whom Pauley describes as a very "able person" who "got on well with Papa and Bill," carried much of the household load when Pauley was away.[25] In the political economy of the South, middle- and upper-class white households had long purchased time for themselves, whether for leisure and social activities or, as in Pauley's case, political work, by relying on African American domestic labor. Such had been the case in Pauley's own life for many years. During her childhood, the family hired an African American cook who also provided a variety of other domestic services, and throughout her adulthood she similarly relied on domestic help. Simply put, in the 1960s Pauley continued to transfer much of the gender labor that was expected of her to an African American woman. She was able to engage in her racial liberalism in part by engaging in the socially conservative practice of domestic service in the racialized, low-wage economy of the South. Pauley readily and gratefully acknowledges Bobby's contribution but never stops to analyze it within the framework of her civil rights activity. In the society in which she lived, it was perfectly acceptable, and not at all noteworthy, for a woman of Pauley's race and class to rely on domestic servants. But it was noteworthy for a woman of Pauley's politics. In that context, this practice points toward a limitation of her racial activism.

The tradition of racialized domestic service on which Pauley relied was part and parcel of the system of segregation that Pauley devoted her council years to dismantling. She undertook numerous campaigns aimed at desegregating employment practices, and she founded welfare rights chapters of the council to advocate the interests of Georgia's poorest citizens. The political economy of the state and the complex relationship of race and employment were ongoing concerns. How, then, did someone who became so acutely aware of race, both as a matter of individual identity and as embedded in social practices, not see it in the intimate context of family? The answer seems to be that Bobby slipped through the cracks of both Pauley's politics and the civil rights movement's, the one compounding the other. In her autobiography, Pauley constructs a self that measures its importance by political acts and by degrees of change in southern society. The family is static, while the world of Georgia and the South changes around it; Pauley organized for social change in the world, not in the home. This tendency to maintain family and politics as separate realms meant that the impetus for making this connection would have had to come from elsewhere.

That impetus did not come from the civil rights movement, at least not during Pauley's years with the council. Only in the latter part of the 1960s, and only through the activism of African American women, did domestic service become defined as a civil rights issue. In 1968, Dorothy Bolden, an African American domestic worker in Atlanta, began organizing black domestics; she eventually founded the National Domestic Workers Union, drawing support from the Urban League and the Georgia Council of Human Relations under Pauley's successor.[26] Pauley, who was active in earlier years, took her cues from black leaders of the early 1960s and was not urged from within the movement to examine this racial relationship. (Moreover her experiences suggest that the gendered nature of leadership in the movement may have had less to do with the differential activities of women and men than with their relative success in defining what goals and objectives defined the movement.) The result was that certain aspects of what a desegregated society would mean remained beyond the scope of the movement. A situation that Pauley might have considered racial and political, and therefore subject to activism, thus remained in the personal and gender realms. Pauley's understanding of domestic service in relation to the movement stands as an example of the limits of her activism—and likewise those of many civil rights leaders.

Conclusion

To understand Frances Pauley's activism we need both autobiography and biography, both her self-presentation of a racial identity and a critical analysis of
that self-presentation that explores its subtexts and silences. Autobiography's
strength lies in capturing personalities, times, and places. Autobiography
promises a plumb line sounding the depths of self and society and unfolding
layers of experience. Autobiographical texts take us into the emotional world
of the civil rights movement, the inner experience of activism, which is still
underresearched and undertheorized in scholarship on the movement. Biography acts somewhat differently. It carries a line not down into a time, but
across times, allowing new contexts to comment on the time frame of a life as
lived. The biographer interprets the life, drawing out new meanings and significance. In this case, I have used a biographical analysis that foregrounds
gender to identify motivations and emotions about which Pauley spoke very
little and only obliquely and to explore further the achievements and limitations of her activism. In the interpretation I have presented here of Pauley and
her life story, a feminist biographical practice guides the analysis. Feminism
counteracts Doris Lessing's "thinning of language against the density of our
experience" because it provides a language and logic for teasing out the subtexts of Pauley's autobiography.

In undertaking such an analysis, my aim is not, however, to replace a "metalanguage of race" with a "metalanguage of gender." Rather, I have sought to
layer biography over autobiography in order to bring one language to bear on
interpreting the other. Pauley's autobiographical text registers the profound
change in her racial identity that accompanied activism in the civil rights movement and documents the power of the movement to transform individuals.
Biographical analysis of Pauley's autobiography not only suggests the ways
that gender inflected her racial identity but also highlights how race could
move to the fore in her own rendering of her life. Attending to gender does not
simply add additional meaning to her story; it suggests how the racial framing
of her life story came to be. In this we learn about Pauley but also about the
social and political context in which she worked, about the civil rights movement that so shaped and influenced her.

Pauley's autobiography documents a particular time, and the biographical
interpretation I offer similarly speaks to a time, the present, when gender has
moved to the forefront in many analyses of the movement, as evidenced by the
growing body of scholarship on women and gender relations. As a framework

for understanding selves and societies, a feminist biographical practice makes Pauley's story interesting and relevant to a generation that came of age when both race and gender were politicized. Pauley's life can, and should, have many meanings, particularly now that her own ability to tell it has ended, and the story has passed from one generation to the next.

Notes

1. Kathryn L. Nasstrom, *Everybody's Grandmother and Nobody's Fool: Frances Freeborn Pauley and the Struggle for Social Justice* (Ithaca: Cornell University Press, 2000), 93–95. All future citations are to this edition and are included in the text. Pauley's life story, as we published it, draws on a range of autobiographical materials and numerous oral history interviews, conducted by myself and others, over a period from 1974 to 1998. By citing the published autobiography rather than the materials on which the published work is drawn, I am referring readers to the most accessible source for Pauley's life story.

2. My interest in this essay for the present volume is with the relationship of autobiography and biography; thus I have not concerned myself with the oral nature of Pauley's autobiography, nor, to any great extent, with my role in creating her autobiography, although all of these are important and complex matters. Moreover, Pauley's published autobiography draws on a range of autobiographical materials such as letters, speeches, and diaries, as well as oral history. Of these, however, oral history is by far the largest component. For a discussion of my selection and arrangement of this range of materials, see "Editorial Method and Commentary," in *Everybody's Grandmother and Nobody's Fool*, 195–204.

3. Frances Pauley to Maxwell Hahn, letter, July 8, 1965, Southern Regional Council Papers [hereinafter SRC Papers], microfilm edition, series IV, State Councils, reel 142 (Ann Arbor, Mich.: University Microfilms International, 1984).

4. On the concept of "bridge leadership," see Belinda Robnett, *How Long? How Long? African-American Women in the Struggle for Civil Rights* (New York: Oxford University Press, 1997), 19–23; Joanne Grant, *Ella Baker: Freedom Bound* (New York: Wiley and Sons, 1998); Septima Poinsette Clark, *Echo in My Soul* (New York: Dutton, 1962).

5. Jim Martin, "Afterword," in *Frances Pauley: Stories of Struggle and Triumph*, ed. Murphy Davis (Atlanta: Open Door Community, 1996), 84.

6. Albert E. Stone, "Modern American Autobiography: Texts and Transactions," in *American Autobiography: Retrospect and Prospect*, ed. Paul John Eakin (Madison: University of Wisconsin Press, 1991), 115.

7. Michael Omi and Howard Winant, *Racial Formation in the United States: From the 1960s to the 1980s* (New York: Routledge and Kegan Paul, 1986), 85–86.

8. Ibid., 66–69.

9. Evelyn Brooks Higginbotham, "African-American Women's History and the Metalanguage of Race," *Signs* 17 (winter 1992): 251–74, especially 253–55. Higginbotham concerns herself with the meaning of race in its social and collective manifestations and in its impact on African Americans. I have borrowed her term as a useful conceptualization for understanding an individual white woman in the context of a racial movement.

10. Doris Lessing, *The Golden Notebook* (New York: Simon and Schuster, 1962), 259.

11. Linda Wagner-Martin, *Telling Women's Lives: The New Biography* (New Brunswick: Rutgers University Press, 1994), 8.

12. Introduction to *The Challenge of Feminist Biography: Writing the Lives of Modern American Women*, ed. Sara Alpern, Joyce Antler, Elisabeth Israels Perry, and Ingrid Winther Scobie (Urbana: University of Illinois Press, 1992), 8.

13. In undertaking this analysis I use the same stories on which Pauley herself bases a racial interpretation of her life. Both Pauley and I work with the text of her life story in fashioning our interpretations, but here I assert the biographer's prerogative of making subtexts of Pauley's stories into a major theme of her biography, and I assume the biographer's responsibility to probe the autobiography, the self-presentation, of her subject and place her in a wider historical context.

14. Joe Hendricks, President, Georgia Council on Human Relations, to Board Members, September 12, 1967, SRC Papers, reel 155.

15. Carolyn G. Heilbrun, in her study of women's autobiography and biography, draws this connection between narrative and life activity: "[W]omen have been deprived of the narratives, or the texts, plots, or examples, by which they might assume power over—take control of—their own lives" (*Writing a Woman's Life* [New York: Norton, 1988], 17).

16. Anne M. Wyatt-Brown, "Introduction: Aging, Gender, and Creativity," in *Aging and Gender in Literature: Studies in Creativity*, ed. Anne M. Wyatt-Brown and Janice Rossen (Charlottesville: University Press of Virginia, 1993), 5, 13. See also, for a case-study approach to this issue, Anne M. Wyatt-Brown, "Another Model of the Aging Writer: Sarton's Politics of Old Age," in *Aging and Gender in Literature*, 49–60, especially 52, 54.

17. Cynthia Griggs Fleming, *Soon We Will Not Cry: The Liberation of Ruby Doris Smith Robinson* (Lanham, Md.: Rowman and Littlefield, 1998), 152, 167; Cheryl Lynn Greenberg, *A Circle of Trust: Remembering SNCC* (New Brunswick: Rutgers University Press, 1998), chap. 6; Charles Payne, "Men Led, but Women Organized: Movement Participation of Women in the Mississippi Delta," in *Women in the Civil Rights Movement: Trailblazers and Torchbearers*, ed. Vicki L. Crawford, Jacqueline Anne Rouse, and Barbara Woods (Brooklyn, N.Y.: Carlson, 1990), 2.

18. Quoted in Greenberg, *Circle of Trust*, 133.

19. Greenberg, *Circle of Trust*, 127–36.

20. "African American Women in the Civil Rights Movement" (paper delivered at the University of Georgia, March 7, 1991), reprinted in *Hospitality* [newsletter of the Open Door Community, Atlanta, Georgia] 10 (May 1991): 1–3.

21. Fleming, *Soon We Will Not Cry*, 153–57; Greenberg, *Circle of Trust*; Constance Curry et al., *Deep in Our Hearts: Nine White Women in the Freedom Movement* (Athens: University of Georgia Press, 2000).

22. Quotations drawn from three letters: Dear Children, n.d.; [no salutation] March 2, 1969; and [no salutation] April 20, 1962, Frances Pauley Papers, Special Collections Department, Robert W. Woodruff Library, Emory University, Atlanta, Georgia, box 1.

23. The question of whether or not SNCC invited King to Albany is a matter of some debate among activists. Pauley, for her part, is quite certain in her memory: "You know, there's a lot of controversy about whether King just went or whether SNCC asked him to come to Albany. Well, I'll have you know SNCC asked him. I heard it. They got on the phone and called him. He said he'd consider and let them know, and he called back and said he'd come" (86).

24. Frances Pauley, interview by Kathryn Nasstrom, May/June 1997, untranscribed, in author's possession.

25. Pauley interview, May/June 1997. In 1997, Pauley could not recall Bobby's last name, and my search of Pauley's personal records did not yield that information.

26. "Organizing Domestic Workers in Atlanta, Georgia: Dorothy Bolden," in *Black Women in White America: A Documentary History,* ed. Gerda Lerner (New York: Vintage Books, 1973), 234–38; "Dorothy Bolden," in Nancy Seifer, *Nobody Speaks for Me! Self-Portraits of American Working-Class Women* (New York: Simon and Schuster, 1976), 138–77; Dorothy Cowser Yancey, "Dorothy Bolden, Organizer of Domestic Workers: She Was Born Poor but She Would Not Bow Down," *Sage* 3 (spring 1986): 53–55.

chapter 4

Anne Braden and the "Protective Custody" of White Southern Womanhood

CATHERINE FOSL

*The true focus of revolutionary change is never merely the oppressive situations which
we seek to escape, but that piece of the oppressor which is planted deep within each of us,
and which knows only the oppressors' tactics, the oppressors' relationships. . . . We
sharpen self-definition by exposing the self in work and struggle together with those
whom we define as different from ourselves, although sharing the same goals.*
—Audre Lorde, 1980[1]

*That's what they always called us, the segregationists, those white people who hated us.
Race traitors.*
—Anne Braden, 2001, reflecting on the post–World War II South[2]

Anne McCarty Braden addressing an anti-Klan rally in Lafayette Park,
Washington, D.C., 1983. Courtesy of Catherine Fosl.

∞

WHEN WE IN the twenty-first century ask, "What did it *mean* to be white and female and to stand up to segregation in the South?" we ponder such matters with an attention to identity politics formed out of the black consciousness and women's liberation movements that spun off from the southern civil rights movement in the late 1960s. Underlying any answer to this question is a troubled awareness of the justifiable critiques that people like Audre Lorde (an African American lesbian feminist poet whose cautionary note appears here) and other radical women of color leveled at white feminists during the 1970s for their failure to acknowledge white privilege and address a broader range of women's concerns.[3]

One of the relatively few white women who joined in those critiques was Anne Braden, a southern activist whose immersion in racial justice causes originated in the late 1940s and continues today without interruption. Although she was often a controversial figure even within the ranks of the civil rights movement in the 1950s, 1960s, and 1970s because of her radical politics and associations with the Communist Party (CP), Anne Braden's life has been fired by a relentless passion to undo white supremacy that is rare indeed among whites, especially white southerners of her generation. In the early 1960s, for example, she nudged the Student Nonviolent Coordinating Committee (SNCC) to hire a white staffer to reach southern white students. Later in the sixties she became one of the most vocal white supporters of the Black Power movement, and she echoed its call for whites to organize other whites. After having observed the mass civil rights movement's early 1960s vision of a "beloved community" founder on the shoals of internal tensions and government repression, she took her message of whites' need to act against racism to the women's, student, antiwar, and environmental movements, all of which her life has touched. Getting whites to confront both their own racism and institutional racism became a focal point of her political philosophy and her rhetorical and organizing strategies and has remained so for four decades.[4]

With a history of continuous white antiracist activism that both predates and postdates the 1960s mass civil rights upsurge, Braden has rooted herself in the black community but has focused much of her more than half a century's work on convincing other whites of the persistence of racism and of their responsibility to eradicate it. She self-consciously claimed a "white identity" long before it was fashionable to do so, in fact well before the emergence of the post-*Brown* mass civil rights movement. Since the early 1950s, her articulations of her own whiteness have been central to her critiques of segregation and racism. She claims forcefully that being white gave her what she has called "credentials"—meaning, as she explained it, "I know what I'm talking about. I'm a white person who's rejected [segregationist] values, and there are other people out there like me." Such white southerners were few in those years, of course; sometimes they "stuck out like sore thumbs." Yet by representing them, Braden hoped to increase their ranks and make visible an alternate white southern identity that countered rather than defended segregation and held the promise of cross-racial solidarity.[5]

Out of the modern civil rights movement and the subsequent social struggles it spawned came moments of that solidarity. A more acute awareness of differences also emerged, however, that led to divisions between even the best-intentioned whites and those labeled "nonwhite." Understanding those differences is crucial to obtaining a fuller history of the unfinished civil rights revolution of the post–World War II era. An anthology such as this one, centering on white women, might seem at first glance to be problematic. As the political scientist Diane Fowlkes has pointed out, "[s]uch a focus reinforces the racial privilege that white women enjoy, consciously or unconsciously." But whiteness has never been the "neutral" or "normal" feature of American identity that it seemed to be for much of our history, and evaluating white women's experiences in the movement presents an opportunity to discern how and to what extent their own racial identities became visible and perhaps shifted as a result of their activism against racism. For some whites—Anne Braden among them—the southern black freedom movement first brought into focus the privileges associated with being white and then prompted a dramatic reevaluation of the system of racial hierarchy. Whites in the movement found that, just as people of color had what W. E. B. DuBois has described as a "double-consciousness" associated with their being thought of as "other" on the basis of their skin color, being *thought of* as white carried certain preconceptions that a particular white person might or might not wish to embrace.[6]

Braden is not representative of white southern women, not even of activists, and certainly not those of her own generation. She made a more thorough break than most with the southern social conventions in which she was reared, and the socialism she embraced earned her fierce ostracism and the label "red." Many of the women of her own age or older profiled in this volume eschewed contact with her until recent decades, either because of real fears about her subversiveness or to avoid the taint that such collaboration might bring to their own reform efforts. Yet out of her radical politics Braden became a kind of harbinger of the multiculturalism that was to come in southern social change: she imparted a new consciousness about race, class, and gender and their intersections to other, younger activists, becoming an important mentor to young women of the 1960s and thereafter.[7]

The radicalism of women active in feminist causes has been examined in various histories of the modern women's movement, but a gendered understanding of radical women's activism in other social movements is less common, as the sociologist Kathy Blee points out in a 1998 anthology on radical female protest. Braden's radicalism has deeply informed her brand of racial identity, and her story offers a connecting point between historians of civil rights and feminism and sociocultural investigators who probe the social construction of whiteness and question the nature of "white" identity.[8]

Anne Braden has written and spoken at length on the relationship of being white and southern and female to racism and privilege. Throughout her adult life she has maintained that "it takes an explosion," individual and societal, to get white people to act against white supremacy. This essay explores the nature and substance of that explosion in Braden's life and employs moments from her life and times as a biographical lens through which to examine the intersecting standpoints of white (privilege) and female (oppression) in relation to civil rights activism. Braden's experiences have particular import for a historical understanding of whiteness in relation to gender and to the civil rights movement, partly because of her sheer longevity as an activist and partly because of her organizing emphasis on white racism and the importance of black leadership. More significant, perhaps, is how thoroughly her identification with left-wing causes and consequent discrediting as "red" affected both her own understanding of her racial identity and others' understanding of her whiteness when they denounced her as a "race traitor."[9]

In the more than fifty years since Anne Braden joined her life to the cause of racial freedom in the South, the implications of being a "race traitor" have shifted and become—in some circles, at least—a positive claim. Not so when she first heard those words hurled at her by opponents in the 1950s. The black consciousness movement of the mid-to-late 1960s yielded a new awareness among many African Americans and other people of color that their racial identity was a positive source of pride rather than something to be given up in order to assimilate and become "simply" Americans. That insight is at the root of "whiteness studies," an emerging interdisciplinary body of literature that represents, in part, a response to the challenges that black racial pride brought to white supporters of the freedom movement, who were left wondering where they fit in and how to think of themselves in relation to race. A key question that arose is whether being white has any meaning other than the racial privilege that it confers. In subsequent decades, social theorists influenced by African American studies and the rise of identity politics have investigated the social construction of whiteness in an attempt to understand the persistence of white identity, its relationship to racism, and its intersections with other structures of power. One such intersection takes place with gender, for example: the normative features of what has been unacknowledged as "white" overlap considerably with the unacknowledged "male." Yet although white women may experience racial identity and privilege differently from their male counterparts, their experiences of race and gender also depend on other variables such as class, ethnicity, sexual orientation, region, and, of course, time.[10]

Although such interdisciplinary "whiteness studies" often refer to or gesture toward the southern freedom movement of the 1960s, they have not been widely employed by historians of the civil rights movement. As Peter Kolchin points out in a 2002 evaluation of the proliferating literature on whiteness, this new approach to addressing an older concept, the social construction of race, has yet to fully "delineate the multiple meanings of whiteness" and the particular contexts in which they arose. Braden's experiences pose an intriguing case study for looking at one context for white identity in the Cold War South. As she became a lightning rod for the ferocity of southern segregationists against "subversion" (by which they meant largely racial change), her notoriety as a "red" seems to have made her, metaphorically, *less white* and thus more subject to ostracism, prosecution, and ongoing threats of violence.

At the very least, Braden's experiences in the post–World War II South steer us away from any monolithic picture of white identity or even of white privilege. Her story reveals a particular variation of whiteness that evoked a peculiarly vehement denunciation from those white southerners who held political and image-making authority in a regional Cold War culture that lingered long after McCarthyism was on the wane elsewhere. Anne Braden's claims to an alternative white identity outlasted the vigor of the opposition she faced but were altered somewhat by her odyssey through several generations of southern racial justice movements. That odyssey offers a window into understanding white women's contributions to racial change in the modern South.[11]

The Making of a Radical

In examining Braden's life in relation to her racial identity, it is necessary first to revisit her youth for the sources of that identity and her young adulthood for the factors that shaped her into what she thought of as a radical and what her segregationist detractors thought of as a "race traitor." Born Anne McCarty in 1924, Braden is part of a transitional generation of American women who came of age as World War II ended. Her college years, 1941–45, coincide precisely with U.S. involvement in the war. She was reared in a middle-class family in the Deep South, mostly in Anniston, Alabama, where her father's work took them when she was seven. Gambrell and Anita McCarty, her parents, were both native Kentuckians, and her mother's side of the family proudly claimed a lineage that dated to the Bluegrass State's earliest white settlers, who had come across the Alleghenies with Daniel Boone. The McCartys were Democrats who, though not politically active, accepted the conventions of Jim Crow wholeheartedly. Earlier generations of both parents' families had backed the Confederacy in a state that was deeply divided internally by the Civil War. The slave South was a centerpiece of family legend, as was the white colonists' early subjugation of native peoples. Those swashbuckling tales of native conquest and slaughter bothered Braden as a child, and years later she identified them as her first racialized memory. The McCartys saw themselves as part of what their daughter later called the "southern aristocracy," and they encouraged her from early childhood to see race as a natural dividing line that placed her and her kind in a status above all people of color, but especially blacks, whom she knew only as servants. Troubled by the wretched Depression-era suffering around her though her own family remained comfortable, Braden was an introspective, devoutly religious child whose upbringing in a social-gospel-oriented Episcopal parish was her only window to a larger worldview.[12]

As a girl, Braden felt most comfortable with her mother, who encouraged her toward academic achievement and a career as a writer. The adolescent Anne was a prolific diarist and a good student, but it was her attendance at two elite Virginia women's colleges (Stratford and Randolph-Macon) that introduced her to strong female mentors and what she has called "the world of ideas." She has described it thus: "Going to women's colleges gave me a chance to find myself, to begin thinking about myself as a woman. I felt like I'd wasted sixteen years of my life—all of the things I hadn't read and wanted to read, that sort of thing." Her college years brought an intellectual awakening and a vague awareness that segregation was wrong, prompted by the racialized crusade of Nazi fascism and by meeting for the first time southern liberals who criticized her region's racial arrangements.[13]

Braden also caught what she later thought of as the "spillover" from an earlier generation of feminists who were now professors or alumnae at her alma maters. When she graduated from Randolph-Macon in May 1945, it was with an expansive sense of her own agency and a determination to become a great newspaperwoman. She took advantage of wartime opportunities for women in journalism to begin her reporting career at the *Anniston Star,* and then moved on to Birmingham, known in the postwar years as the "Johannesburg" of the American South for its savage, government-sanctioned repression of its African American population. A brief stint covering the courthouse for the *Birmingham News and Age-Herald* made it plain to the novice reporter that blacks had no hope of justice there. The rigidly separate worlds blacks and whites inhabited left her ignorant of the small postwar wellspring of labor and civil rights activism that persisted locally amid extraordinary racial violence. Sickened by the harsh divisions of segregation and the limitations imposed by southern white culture, where well-to-do women seemed destined for lives hosting bridge parties and going to the country club, Braden fled the Deep South and returned to her native Louisville for a job on the *Louisville Times,* afternoon companion to the South's most respected newspaper, the *Courier-Journal.* "What happened to me wasn't that different from what happened to a lot more people in later generations," she has reflected. "I had become totally disillusioned by the society I grew up in, and I had to get away from it. I knew that the place to be a successful newspaper writer was in New York or Chicago, so it was partly ambition and partly running away." She ran only as far as the South's northern border, drawn initially by her family ties there, but Louisville's prestigious newspapers also appealed to her as a steppingstone for a job with one of the nation's leading papers outside the region.[14]

Although its buses and streetcars were desegregated and African Americans retained voting rights, Louisville, a commercial river city known as the "gateway to the South," was only marginally less segregated than Alabama in 1947. Yet there was one important difference: Louisville had a feeling of possibility, particularly in the visibility of dissent from the racial status quo. Braden's arrival coincided with a new crusade headed by the Louisville branch of the National Association for the Advancement of Colored People (NAACP) to integrate public parks. The weekly *Defender,* an African American newspaper, publicized these campaigns and nudged the mainstream press toward more sympathetic coverage of desegregation activities. Braden was assigned to cover the legal challenge that ultimately desegregated the University of Kentucky. Farther north and out of her parents' oversight, she sought out NAACP activists on her own and tentatively began to make friends across the color line. In doing so, she had to unlearn old habits: even pronouncing *Negro* correctly was a challenge after having grown up in a household in which *ni-gra, colored,* and *nigger* were used interchangeably. "Just hit your knee and tell it to grow!" was one African American friend's joking recommendation to her that year.[15]

Through her friendship with fellow *Times* reporter Carl Braden, a left-leaning trade unionist whose socialist parents had named him after Karl Marx, the
young journalist also began covering the post–World War II upsurge of organized labor. She met leaders of the labor left that had evolved during the 1930s–
1940s "Popular Front" uniting liberals, socialists, and Communists in reforms
to end the Depression. They included both blacks and whites critical of segregation and the "empire thrust" of U.S. foreign policy, some of whom were
members of or sympathetic to the Communist Party. The Cold War was taking
shape in the ashes of Hitler's fascist campaign during Braden's early months in
Louisville, and it would soon demonize not just CP members and supporters
but any who failed to disassociate from them, wreaking a domestic anticommunist "purge" that all but silenced dissent, especially in the South. Yet the buds
of opportunity for southern racial and social change that had opened in the
New Deal years were still in bloom in late 1947, and they beckoned to Anne
Braden as she saw the energy that commitments to racial and working-class
justice inspired. She came to know Communists like Charles Gibson, a white
man who was president of the local Farm and Equipment Workers' Union, and
Ernie Thompson, an African American who headed Louisville's Negro Labor
Council, not as menaces to society but as model citizens dedicated to racial
equality. Something in her responded deeply to the vigor that emanated from
the labor and civil rights organizers she met that year, and as 1947 ended, her
view of the "good life" enlarged with her dawning awareness of social change
movements and the passionate lives lived within them.[16]

At the age of twenty-three, Braden, like other southern whites before her
who had rejected the lessons of their Jim Crow upbringing, underwent a personal and political transformation of several months' duration that she later
described as "turning myself inside out." That experience is one she thinks
white southerners of her generation, and earlier ones reared under segregation,
had to go through as they became active for racial change: "I had to come to
terms with the fact that my whole society—one that had been very good to
me—my family, friends, the people I loved and never stopped loving—were
just plain wrong—wrong on race. It's a searingly painful process, but it's not
destructive, because once you do it, you are free."[17]

Her disgust with segregation and racial hierarchy was the opening wedge
that exposed the hypocrisy that infused the culture in which she had grown
up. She began to view her old life as a prison she desperately wanted to escape
in order to forge a more creative future free of the barriers segregation had
erected. Her motives were not sympathetic or other-directed as much as they
involved curing what felt like a sickness inside her. Yet Braden's views on race

had already begun to shift before she left Alabama and only intensified once she met civil rights crusaders in Kentucky. The painful transformation she endured from 1947 to 1948 widened as she also changed her class allegiance. To do so, she had to make an even more fundamental break with the values of her upbringing than those governing racial norms: "Like most people who identify with the upper class," she later recalled,

> I didn't think there were any social/economic classes. Essentially I came to identify with the oppressed instead of the oppressor, which changed my whole worldview. When I realized that I had grown up part of a privileged class that enjoyed its place in society because not only black people but ... most of the rest of the population was subjugated, I really had to turn the world as I saw it and the world within myself [inside out]. It was a lot to manage all at once. ... I had a very emotional feeling about [our country's] democratic rights, and now I was coming to terms with the fact that these things really weren't rights but were privileges I had gotten because of my class. I remember crying—and I don't cry easily—wondering whether I was turning against my own people.

That change hurt: it threw all of her assumptions into question. Unlike race, class had no uniformly observable dimension. To see her own class privilege, Braden had to rethink the most basic assumptions that had shaped her self-understanding. "You assume your place in society is eternal," she has reflected. "You assume—and you don't even think about it—that people like you run things because they're more intelligent, more capable, of 'superior stock.'"[18]

Her co-worker Carl Braden, ten years her senior and more politically active and informed than she, had become her closest friend and political mentor during the turbulent months when Anne turned her values inside out. Friendship turned to romance, and her feelings for him provided what was perhaps the critical impetus for the wrenching changes she underwent that year. "It took something as strong as the emotional pull to him to shake me loose from my past," she later reflected, with some embarrassment about what a "savior" he was for her in their early days together. When she moved in with Carl and in mid-1948 married him, she saw herself as marrying not just a man but a movement. Both wanted from the partnership not only personal fulfillment but a way to enact their shared ideals. As she described it,

> There was a real sense when Carl and I decided to get married that we were joining our lives to bring about a new world. ... The idea of being a successful newspaperwoman didn't even appeal to me anymore. I had a feeling that I

could contribute a little something; I didn't expect to contribute a great deal, but I was going to be on the side of history that represented life instead of death.

The zeal that had characterized her devout faith as a young girl was reborn as a desire to move society in a more humane direction.[19]

She was conscious enough of the looming domestic Cold War to know that she was joining an "outlaw movement." Yet those emotionally difficult months that set her life course on social change remain etched in her memory as a powerful formative moment: "In anybody's life there is a time that's a turning point. I hope I've grown since then, but for me the real change was from being a woman of the white privileged class in the South to being what I consider a revolutionary." Although she had returned to Louisville with a vaguely liberal sensibility, she had never been politically active for liberal causes. Her metamorphosis into a political activist was molded more from the working-class, militantly interracial, anticapitalist, and internationalist ideology of the postwar left that she discovered there—currents that meshed with Christian ideals she had first absorbed growing up in the Episcopal church. Over the next few years she and Carl left mainstream journalism and worked in the left wing of the labor movement. Through a variety of national organizations that faced increasing stigmatization as "communist fronts," they challenged the spread of what became known as McCarthyism. Braden embraced what she has called a "working-class perspective" that gave her an affinity with all who were dispossessed. That view, she still maintains, differentiated her from liberals, although she collaborated with them wherever possible.[20]

As she grew more confident in her politics and became more immersed in what remained of the interracial subculture of the post–World War II left, opposing segregation became more of a "compulsion" for her, and she urged her husband toward racial activism too. She no longer wanted to leave the region of her birth; she wanted to transform it. It was not so much that she believed that ending segregation would end racism. In those years, in fact, she rarely heard or spoke the word *racism*. But southern segregation was so blatant that it was hard to think beyond it. Ending Jim Crow seemed the logical first step toward greater social justice.[21]

Braden recalled later that "the feeling of people like us was that our destiny rested with the freedom movement of blacks. . . . [I]t wasn't that we were 'helping those poor blacks' . . . it was our struggle too." The postwar years were not an auspicious time for revolutionary action, and the Bradens concentrated on fairly modest racial reforms, becoming among the few local whites to plunge into initiatives to desegregate Kentucky hospitals and schools. "I hadn't rejected the people in that white world, but I had rejected its values, its standards," she has explained. "I had this feeling that I had been liberated from a world that was wrong, and that I needed to share that vision with others."[22]

To Be White, Southern, and Female

In May 1951, three years after she had undergone what literary scholar Fred Hobson has called a "racial conversion" in recognition of its quasi-religious intensity, Anne Braden went to jail for the first time. She had traveled to Laurel, Mississippi, one of only three southerners to participate in a white women's delegation to protest the impending execution of Willie McGee, an African American convicted of the 1945 rape of a white woman. Perhaps because of her broad Alabama accent, Braden was chosen as spokeswoman for the group, and her statement that day declared, "We are here because we are determined that no more innocent men shall die in the name of southern white womanhood."[23]

Mississippi officials were horrified by the delegation, seeing it only as the work of "reds" because the sponsoring organization was the Civil Rights Congress (CRC), a group containing both liberals and leftists that was currently under government attack for its refusal to register as a "Communist front." Instead of meeting with the governor, as they wished to do, the women were taken into what local officials called "protective custody." The irony of that phrase was not lost on Braden when she found herself behind bars. Mississippi jails were strictly segregated, but the women knew that McGee was being held somewhere in the building and were determined to make their presence known to him. As a gesture of their solidarity, they began singing, "Hallelujah, I'm A-travelin' Down Freedom's Main Road," and some of the other freedom songs a younger generation would again employ in Mississippi jails a decade later. That afternoon she and her colleagues were ordered to leave the state. Three days later, after a protracted legal battle and in spite of new evidence suggesting that the alleged victim had been McGee's lover for years, he was hanged in front of a cheering crowd of seven hundred.[24]

Braden's rough treatment at the hands of a Mississippi policeman provoked a visceral awakening in her of how precarious was the southern white chivalry accorded to a "lady." When he discovered that Braden was a native southerner, the officer grew enraged by her defense of McGee and told her she "ought to be shot." Braden was aware, in general terms, of the link between white women and white supremacy that loomed large in southern history; it was first articulated by proslavery ideologues of the 1830s, who wrote that the elevation of white women depended on the availability of slave labor. Thinkers like the antebellum Virginia publicist George Fitzhugh held that abolitionism and women's rights were twin evils that endangered any southern white woman who dared to contemplate them. "Women," he argued, "like children have but one right, and that is the right to protection." By the dawn of the twentieth century that "protection" had been exposed by the African American journalist Ida B. Wells as merely a rhetorical strategy through which southern whites deployed gender as a rationale for violence against blacks.[25]

Knowledge of that history was the basis, at least rhetorically, for the CRC's recruitment of white women for the McGee protest. Braden already possessed a well-honed critique of race and class hierarchies and of "male supremacy," a phrase she and others on the left used to name and deplore sexism. Yet, as a middle-class southern white woman in the postwar era, Braden's class privilege, enmeshed with her race, gender, regional background, and perhaps even her marital status, had thus far created a kind of shield that many other activists simply did not enjoy. Up to a point, she was freer to criticize regional conventions, and she maximized that discursive space, inadvertently benefiting from the kind of male "protectionism" toward elite southern white women that she herself decried. Braden's encounter with the police officer on her way to jail was the first time she ever found herself stripped of the privileges her gender and class had accorded her in southern culture. Had it not been for race privilege, she might well have experienced consequences more severe than a threat for speaking out in Laurel: white southerners defying regional racial practices "ought to be" shot, but black ones might well *be* shot. The confrontation, together with the grotesque spectacle surrounding McGee's execution, graphically demonstrated to her the ugly underside of southern paternalism. The failed mission to save his life bolstered her conviction that southern whites had a unique responsibility to oppose racism.[26]

This consciousness concerned gender as well as race. Braden felt that southern white women, *especially,* should speak out because of their part as the "protected" in the mythology that led to violence against black men. Her view of southern white women's responsibility to act was heightened by her belief that, as she wrote later, "women—if they don't suppress it—have a [special] kind of compassion that the world needs." That sort of thinking, which attributes certain essentialized qualities to women as a whole, was common among female reformers of the early and mid-twentieth century. In the postwar years, it constituted what some feminist historians have called "left feminism," referring to women's groups on the left that united women for social action on the basis of their shared womanhood and, often, female care-giving qualities that stemmed largely from women's child-bearing and -rearing abilities.[27]

On her return to Louisville, Braden spoke at several black churches about the McGee case and wrote about it in the *Louisville Defender*. Later she reported on her activities in a letter to William "Pat" Patterson, an African American Communist who headed the CRC and had spearheaded the campaign to save McGee. Instead of lauding her efforts, Patterson gently chided her, "Blacks don't need you to tell them they're oppressed." It was white people, he suggested, whose minds needed changing.[28]

By that point, Patterson was a menacing figure to U.S. government officials and was shunned by liberals in the NAACP and the American Civil Liberties Union for his strident anticapitalist rhetoric and unabashed CP membership. But Anne Braden respected Patterson enormously. She took his advice seriously, and it prompted in her an epiphany about what being white meant. Because her introduction to social reform had taken place through the postwar "Old Left," which was still vibrant even as Cold War anticommunism began to eclipse it, Braden was exposed early on to a generation of African American labor and civil rights leaders who welcomed whites as allies but did not hesitate to challenge racist or paternalistic comments. Patterson's suggestion resonated with the sense of liberation Braden had felt when she rejected segregation. Rather than seeing her skin color as a source of guilt, she began to think of her whiteness as a mandate for what became a lifetime of outreach to enlist other whites in campaigns for racial freedom, always in close conjunction with African Americans.[29]

Black, White, and Red

By the 1950s, anticommunism was as much a defining feature of liberalism, North and South, as it was of the larger cultural and political landscape. The broad-based "Popular Front" coalitions of New Deal–era southern reforms had been decimated by the hysterical fear of internal communist subversion that engulfed American culture in the postwar period. The post–World War II red scare gripped the South with particular force as it meshed with white southerners' fears of racial changes demanded by a new generation of African American veterans and increasingly supported by the federal government. "Red-baiting" was not new to segregationist zealots, but cultural anticommunism gave new legitimacy to their crusade to defend segregation as it came under increasing assault. The red scare infected even liberal reform organizations such as the NAACP, which purged suspected Communists from its ranks as its members fought off charges of being Communists themselves. The southern political establishment's attempt to stave off civil rights crusades by decrying them as "red" reached new heights in the period following the U.S. Supreme Court's *Brown v. Board of Education of Topeka* decision, which symbolically aligned the federal government with the gathering movement against legal segregation.[30]

In the months surrounding *Brown,* Anne Braden's sharp-edged challenges to southern racism, lodged through groups like the CRC, landed her in jail and brought her regional and national notoriety as a woman diametrically opposed to white southern conventions. When she and her husband flung a dramatic challenge to housing segregation in Louisville, also in 1954, they unwittingly triggered a series of events that would follow them across the South for many years to come.

That spring, Andrew Wade, an African American World War II veteran and prospective homeowner repeatedly rebuffed by racially restrictive real estate policies, sought out the Bradens and asked them to act as "fronts" for him in his quest to buy a suburban home. Without much thought to the repercussions of doing so, the couple agreed to use the privileges granted to them as whites in order to facilitate the purchase. Only one day before the Supreme Court ruled on the *Brown* case, a burning cross and bullets shot through their windows greeted Wade and his family in their new neighborhood. Six weeks of violence followed, culminating in the house's destruction by dynamite and a grand jury investigation into the blast.[31]

In a region rife with tension over the racial changes *Brown* portended and in a nation on its guard against the threat of internal subversion, the Bradens had openly defied segregation. Their defiance looked to many like treason, especially once their history of left-wing associations became public, and the grand jury concluded that they must be members of the Communist Party, or at least "fellow travelers." Their refusal to disassociate themselves from CP allies and causes together with their flagrant transgression of racial boundaries was enough to condemn them. In October 1954, Anne and Carl Braden and five other supporters of Wade (three men and two women, all of them white) were indicted and jailed on sedition charges after the grand jury determined that the Bradens and their fellow conspirators had undertaken the purchase of a home for the Wade family as part of a devious communist plot to stir up discontent among blacks. Those charges sound preposterous in retrospect, considering Wade's repeated testimony that he had sought the couple out and initiated the subterfuge, but at the time they were deadly serious. A sensationalized criminal trial packed with spectators generated banner headlines and courtroom television coverage that held Louisvillians spellbound as FBI witnesses and former CP members from around the nation testified to the evils of Communism. On December 13, 1954, although no evidence substantiated the prosecution's theory of a "Communist plot" or in any way linked him to the destruction of the house, Carl Braden was convicted of sedition in a Kentucky court and sentenced to fifteen years' imprisonment.[32]

Although none of the other defendants was ever tried, the sedition case devastated the Bradens' personal lives: Carl was remanded to prison, and Anne faced a similar fate. Their two young children had to be placed in their grandparents' care for nearly a year, and the couple fought the conviction and lingering charges until a federal ruling in 1956 invalidated state sedition laws and ultimately voided the initial conviction. The Bradens and their co-defendants, the subjects of intense press scrutiny that became regional and national after the trial, found themselves utter pariahs, particularly among whites but eventually among many in the African American community as well.

It is worth noting that only whites were indicted in the sedition case, and that all members of both the grand jury and the criminal jury were white, as were the judge and prosecutors. Although Andrew Wade had also been active in left-wing politics, it was more comfortable, perhaps, for these whites to think of Wade as a "dupe" than to see him as a co-conspirator. Also, if we consider whiteness as socially constructed, the racial dynamics in this case clarify some of the processes through which the boundaries of whiteness were policed during this period. The *Brown* decision appears to have prompted a large number of whites to rally for the first time *as whites,* as evidenced by the birth of the White Citizens' Council movement. Wade's 1954 purchase of a house in an all-white neighborhood provoked a similar upsurge of white-identified reaction. Three weeks before dynamite exploded Wade's home, for example, one letter writer to a suburban Louisville newspaper expressed his opposition to the neighborhood's desegregation by calling for "loyal white people" to join his newly established "American White Brotherhood."[33]

Although public censure of blacks as "communistic" was not unheard of in the 1950s South, that label was far more commonly applied to whites. As the Louisville grand jury transcript reveals, many white southerners of the Cold War era were so mystified by those of their own race who crossed the color line that they could attribute such behaviors only to "traitors." "Colored" Americans were already "other," but once she and her husband were publicly colored "red," Anne Braden was effectively stripped of at least some of the privileges accorded to those who were not colored—that is, other "whites." And although the charges against her and Carl concerned only their beliefs and associations—as opposed to any particular act of wrongdoing—she heard whispers in the courtroom that they should be lynched, and people she had known for years refused to speak to her on the street.[34]

The Bradens never stopped being white, of course. Their skin identified them as such, and they could have simply moved away, changed their names, and begun anew without the "red" label they had earned in Louisville, at least until or unless someone recognized them. But this they did not do. In fact, perhaps the couple's most damnable quality, from the segregationists' perspective, was their stubborn unwillingness to cease their crusades against racial inequality. After 1954, they simply used the media skills they had employed in fighting the sedition charges in service of the burgeoning civil rights movement farther south.

Their activities were frequently derided in the southern press, however, and used to link the civil rights movement with communism in the public imagination. A nationally syndicated columnist, David Lawrence, suggested in 1958 that the Bradens might be responsible for the wave of bombings ripping apart southern synagogues and black churches. Alabama newspapers periodically resurrected the details of the sedition case to castigate local civil rights activists for allowing Anne Braden to address their gatherings. At the movement's height in 1963, Governor George Wallace of Alabama waved a photo of Anne Braden standing next to Martin Luther King Jr. and ranted about the Bradens' communism on the *Today* show in a frenzied defense of Birmingham segregationists.[35]

Prior to the 1960s, most southern white women and men who dissented from the region's racial conventions had located themselves within a liberal reform tradition that was in part an outgrowth of the social gospel message in southern Protestantism. Having found a collective voice only through the distress of the Great Depression, southern liberals championed Franklin Roosevelt's New Deal and criticized racial hierarchy as part of an economic development agenda that sought to reform rather than overthrow capitalism. They sought cooperation with African American activists, and they sometimes joined coalitions that included Marxists of diverse persuasions (some members of the Communist Party or the Socialist Party, and some not). Yet white liberal reformers of the New Deal–World War II era varied widely in their willingness to confront segregation and to level racial hierarchies. Some, like the trade union organizer Lucy Randolph Mason and the New Deal administrator and Alabamian Aubrey Williams, worked at dismantling Jim Crow; others, such as the antilynching activist Jessie Daniel Ames and the *Atlanta Constitution* editor Ralph McGill (among the founders of the Southern Regional Council in 1944), focused on bettering race relations within segregation.[36]

By the 1950s, however, the Cold War had created a void between southern liberals, already relatively few in number, and more radical voices like Anne Braden's, who had been influenced by what historians know as the "Old Left." In practical terms, throughout the Cold War years but particularly after the 1954 sedition case, the "red" label colored Braden every bit as much as her being white ever had. It would take years—decades, really—for her civil rights commitments to be seen as genuine and not as some subversive attempt to "use" racial discord to promote the aims of Soviet communism.[37]

White Woman, Black Power

By 1957, William Patterson's advice to "change white minds" had become Braden's life work. She and her husband became full-time field organizers for the Southern Conference Educational Fund (SCEF), a World War II–era reform group now attempting to build white southern support for the civil rights cause. Instead of silencing her with the "red" label, the sedition fight had galvanized Braden into greater activism after she observed the dearth of white voices in the Cold War South who would support the African American freedom movement that was blossoming around her. In those years Anne Braden edited SCEF's newspaper, the *Southern Patriot,* and she and Carl canvassed the South for news of the few whites willing to act in support of racial integration, which they eagerly publicized.[38]

Student sit-ins in the spring of 1960 ignited a new generation of young dissenters from the racial status quo—black and white. While they were still a tiny minority in relation to southern society at large, pro–civil rights whites were considerably more visible by 1961 than they had been in 1948 when Braden had turned herself inside out and joined African Americans in opposing segregation. Like her, that next cohort of young white women of the early 1960s, who were drawn to join SNCC and the student civil rights movement, immersed themselves in the vibrancy of black culture and cherished a vision of a "beloved community" not unlike the postwar interracialism that had so appealed to Braden. A point of continuity between their generation and the postwar "left" culture into which she had come of age was in the strong black leadership evident in each. Braden has recalled of the early mass movement years: "I don't remember any great debates of 'will whites follow black leadership?' It was just so clear in the sixties that the whole country was following black leadership. Blacks never held political power in the sixties, but they set the agenda for the country in that decade and all of us in the movement knew it."[39]

The 1964 Freedom Summer brought a massive influx of whites into the movement, and with them came new race and gender tensions. The Mississippi Freedom Democrats' abortive challenge at the Democratic Convention that fall brought a great deal of disillusionment into the southern freedom movement. The rise of Black Power soon afterward spelled the end of the idealistic "beloved community" phase of the early student civil rights movement. African Americans in SNCC began to suggest that whites should be working primarily with others of their own race for new civil rights recruits. The years spent acting on Patterson's advice left Braden receptive to that message when black leaders in SNCC essentially reprised it from late 1964 to 1966. While many of SNCC's earliest white staffers found that suggestion emotionally devastating, Braden—a close collaborator with, yet a generation removed from, the students—did not. She became among the few white journalists to give it unqualified support, again differentiating herself from most liberal southerners. She endorsed the new proponents of Black Power and wrote in the *Southern Patriot* in May 1966 that "white people who really believe in a united human race should not be frightened when SNCC and other groups talk about 'black power.' Our society has lived by white power. Unless black people create their own power, there can never be a meeting ground."[40]

Widespread resistance to Black Power was evident in the civil rights movement itself, but it was much more pronounced in the larger society, which reacted hyperbolically, much as it had done in the red scare a decade earlier. Major news organs all around the nation castigated black nationalism, and the government's COINTELPRO operation went to great lengths to crush this imposing new brand of black leadership. Such currents convinced Braden that racism was a more insidious and immovable force than she had previously reckoned it to be.[41]

Although the southern manifestations of the Cold War limited and divided the civil rights movement, opposition to "red-baiting" within the movement also grew as the 1960s unfolded. Anne and Carl Braden were no longer the pariahs among southern youth of the 1960s that they had been among their own age group. Young white supporters of racial change who left SNCC in the middle to latter part of the decade often made their way into SCEF, for which the Bradens served as co-directors after 1966. The couple had worked hard to keep SCEF interracial throughout the late 1950s when whites were particularly hesitant to support civil rights. But they saw the group become increasingly—

even predominantly—white as the 1960s ended and SCEF attracted disillusioned whites departing SNCC. Young white southerners who sought through SCEF to use the tactics of the civil rights movement on other whites failed in part because of what Braden called a "reentry problem." "Some whites who had been in Mississippi where every white face was an enemy just didn't like white people," she observed. "You can't organize people if you don't like them!"[42]

Carl Braden left SCEF in 1973 after a bitter internecine dispute among factions of young, mostly white, radicals; Anne left soon afterward and vowed never again to be a part of an all-white group—and she has not. Her consciousness about whiteness and the blinders it could impose was now such that she would position herself in the movement in relation to her race. "Long before I began putting it into words, I sensed that the black freedom movement was the key to really changing the society," she reflected on that period. "But after we saw the movement of the sixties destroyed, it was so clear that only a strong people-of-color-led movement could bring us to the point where there could be a real beloved community."[43]

As youths who had helped to bring the civil rights movement to national attention went on to launch other social movements later in the 1960s and 1970s, the racial divides that too often characterized those movements became a foundation stone of the rhetorical emphasis on white racism that has characterized Braden's subsequent racial justice campaigns. She began to view overcoming racism, for whites, as a lifelong process. "No white people in a society founded on racism ever totally free themselves of this prison," she wrote later. Black activists, though they frequently opposed the Vietnam War and other injustices, kept their sights on racial freedom in every social movement of which they became a part, while many whites flocked to campus antiwar organizing and various other new causes, leaving behind the antiracist impulse that had first ignited their social activism. Although Braden supported blacks who organized separately from whites, she fought what was often a losing battle against whites' tendency to do the same, convinced that exclusively white groups were all too likely to disregard racism or paternalism in their organizations and in the larger society.[44]

The women's liberation movement that emerged in the late 1960s, just as government repression against black radicalism was fiercest, is a case in point. Braden was initially enthused about the resurgence of feminism. Its early initiators included many of her friends and co-workers, some of whom had first become activists through the civil rights movement. Having developed a gendered consciousness during her years at women's colleges and enjoyed a supportive marriage that nurtured her independence, she had long considered herself a feminist and had routinely worked in women's organizations such as the Women's International League for Peace and Freedom. She had functioned as a mentor to many young women in SNCC and took pride in what she thought of as her "mission to get women out of the kitchen and involved in things." (One of those women was Coretta Scott King, who was included in the Bradens' strategy meetings with Martin Luther King Jr. only at Anne Braden's request.) But she soon became disenchanted with the new women's liberationists, who were overwhelmingly white and focused too narrowly on what she and other critics saw as white women's concerns.[45]

Braden's *Letter to White Southern Women,* published in 1972 as a public conversation with the women's liberation movement, recalls the pathos and malice she witnessed surrounding Willie McGee's execution twenty-one years earlier. The letter (actually a mass-produced SCEF pamphlet), aimed at feminists active in the antirape movement, cautioned them to remember the history of black male–on–white female rape in the South and to challenge rape cases that contained a racial injustice

> I am aware that my appeal to you . . . comes at a time when the women's movement . . . is struggling to make our society . . . deal with the crime of rape. My position is not at odds with this struggle; it is simply another dimension. For the fact is that rape has traditionally been considered a crime in the South—if the woman was white and the accused black. But it has not been seen as a crime—and is not now—if the woman is black. . . . [W]e who are white will overcome our oppression as women only when we reject once and for all the privileges conferred on us by our white skin.[46]

That sort of appeal aligned her with other movement critics—mostly radical women of color—of the new women's liberationists. Although she attended feminist gatherings and supported feminist goals and programs, most of Braden's activism within that movement consisted of nudging it toward greater inclusivity, especially with regard to race, class, and antiwar concerns. "They left race behind," she has maintained of 1960s and 1970s feminism in the decades since. That is not altogether true, however: through the intervention of feminists like Audre Lorde, Anne Braden, and numerous other critics, a more multicultural feminism had emerged by the late 1980s.[47]

Race Traitor

When Anne Braden came of age politically in the postwar South, her radical economic critique, coupled with her relentless challenges to segregation, marginalized her and set her apart from many race dissenters of her own age or older, especially those who were white. But a new generation of young people in the 1960s brought new allies to the struggle to dismantle Jim Crow, and the civil rights movement succeeded in breaking through the southern "police state," as she has described it, to make dissent of all kinds more possible. At the most basic level, Braden outlasted the southern Cold War and its cultural on-slaught against what southern politicians described as her "common-istic" tendencies. Beginning with her mentoring of young 1960s SNCC activists such as Jane Stembridge, Dorothy Dawson, and Sue Thrasher, and continuing with subsequent generations of southern reformers, Braden was able to tran-scend her marginalization as "red" and to shape an alternative ethos of white-ness that included antiracism as a key ingredient.[48]

She has also been remarkably consistent in her critique of white privilege. Her rejection of racism was born in the World War II–era left, which was overly simplistic in its "Negro and white, unite and fight" ideology but laid important groundwork for what became, for Braden, a lifetime of thinking and acting against white supremacy. Considering her unbroken white antiracist activism over six decades, it seems that her radicalism has been most thoroughgoing with regard to race. Very few whites of any generation or region have chosen to foreground race in their own lives to the extent that she has. Since the 1950s, although she has lived in and found much of her affirmation in the African American community, Braden has chosen not to relax into black community life and "pass," so to speak. Instead she has consistently directed her crusades against white supremacy at other whites.[49]

Braden has based her antiracist appeals, above all else, on her identity as a white woman. Her strong self-identification in that regard offers new insights into the history of white female reformers, but it also provides a fascinating vantage point from which to assess a number of controversies in whiteness studies. In general, social theory on whiteness tends to revolve around two dis-tinct responses to the notion of whiteness as a social category. The central question in this regard is: Does a white identity amount to anything more than the racial privilege it confers? If whiteness is a category that is devoid of any meaning save white privilege, the implication is that deconstructing it is not enough. The only path to justice, then, lies in destroying whiteness. This perspective is reflected in the scholarly/activist journal *Race Traitor: Journal of the New Abolitionism,* whose slogan is "treason to whiteness is loyalty to humanity," a postmodern adaptation of an old saying by Susan B. Anthony. Ian Haney Lopez, a critical race theorist and proponent of this view, suggests that "for Whites even to mention their racial identity puts notions of white supremacy into play." Other scholars, such as the legal theorist Barbara Flagg, argue that abolishing whiteness is impractical, either materially, since differences in skin color can still be observed, or conceptually, since cultural, familial, and historical signals have strongly ingrained whites with an awareness of being white that is simply too powerful to give up. Flagg focuses on the need to develop a more positive, holistic white identity that acknowledges that whites too are raced yet rejects racism and racial hierarchy.[50]

Anne Braden's lived experiences suggest that these two approaches are not necessarily dichotomous but rather are strategies that may be utilized in differing circumstances without fully embracing either of the two philosophies. At different moments, Braden has put into practice both schools of thought. Like most current social and cultural theorists of whiteness, she rejects the "melting pot" thesis that once governed American notions of what is today called "diversity." In recent years she has observed that color will, in all likelihood, "always be important." Unlike Lopez, she has found it not just expedient but crucial in her organizing to discuss white privilege openly with other whites in the hope of evoking a "racial conversion" similar to the one she experienced in 1948. "You can't change the color of your skin," she has reiterated, "and guilt is not productive." Action is demanded. Braden balks, however, at the notion of a positive white cultural identity: "The culture I grew up in was fascist. I had to reject it. That doesn't mean I rejected white people. There's a big difference." Her formula for undermining racial hierarchy and working through differences is uncannily similar to that suggested by Audre Lorde (whose passage opened this essay), although the two never conversed or read each other's work, as far as we know. Braden's experiences force both her allies and her opponents in the many social movements of which she has been a part to meditate on the meanings of whiteness because she challenges dominant conceptions of what being—or even being thought of as—white may consist of.[51]

In speeches and writings spanning several decades, Braden has chosen to emphasize her own white privilege mainly for the purpose of deploying it in continuous efforts to topple white supremacy, undertaken always in close collaboration with African Americans and, more recently, other people of color. In delineating herself as a white southern woman, she has long been careful to add that she and all other whites continue to benefit from white privilege and must continually combat their own racism. From the failed 1951 white women's delegation to save the life of Willie McGee, to her role as a "front" for the 1954 desegregation of a Louisville neighborhood, to her championing of Black Power in the late 1960s and 1970s, to more recent campaigns against police abuses in her native Louisville, Braden's radicalism has advanced a broad array of civil rights and civil liberties causes. Her life's radical course also offers historians and social theorists an alternative view of whiteness that, while remaining intimately bound up with the complexities of race, class, and gender, necessarily takes a stand against white supremacy and demonstrates that differences—whether racial, political, or otherwise—do not always divide.[52]

Notes

I would like to thank Tracy K'Meyer, my friend and colleague at the University of Louisville, and Peter Fosl, my philosopher-husband, for helping me to think through some of the ideas on whiteness explored in this essay.

1. Audre Lorde, "Age, Race, Class, and Sex: Women Redefining Difference" (paper delivered at the Copeland Colloquium, Amherst College, Massachusetts, April 1980).

2. Anne Braden, interview with the author, November 2, 2001, Louisville, Kentucky.

3. *This Bridge Called My Back: Writings by Radical Women of Color,* ed. Cherríe Moraga and Gloria Anzaldúa (Watertown, Mass.: Persephone Press, 1981), is probably the best anthology synthesizing various strands of this criticism. My points about white identity in this essay should not be taken to suggest any sort of monolithic or ahistorical white identity, but it is beyond the scope of this essay to unpack fully the multiplicity of meanings therein. I am most interested in Anne Braden's understanding of whiteness, how her politics influenced others' understanding of it, and how those factors have influenced southern social movements of the past half century.

4. Clayborne Carson discusses Braden's initiative in the SNCC white student project in *In Struggle: SNCC and the Black Awakening of the 1960s* (Cambridge: Harvard University Press, 1981), 52–53; Carson examines Braden's relationship to Black Power on pp. 205–6.

5. Anne Braden, interview with the author, November 18, 2001, Louisville, Kentucky; Anne Braden, *The Wall Between* (New York: Monthly Review Press; reprint, Knoxville: University of Tennessee, 1999), epilogue, 335.

6. Diane Fowlkes, *White Political Women: Paths from Privilege to Empowerment* (Knoxville: University of Tennessee Press, 1992), 2; W. E. B. DuBois, *The Souls of Black Folk* (Mineola, N.Y.: Dover Thrift edition, 1994), 2–6; my thinking in this paragraph was influenced by Vron Ware's *Beyond the Pale: White Women, Racism, and History* (London: Verso, 1993, 1996). Ware differentiates between *being* white and *being thought of as* white on p. xii.

7. Braden's voluminous manuscript collection in Wisconsin details her encounters with a variety of southern white liberal women, including some of the individuals profiled in this collection. Most were cordial but distant, as is reflected in Braden's letters regarding the wariness with which she was received during visits with activists in Memphis in 1958; see Anne Braden, miscellaneous correspondence, Carl and Anne Braden Papers, MSS. 6, State Historical Society of Wisconsin, Madison [hereinafter Braden Papers, SHSW], box 29, folder 1. In recent conversations, Braden has also told me of her difficulties establishing correspondence or collaborative initiatives during the 1960s with some of the women profiled here. It should be noted, however, that Braden had an extremely close friendship with Virginia Durr of Montgomery; another exception is her positive association with Alice Spearman; both women are discussed in this volume. On Braden's influence as a role model, see, for example, Sara Evans, *Personal Politics: The Roots of Women's Liberation in the Civil Rights Movement and the New Left* (New York: Vintage Books, 1979), 49–50. Dianne McWhorter also locates Braden as ahead of her time, someone who had to "wait for the zeitgeist to catch up," in "The Connection," *New York Times Book Review,* January 19, 2003, 13.

8. See Kathleen Blee's introduction to her edited volume, *No Middle Ground: Women and Radical Protest* (New York: New York University Press, 1998).

9. Anne Braden, interview with the author, June 3, 1997, Louisville, Kentucky (unless otherwise specified, interview tapes are in the author's possession).

10. Social science research into white identity began, in part, with the questions raised in Michael Omi and Howard Winant, *Racial Formation in the United States: From the 1960s to the 1980s* (New York: Routledge and Kegan Paul, 1986). During the 1990s the scholarship on whiteness proliferated in both the social sciences and in literature, the latter somewhat prompted by the challenge presented by Toni Morrison's *Playing in the Dark: Whiteness and the Literary Imagination* (Cambridge: Harvard University Press, 1992). As this research blossomed throughout the 1990s, scholars began addressing other variables (class, gender, sexual orientation) in increasing depth. Some of the most relevant studies focusing on white women include Ruth Frankenberg's *The Social Construction of Whiteness: White Women, Race Matters* (Minneapolis: University of Minnesota Press, 1993) and Vron Ware's *Beyond the Pale*; the latter is among the most historical but focuses more on the nineteenth century and on Britain than on modern U.S. history. The study that I have found the most insightful with regard to modern southern civil rights history is Becky Thompson's *A Promise and a Way of Life: White Anti-racist Activism* (Minneapolis: University of Minnesota Press, 2001). Thompson's work, which advanced my thinking significantly on the ideas explored in this essay, profiles thirty-nine white U.S. antiracist activists, male and female; among them are Anne Braden and several others whose work was grounded in the civil rights movement. My focus here is on the social and cultural studies research because its content is most relevant to civil rights studies. The journal *Race Traitor* was an early source of much of this investigation.

11. Peter Kolchin, "Whiteness Studies: The New History of Race in America," *Journal of American History* 89.1 (2002): 154–73; quoted material from p. 172.

12. Anne Braden, interview with the author, November 18, 2001; I have borrowed the phrase "transitional generation" from Susan Hartmann, "Women's Employment and the Domestic Ideal in the Early Cold War Years," in *Not June Cleaver: Women and Gender in the Post-war America, 1945–1960,* ed. Joanne Meyerowitz (Philadelphia: Temple University Press, 1994), 84; the phrase "southern aristocracy" is from Reminiscences of Anne Braden, told to Lenore Hogan, June 23, 1972, p. 2, in the Columbia University Oral History Research Office Collection, New York City [hereinafter Braden interview with Hogan, CUOHROC]. Biographical material on Braden not otherwise referenced is drawn from my book, *Subversive Southerner: Anne Braden and the Struggle for Racial Justice in the Cold War South* (New York: Palgrave Macmillan, 2002).

13. Anne Braden, interview with the author, March 10, 1989 (tape 6), Louisville, Kentucky.

14. Ibid.

15. For more detail on postwar Louisville civil rights campaigns, see Wade Hall, ed., *The Rest of the Dream: The Black Odyssey of Lyman Johnson* (Lexington: University Press of Kentucky, 1988), especially 127; Patrick McElhone, "The Civil Rights Activities of the Louisville Branch of the NAACP, 1914–1960" (master's thesis, University of Louisville, 1976), iii; Kentucky Commission on Human Rights, *Kentucky's Black Heritage* (Frankfort: Commonwealth of Kentucky, 1971), 92–93; Anne Braden, interview with the author, March 8–9, 1989 (tape 3), Louisville, Kentucky.

16. Braden interview with the author, March 8, 1989 (tape 2); on the left wing of the Congress of Industrial Organizations (CIO), see Steve Rosswurm, ed., *The CIO's Left-Led Unions* (New Brunswick: Rutgers University Press, 1992); the idea of the Cold War "purge" comes from David Caute, *The Great Fear: The Anti-communist Purge under Truman and Eisenhower* (New York: Simon and Schuster, 1978); these Louisville unionists were active in the Farm and Equipment Workers' (FE) Local 236 and are discussed at length in chapter 5 of Toni Gilpin's "Left by Themselves: A History of the United Farm Equipment and Metal Workers Union, 1935–1955" (Ph.D. diss., Yale University, 1992).

17. Anne Braden to author, June 11, 1997, personal correspondence in the author's possession.

18. Ibid.; Braden interview with the author, March 8–9, 1989 (tape 3); Anne Braden to author, n.d., circa December 28, 2001, 15–17, handwritten correspondence in the author's possession.

19. Braden interviews with the author, June 17, 1999; March 8–9, 1989 (tape 3); Braden interview with Sue Thrasher, April 18, 1981, Louisville, Kentucky (held by Highland Center, New Market, Tennessee), tape 7, side 1, 184–85.

20. Braden interview with Thrasher, tape 6, side 1, 161. Braden has spoken to me of

her working-class perspective in many of our interviews and conversations. Her letter to me of December 28, 2001, 15–17, explicates her view of liberalism, and *Wall Between,* her memoir, alludes to this point in several places. In our final conversations as my book, *Subversive Southerner,* went to press, she differentiated herself from liberals and discussed her views on religion in some depth: see the book's epilogue, p. 338.

21. Braden mentions her compulsion to end segregation in *Wall Between* (1999), 34; Anne Braden, interview with Bud and Ruth Schultz, Louisville, Kentucky, September 2, 1984, interview 1, 43 of transcript.

22. Braden interview with Hogan, CUOHROC, December 7, 1978, interview 2, 105 of transcript; the final quotation is from Braden interview with the author, November 18, 2001.

23. Fred Hobson, *But Now I See: The White Southern Racial Conversion Narrative* (Baton Rouge: Louisiana State University Press, 1999); *Jackson Daily News,* May 6, 1951.

24. For a thorough discussion of the CRC and the McGee case, see Gerald Horne, *Communist Front? The Civil Rights Congress, 1946–1956* (Rutherford, N.J.: Fairleigh Dickinson University Press, 1988); Anne Braden, interview with the author and Michael Honey, Louisville, Kentucky, November 10, 1994; John Dittmer, *Local People: The Struggle for Civil Rights in Mississippi* (Urbana: University of Illinois Press, 1994), 21–22.

25. "City white woman told she should be shot for attempting to defend Negro man's life in Mississippi," *Louisville Defender,* May 12, 1951; this mission is described in full throughout Braden interview with Hogan, CUOHROC, December 7, 1978, interview 2; Fitzhugh quoted in Virginia Kent A. Leslie, "Myth of the Southern Lady," *Spectrum* 6 (1986): 28–29.

26. Dittmer's *Local People* discusses how routine was violence against blacks in Mississippi; LeeAnn Whites's essay, "Rebecca Latimer Felton and the Problem of 'Protection' in the New South," which appears in *Visible Women: New Essays on American Activism,* ed. Nancy Hewitt and Suzanne Lebsock (Urbana: University of Illinois Press, 1993), discusses "protectionism" as having shaped southern gender relations since the Civil War.

27. Anne Braden to author, "Feminism and My Relation to It," January 3, 2002, typescript manuscript in the author's possession. For more on left feminism of this period, see, for example, Amy Swerdlow, "The Congress of American Women: Left-Feminist Peace Politics in the Cold War," in *U.S. History as Women's History: New Feminist Essays,* ed. Linda Kerber, Alice Kessler-Harris, and Kathryn Kish Sklar (Chapel Hill: University of North Carolina Press, 1995). Left feminist activism might take aim at women's subjugated status or it might be directed at a wider social injustice, and such campaigns might or might not actually articulate the source of participants' unity as women.

28. Anne Braden, interview with the author, March 8–9, 1989 (tape 3): Patterson's comments, quoted here, are Braden's recollections of his statements in this interview.

29. The sort of ideology that influenced Braden in post–world War II Louisville is examined most thoroughly in Bob Korstad and Nelson Lichtenstein, "Opportunities Lost and Found: Labor, Radicals, and the Early Civil Rights Movement," *Journal of American History* 75.3 (1988): 786–811.

30. On the origins of the Popular Front uniting Communist Party members and supporters with liberals, socialists, and other Marxists, see Harvey Klehr, *Heyday of American Communism: The Depression Decade* (New York: Basic Books, 1984). On New Deal–era southern reform and the Popular Front, see Patricia Sullivan, *Days of Hope: Race and Democracy in the New Deal Era* (Chapel Hill: University of North Carolina Press, 1996), especially her final chapters on Cold War silencing of dissent. A number of studies address the southern manifestations of Cold War anticommunism: see especially Anthony Dunbar, *Against the Grain: Southern Radicals and Prophets, 1929–1959* (Charlottesville: University Press of Virginia, 1981). Examples of liberal reform groups that established anticommunist policies include the NAACP, ACLU, and CORE. The *Brown* decision as a watershed in civil rights history is discussed in various works: see, for example, Patricia Sullivan, "Southern Reformers, the New Deal, and the Movement's Foundation," in *New Directions in Civil Rights Studies,* ed. Armstead Robinson and Patricia Sullivan (Charlottesville: University Press of Virginia, 1991). Numan Bartley's *The Rise of Massive Resistance: Race and Politics in the South during the 1950s* (Baton Rouge: Louisiana State University Press, 1969) has relatively little to say about the links between anticommunism and the torrid defense of segregation that sprang to life after *Brown,* but his conclusions are similar to mine: see, for example, p. 185.

31. A primary account of these events is available in *The Wall Between,* Anne Braden's 1958 memoir of the sedition case.

32. For details, see miscellaneous newspaper clippings and documents relevant to the sedition case in Braden Papers, SHSW, box 12; or see grand jury transcript, Braden Papers, SHSW, box 2, folder 2. Note: I capitalize the words *communism* and *communist* in this essay and in my book only when the reference pertains to the Communist Party–USA. It is interesting to notice, however, that although their relations with the party were a basis for the proceedings against Anne and Carl Braden in this case, a lower-case *c*—thus, in my mind, a more generic form of communism—was used in the text of the sedition charge that mentions that word (the second of two sedition counts lodged against the Bradens). Though Carl Braden testified under oath that he was not a Communist, Anne Braden—partly as a result of the sedition fight—did not (and still will not today) admit or deny membership in the Communist Party, feeling that such an answer served only to legitimate or delegitimate social activism. Their failure to denounce the party, coupled with their civil rights activism, held the Bradens up to continued harassment by southern authorities. Any form of cooperation with the party was sufficient to

demonize a reformer in the Cold War South and suggest Soviet espionage without any evidence or even mention of such.

33. For a more thorough examination of the events surrounding Wade's purchase, see my *Subversive Southerner,* chap. 6 (especially p. 151 in relation to the letter cited here).

34. I am aware of no comparative study of either white and African American Communists in the South or of the red-baiting assaults against activists in relation to their race, but I base this assertion on an informal assessment of those persons hauled before southern legislative committees or federal un-American investigative hearings held in the postwar years. Such witnesses tended to be white, although there are a few instances of African Americans who became infamous in this regard, including Hosea Hudson in Birmingham and Jack O'Dell in Atlanta. Their cases are discussed, respectively, in Nell Irwin Painter with Hosea Hudson, *The Narrative of Hosea Hudson: His Life as a Negro Communist in the South* (Cambridge: Harvard University Press, 1979); and Taylor Branch, *Parting the Waters: America in the King Years, 1954–1963* (New York: Simon and Schuster, 1988).

35. Clippings and items related to the David Lawrence column referred to here are in Braden Papers, SHSW, box 29, folder 1; Braden Papers, SHSW, box 32, folder 2 (see, for example, clippings from *Montgomery Advertiser* and *Birmingham News,* n.d. [circa December 1959], regarding Anne Braden's speech to the Tuskegee Civic Association); *Today* program transcript, September 27, 1963, in Braden Papers, SHSW, box 56, folder 10.

36. This discussion of the varieties of southern liberalism is much abbreviated: for a more thorough understanding of this topic, see, for example, John Egerton, *Speak Now against the Day: The Generation before the Civil Rights Movement* (New York: Knopf, 1994), 175–89, 305–16. The two primary vehicles for southern (white and interracial) liberalism in the 1930s and 1940s were the Southern Conference for Human Welfare (the more left-leaning and critical of segregation) and the Southern Regional Council (the more moderate).

37. On the Old Left, see Maurice Isserman, *If I Had a Hammer: The Death of the Old Left and the Birth of the New Left* (New York: Basic Books, 1987); on the effects of anticommunism on liberal reform, see Daniel Horowitz, *Betty Friedan and the Making of the Feminine Mystique: The American Left, the Cold War, and Modern Feminism* (Amherst: University of Massachusetts Press, 1998); on the evolution of southern liberalism, see, for example, Morton Sosna, *In Search of the Silent South: Southern Liberals and the Race Issue* (New York: Columbia University Press, 1977). Various studies touch on the difficulties southern anticommunism posed for regional race and economic reforms: see for example my discussion of Bartley in n.30; on the power of cultural anticommunism to marginalize Anne and Carl Braden and other "Old Leftists" even within the civil rights movement, see Anne Braden, "A View from the Fringes," *Southern Exposure* 9.2 (1981): 68–73. Taylor Branch's discussion in *Parting the Waters* of the experiences of Jack O'Dell and Stanley Levinson in their work with Martin Luther King Jr.

and the SCLC explores this pattern. Though it declined by the late 1960s, notoriety and marginalization on the basis of having been identified as "red" continued to plague Braden's activism until well after Carl Braden's death in 1975 and in lessening form until the end of the Cold War at the beginning of the 1990s.

38. For an explanation of how the sedition case affected her feelings about whites in the movement, see Braden interview with Thrasher, tape 9, side 1, 268–69.

39. Anne Braden, interview with the author, November 18, 2001. This observation is consonant with comments on this subject expressed by various contributors to Constance Curry et al., *Deep in Our Hearts: Nine White Women in the Freedom Movement* (Athens: University of Georgia Press, 2000).

40. For more on the emotional difficulties of SNCC's turn to black nationalism, see especially the essays by Penny Patch and Emmie Schrader Adams in Curry et al., *Deep in Our Hearts,* pp. 165, 331 (respectively); Anne Braden, "The SNCC Trends: Challenge to White America," *Southern Patriot* (May 1966): 1–2. It should also be noted that Braden took a good deal of heat for what was seen by some radicals at the time as a reformist view of black nationalism as a mere stage rather than as an end in itself: see, for example, Carol Hanisch, "Blacks, Women, and the Movement in SCEF," in *Feminist Revolution* ([New Paltz, N.Y.:] Redstockings, 1975), 188–91.

41. Clayborne Carson details the reaction to SNCC's turn to Black Power in *In Struggle,* 191–228; for a fuller discussion of COINTELPRO, see, for example, Kenneth O'Reilly, *"Racial Matters": The FBI's Secret File on Black America* (New York: Free Press, 1989).

42. Anne Braden, interview with the author, October 21, 2001, Louisville, Kentucky.

43. Ibid.

44. The final chapters of Carson's *In Struggle* document some of this history; the quoted statement is from Braden, *Wall Between,* 339. Braden's views are drawn from her interviews with the author in 2001 and her unpublished writing (written to author), "Integration and Black Power," January 3, 2002, copy in author's possession.

45. Braden quoted in Evans, *Personal Politics,* 50. Her correspondence during the late 1950s verifies that this mission dates back to at least 1957: see miscellaneous correspondence, Braden Papers, SHSW, boxes 31–34.

46. Anne Braden, *Free Thomas Wansley: A Letter to White Southern Women* (Louisville: SCEF Publications, 1972), pamphlet in author's possession.

47. A thorough critique of racism in the women's liberation movement can be found in various essays in *This Bridge Called My Back*; Braden interview with the author, November 2, 2001. Examples of more inclusive feminist writings abound in women's studies and women's history anthologies that began appearing in the late 1980s. This history is detailed somewhat in the later chapters of Ruth Rosen, *The World Split Open: How the Modern Women's Movement Changed America* (New York: Penguin, 2000). A fuller account can be found in Becky Thompson, "Multiracial Feminism: Recasting the Chronology of Second Wave Feminism," *Feminist Studies* 28.2 (2001): 337–60.

48. This phrase is adapted from Michael Honey's colloquial southern usage of

"common-ist" in *Southern Labor and Black Civil Rights: Organizing Memphis Workers* (Urbana: University of Illinois Press, 1993), 54. In *Personal Politics*, pp. 49–50, Sara Evans writes of Braden's mentoring role in SNCC, and I base these observations also on various conversations I have had with these three women and others. With regard to subsequent generations, it is beyond the scope of this essay to discuss Braden's influence on white antiracist women activists who came after her, but two who come to mind include Mab Segrest of North Carolina (author of a 1994 book entitled *Race Traitor*) and Carla Wallace of Louisville.

49. The relationship of African Americans to the CP and the left generally is explored in various works: one that was most influential in shaping my analysis is Robin D. G. Kelley, *Hammer and Hoe: Alabama Communists during the Great Depression* (Chapel Hill: University of North Carolina Press, 1990).

50. The scholarship on whiteness is too large to detail here, but this synthesis is drawn from Thompson's introduction to *Promise and a Way of Life,* xix–xxi. The quoted material is from Lopez, *White by Law: The Legal Construction of Race* (New York: University of New York Press, 1996), 189: quoted on Thompson's p. xx.

51. Braden interview with the author, October 21, 2001.

52. Braden writes at some length of her own racism in the 1999 epilogue to *Wall Between,* 338–41.

chapter 5

"How Shall I Sing the Lord's Song?"

United Church Women Confront Racial Issues in South Carolina, 1940s–1960s

CHERISSE R. JONES

We came from seventeen states, represented many denominations, and faced multiple problems. But one question and one purpose drew us close together: How shall I sing the Lord's song? Our days of working and thinking together helped to answer that burning question. We learned that while the problems may vary in degrees in different states, all of us face similar situations. New courage is found in the knowledge that one is not alone. We who carry the responsibility of leadership in these crucial days, found the power which flows from such companionship.[1]

※

Caroline Lu Gillespie of South Carolina relayed these sentiments after attending a conference of the Christian Social Relations Departments of United Church Women from the southern, border, and midwestern states in Atlanta, Georgia, on June 21, 1954. The churchwomen had gathered to discuss the implications of the Supreme Court's recent *Brown* v. *Board of Education of Topeka* decision. On returning to South Carolina, members of United Church Women had not only to deal with school desegregation but also to confront the state's pervasive racial discrimination and the poverty it engendered.[2] Southern white churchwomen looked to religious inspiration as motivation for their activism, as Gillespie made clear when she asked, "How shall I sing the Lord's song?" She recognized that similar problems confronted white women in other southern states and emphasized the "courage" of those who had found the "power" to pursue changes. An examination of the efforts of South Carolina's United Church Women to combat segregation and discrimination highlights both the possibilities and the limitations of white women's advocacy for racial justice in southern states in the post–World War II era. This essay illuminates the conservative stance that most white South Carolinians, even those motivated by principles of Christian brotherhood, took toward dismantling segregation and opening political rights to African Americans in the period between World War II and the end of the 1960s. Because records for the rest of the state are sparse, this examination of the United Church Women of South Carolina focuses heavily on the Columbia, South Carolina, chapter.

United Council of Church Women and Racial Activism

During and after World War II, many Americans were forced to reckon with a paradox: they were fighting a war for democracy in Europe while failing to fully practice participatory democracy at home. The war stimulated racial militancy among African Americans and prompted liberal-minded white Americans to evaluate the country's racially discriminatory practices. Women in particular joined voluntary organizations in increasing numbers during the postwar years, especially the American Friends Service Committee (AFSC), the National Council of Jewish Women (NCJW), the National Association for the Advancement of Colored People (NAACP), the Young Women's Christian

Association (YWCA), and United Church Women (UCW), all of which were committed to fight racial injustice in the United States.[3]

The United Church Women, composed predominantly of women from Protestant denominations, was established in 1941 as the United Council of Church Women (UCCW) bringing together three women's groups: the National Council of Church Women, the Council of Women for Home Missions, and the Committee on Women's Work of the Foreign Missions Conference. Its purpose was to "unite church women in their allegiance to their Lord and Savior, Jesus Christ, through a program looking to their integration in the total life and work of the church, and to the building of world Christian community."[4] In 1950, the UCCW became the General Department of United Church Women under the umbrella of the National Council of Churches of Christ, but was commonly called United Church Women (UCW). Growing discontent with their status under the National Council of Churches prompted UCW members to sever their ties with that organization and become an independent organization, Church Women United (CWU), in 1966.[5]

Religion had historically provided an arena for southern women to come together to discuss common concerns. Female leaders like Jessie Daniel Ames, for example, founder of the Association of Southern Women for the Prevention of Lynching (ASWPL), used the best resources of black and white women's religious organizations—such as the Methodist missionary societies and the YWCA, which traced their racial consciousness back to the nineteenth century—to promote racial justice throughout the South. Ames also drew on the experience of the integrated Commission on Interracial Cooperation for support.[6]

Many white women, however, chose segregated organizations to facilitate their activism. The ASWPL, for example, was created as a white women's organization and deliberately excluded black women. Ames felt that middle-class southern white women had "extraordinary moral authority" and that their position against lynching in the South would have more impact than would an organization whose membership was biracial or predominantly African American. Further, when black and white women did meet together, there was often a great deal of mistrust because many black women were hostile toward white women, who were unable to understand the significance of legal segregation and the depth of racial discrimination.[7]

The national UCCW, however, was never in doubt about whether or not it would exist as an integrated organization. At its founding, the UCCW National Assembly debated whether a stipulation about integration should be included in the new constitution. The consensus was that "interdenominational un-questionably meant interracial," thus rendering any specific wording unneces-sary. The national council assumed that membership in local councils would include women from black churches, and in the 1940s it refused to recognize local chapters that were not integrated; consequently, some local chapters of UCCW existed without officially affiliating with the national council.

The national UCCW urged Christian women to examine their own atti-tudes concerning race relations in the United States and to expand their knowledge of other cultures and races internationally. Like other Christian women's organizations of the time, the national organization urged local UCCWs to form "Interracial Clubs" to provide forums for race-related discus-sions in their communities. It mandated that the UCCW become and remain a part of the crusade to eliminate racial discrimination.[8] The national UCCW supported its position on antidiscrimination by its actions. For example, when a Washington hotel refused to accommodate black women delegates to the UCCW board meeting in 1945, all of the meeting's participants left the hotel and stayed in private Washington homes.[9] Annual and regular meetings were held under conditions that tolerated no discrimination.[10] The organization mandated not only racial integration but also religious integration, and opened membership to Roman Catholic and Eastern Orthodox women. In fact, the UCCW worked closely with Jewish women's organizations as well and en-couraged ecumenical cooperation.[11] By adopting an international focus through its World Day of Prayer, the UCCW worked to decrease prejudice and racism among its white members and to increase racial sensitivity and under-standing.[12]

Even during World War II, while the organization's primary focus was on the war effort, an article in its magazine, the *Church Woman,* revealed a con-tinuing commitment to addressing race problems in America. The article called on members to combat racial discrimination, whose effect was to "wipe out the sacredness of individual personality." It criticized stereotypes that treated minorities as categories and prevented one from seeing individuals, even though white Americans understood and acknowledged differences among themselves. Racial discrimination led to "dangerous propaganda" and to even greater misunderstandings among various groups in the United States. Furthermore, and indeed this sentiment is identical with that expressed by black activists during the war years, the UCCW recognized that America could not be an effective world leader or support peace and democracy if democracy was not practiced at home. Finally, the group understood their work as a "Christian movement" of women to counteract racial inequalities in America.[13] Although UCCW members discussed such wartime problems as labor relations and juvenile delinquency, the organization increasingly turned its attention to the racial issues that would consume a considerable portion of its attention over the next two decades.[14]

Churchwomen in Columbia, South Carolina, originally organized as the Woman's Interdenominational Missionary Union, which first considered affiliation with the UCCW national council in early 1944.[15] Although locals knew that the UCCW was integrated nationally and expected its local councils to follow suit, the United Council of Church Women in Columbia does not appear to have had any black members. It moved cautiously to pursue racial change in the 1940s, and most of its efforts in that period focused on public welfare, migrant workers, Native Americans, and industrial schools known as "Opportunity Schools."

Designed to fight illiteracy in the state, Opportunity Schools were originally developed as adult vocational schools by UCCW member Wil Lou Gray. Sessions typically lasted a month, with students ranging in abilities from those who could not read to college graduates working on special projects. A similar school organized for African Americans at Seneca Junior College in Clemson, South Carolina, offered essentially the same curriculum as the white Opportunity Schools.[16] Other UCCW-Columbia projects to assist black women and girls included sponsoring three women to attend the Annual Christian Conference of Negro Women at Benedict College, a historically black institution. The group also supported a day nursery at the college. Black women were sometimes suspicious of whites' efforts to assist their endeavors. Not many, for example, used the Benedict College day-care center, a point that white UCCW members noted in their meeting minutes. Understandably, some black women felt that white women's efforts for "Negro betterment" often amounted to nothing more than a concern for "better" servants.[17]

Despite the mistrust that limited interracial cooperation among black women and white women, UCCW-Columbia established a social service committee and worked at the Girls Industrial School and the Negro Boys School, both founded for wayward black youth and to fight juvenile delinquency. Nationally, juvenile delinquency attracted social reformers throughout the 1940s and 1950s, and South Carolina women were no exception. UCCW-Columbia members worried about the unsupervised children of the many parents employed at Fort Jackson, the city's army base, or serving in the armed forces. This situation heightened concerns about women "deserting" domestic life and their children, who might then become involved in juvenile delinquency. The national UCCW addressed this issue in tandem with the federal government and waged a campaign to end "sex delinquency" in war production industries. Accordingly, UCCW-Columbia members pressured their city officials for action, writing to the mayor pro tem regarding the seriousness of the issue.[18]

Like the national council, the UCCW of Columbia also turned a programmatic eye toward the racial injustices and child welfare issues that pervaded the state. Meetings often featured such themes as "Our Concern, Every Child in Our Town" and "Our Town's Responsibility and New Frontiers in Our Town."[19] A 1946 UCCW-Columbia program showcased a minister who presented a lecture on "Christians and Race" that included "definite information about conditions in South Carolina."[20] The women ended the meeting with a devotional that focused on the theme of "brotherhood," seemingly unaware that they did not truly practice it.

The State Council of United Church Women worked with organizations such as the integrated Southern Regional Council (SRC), which called for leaders from women's groups to discuss women's role in the creation of better "Human Relations."[21] Formed in 1948, the state council did slightly more than the local affiliates to make members aware of racial injustices in South Carolina. After its formation, publicity chair Edith Dabbs of Mayesville wrote to the *Church Woman* acknowledging churchwomen's commitment to Christian democracy and to changes yet to come: "The Council of Church Women of South Carolina is two years old but at the state meeting recently the skeleton organization was finally completed with constitution and working regulations. It is still in the throes of its infancy but the women enlisted hold the conviction that Christianity is the only answer to world confusion and are ready to meet the challenge."[22] The State Council of United Church Women and the Columbia branch worked to make changes even as they upheld the law of Jim Crow, advocating slow and conservative change. Throughout most of the 1940s, both organizations limited their activism to efforts that merely informed the membership about racial injustice in the state and provided limited and segregated services for blacks.

United Church Women of Columbia and *Brown*

At a meeting in 1951, UCW-Columbia members suggested that "local Negroes should be urged to organize a council." No records indicate that such a segregated branch was formed, yet the organization clearly assumed a more proactive role in improving race relations in South Carolina in the 1950s, particularly during the furor that surrounded the pending decision of the *Brown* v. *Board of*

Education of Topeka case.[23] Indeed, South Carolina had played a pivotal role in this court case. One of the two legal challenges to school segregation to originate in the twentieth-century South was from Clarendon County, South Carolina.[24] The state council of United Church Women determined that regardless of the decision of the Supreme Court, it was necessary to preserve the spirituality of Christian people, black and white, in South Carolina by working to promote racial harmony, and assumed the lead in preparing its members for whatever changes might be mandated by the pending decision. In 1951, Edith Dabbs, whose husband, James McBride Dabbs, was president of the SRC, issued a letter to local branches announcing a meeting in Columbia with Esther Stamats of the national UCW. Although the outcome of the meeting is unclear, Stamats urged white women to discuss "big implications of which we are a part," thus preparing them to examine closely the pending *Brown* decision as well as the inequities of separate schooling in South Carolina.[25]

The state council pursued this direction in 1953 when it called on churchwomen to investigate conditions in South Carolina public schools using a pamphlet called *A Check List for Your Local Schools.* The checklist, published by the SRC, suggested conducting a statistical and comparative study of black and white schools in the state by asking such questions as

What is the average salary of white and Negro teachers with comparable training and experience? What is the current operating expenditure per white and Negro pupil? How do white and Negro school buildings compare in age, appearance, type of construction, toilet facilities, lighting, ventilation, heating, auditoriums, gymnasiums, athletic stadiums, cafeterias, and libraries?[26]

The fact that the exercise was conducted at the level of the state council, which was often more progressive than local councils, forced white churchwomen to confront inferior conditions in South Carolina's black schools.

Caroline Lu Gillespie, chair of the Christian Social Relations Committee of the United Church Women of South Carolina, stressed the seriousness with which the organization regarded the school desegregation case. Members of the state council felt that Christian people should be informed and prepared to give guidance concerning changes that might result from the outcome of *Brown* v. *Board of Education,* such as school integration and equal access to public facilities for blacks.[27] Gillespie further asserted that southern churchwomen were "nearing the threshold of an historic moment in the history of our nation and indeed of the world. Regardless of the decision of the Supreme Court, Christian people will have to be acquainted with the moral and spiritual issues which are at stake."[28] Thus, the state council strongly encouraged white women to become familiar with racial inequities throughout the state.

The *Brown* decision was met with tremendous hostility throughout much of the South. According to one historian, many white southerners "came to perceive segregation and integration as polar opposites, such that one could not exist in the presence of the other, regardless of the experiences to the contrary."[29] Furthermore, some liberal whites who had been sympathetic to African Americans' call for justice perceived forced school desegregation as a threat to local authority and white privilege. Consequently, many of those who had pushed for moderate racial improvements withdrew their support from race relations organizations.

The Supreme Court's decision generated varied reactions in South Carolina, including "shock, disbelief, anger, [and] rage," according to South Carolina historian Walter Edgar. A "Committee of 52," which included businessmen, authors, clergy, and politicians, published a declaration supporting separate schools to preserve "public education and domestic tranquillity."[30] Echoing the nineteenth-century words of John C. Calhoun, they called on state officials to "interpose the sovereignty of the State of South Carolina between Federal Courts and local school officials." They vowed to resist the "clear and present danger" to state sovereignty "without resort to physical strife, but without surrender of our position."[31]

Edith Dabbs, now president of the state council, immediately sent a letter to Governor James F. Byrnes expressing the position of United Church Women of South Carolina: "Both on a national level and statewise, we have always maintained that enforced segregation had no place in Christian activity and constituted a very real threat to our Democracy."[32] Byrnes had previously supported controversial New Deal legislation in South Carolina and had established himself as a political moderate in doing so. He did not, however, support the *Brown* decision, and on leaving office in 1955 urged white South Carolinians to massive resistance.[33] In sum, state leaders were clearly dedicated to maintaining segregation in South Carolina. Thus, when United Church Women looked to them to foster change, they most often found them reluctant to do so.

Under Edith Dabbs's presidency in the 1950s, the state council held annual meetings in Columbia that involved equal numbers of black and white women. By the late 1950s, however, only members of the board of directors were invited to attend the state council meetings, although the bylaws prescribed that *all* members were welcome. Because only one black woman sat on the board (as secretary), the board of directors' meetings became almost exclusively white.

Some members who supported a positive response to *Brown* and wished to see South Carolina schools peacefully integrated attended a conference of the Christian Social Relations Departments of United Church Women from southern, border, and midwestern states in Atlanta, Georgia, on June 21, 1954. At the two-day conference, held just a month after the *Brown* decision, they debated the implications of desegregation. It is not clear if any black women attended this conference; the evidence suggests quite a cautious tone to the discussion. Some attendees worried about the amount of time necessary for whites to adjust to integrated schools and wondered if the Supreme Court decision required immediate integration. The women studied strategies, techniques, and organizational procedures they might adopt to facilitate peaceful integration in each state. Many of these women were struggling to overcome their traditional upbringing in conservative, racially segregated communities; at the same time they recognized that segregated schools perpetuated prejudices in their own (white) children. Churchwomen also wondered about the plight of black teachers who might find themselves unemployed in integrated schools. (They did not consider that some black parents might want only improved conditions in black schools rather than forced enrollment of their children in previously all-white schools.) Some attendees openly criticized southern ministers and churches that failed to speak out in favor of the *Brown* decision. Indeed, they thought it imperative to encourage the clergy to take a positive Christian stand on this issue and help Christian women find solutions to the "bitter climate of opinion."[34] Finally, however, those at the conference reaffirmed their belief in human brotherhood and the inclusiveness of Christian fellowship, and thus committed themselves to promoting a Christian society free of segregation.

The South Carolina members who attended this conference returned home to reaffirm their commitment to work for racial change in their home state. They supported the Supreme Court's decision because it gave them an opportunity to translate Christian beliefs into democratic ideals. Caroline Lu Gillespie summarized their sentiments: "We came [to the Atlanta conference] from seventeen states, represented many denominations, and faced multiple problems. But one question and one purpose drew us close together: How shall I sing the Lord's song?"[35] South Carolina churchwomen realized that they were not alone in combating the injustices of racial and social discrimination. Although the problems varied in degree, churchwomen from other southern states faced similar situations. And although they were ambivalent about the shape their activism would take and the risks it would involve, the churchwomen realized that Christian doctrine mandated that they do something to bring about more harmonious race relations and that, as churchwomen, they were charged with this responsibility.

Members of local UCW chapters struggled to determine what changes to the racial status quo might mean locally.[36] At a meeting in Columbia, South Carolina, in May 1956, Dorothy Tilly, of the Southern Regional Council in Atlanta, gave a lecture on the history of women who had come together in previous decades for racial and social reform. The meeting also included male speakers such as Marion A. Wright of Linville Falls, North Carolina, president of the Southern Regional Council and a legal expert on the *Brown* v. *Board of Education* case, who asserted that "the disease, which afflicts us, is called intolerance."[37] Wright would later marry South Carolina UCW member Alice Norwood Spearman, thus joining two individuals with a long history of civil rights activism.

Among those who recognized the importance of the United Church Women's role in racial activism in South Carolina was Father Maurice V. Shean of "The Rectory" in Rock Hill, South Carolina. Though he was not actually present at the 1956 meeting, he sent a suggestion with his secretary, Mrs. Joseph Bonetti, that United Church Women petition Governor George Bell Timmerman Jr. to appoint a biracial council of women to study implementation of desegregation in the state. In addition to discussing this suggestion, meeting participants met in discussion groups with such titles as "What Can You Do?" and "What Is the Church's Responsibility and Place?" The groups further queried how they might translate their findings into local communities and concluded that it was necessary to get blacks and whites to meet together for discussions to clarify the problems that existed between the races.[38]

Those in attendance were well aware of the obstacles to organizing such a biracial meeting. Grace T. Kennedy of Bennettsville, South Carolina, the secretary of UCW Christian social relations, lamented that whites in her community had refused to meet with blacks for discussions of any kind. Moreover, five UCW members in attendance asked not to receive further information about desegregation, claiming they were "unprepared for it at present."[39] The fear of reprisal was indeed real for some South Carolina churchwomen. Former UCW-SC president Edith Dabbs and her husband faced scathing attacks for their activism from the conservative *Charleston News and Courier*.[40]

The national council, adamant about promoting civil rights throughout the South, encouraged South Carolina churchwomen to help facilitate desegregation and racial understanding. In November 1956, Esther C. Stamats, director of the Department of Christian Social Relations for the national UCW, again came to South Carolina and held a workshop for UCW-Columbia on "Human

Relations." (Interestingly, the national United Church Women referred to such meetings as "race relations" workshops, but churchwomen in Columbia changed the name to "human relations" to encourage attendance and deflect unwanted opposition.) Stamats offered specific tactics to deal with racial issues and organized small groups to discuss the questions "What holds us back?" and "What next steps can you take in your community?" The attendees outlined such obstacles as the breakdown in communication, fear of reprisals, pressures to conform, and threats to freedom. The minutes for this workshop reveal the anxiety some women felt. The secretary reported that "attendance was very poor" at this workshop, but she also affirmed optimistically that everyone who did attend "was exceedingly interested."[41]

The national council also pressured United Church Women in South Carolina to take the obvious step toward integration by welcoming African American women into their local organizations. In 1957, when Mrs. David Baker, editor of the *Church Woman,* spoke to the Columbia organization about her experiences with a team of Christian women who had traveled abroad, she emphasized the "interdenominational, interracial and intercolor composition" of its teams with churchwomen around the world.[42]

Despite the model of integration practiced by the national UCW and the various programs it promoted, white hostility toward desegregation and the increasing local racial tensions limited white women's attempts to integrate their organizations and their communities. According to summaries of reports from UCW state and local councils between 1957 and 1959, only two of the South Carolina councils were involved in economic and industrial relations programs, and none was involved in race relations or civil liberties work. As of 1959, only one council was actively involved in the aforementioned endeavors.[43]

This was not an unusual position for southern chapters of United Church Women. The president of United Church Women of Mississippi resigned in 1958 after declaring that the national UCW had let "integration become its one absorbing interest." She further asserted that she had not resigned "because of integration, but because of the group's absorption with the issue."[44] UCW-Columbia's leadership broke away from the national council's policies supporting racial activism and adopted a defensive position toward race relations in the 1960s. In addition, they refused to support the South Carolina Council for Human Relations (SCCHR) with its emphasis on interracial cooperation and racial justice.

Not all members of UCW-Columbia accepted their organization's intransigence on racial issues, however. Alice Norwood Spearman, a member of UCW-

Columbia as well as the executive secretary of the SCCHR and a former president of the South Carolina Federation of Women's Clubs, refused to be intimidated by white critics and local racial tensions. She urged the organization to follow national bylaws mandating interracial cooperation and racial understanding. In her estimation, "No one has the right, not even an officer, to set aside the provision in our by-laws that annual membership meetings be held." Spearman encouraged all UCW members to attend a joint meeting with the SCCHR at Saint John's Episcopal Church in Columbia, South Carolina, to discuss racial justice.[45] In a confidential letter to black member and officer Sarah Z. Daniels of Morris College, Spearman urged Daniels to bring other black women who would be sympathetic to the SCCHR's agenda, asserting, "it has occurred to me that it would be fine to have you bring with you any of the fine Negro women whose interests would make them natural participants in the council program." Spearman, who hoped to encourage United Church Women of South Carolina to continue following the national policy mandating integration, was adamant about maintaining biracial organizations such as the UCW, arguing, "[S]urely in these trying times we should not permit any organization which is able to function bi-racially to diminish its efforts."[46] Individuals such as Alice Norwood Spearman and black churchwomen in general understood not only the importance of UCW locally, but also its importance as a national force fighting racial injustice, and urged all Christian women in South Carolina to put "cause above personal prestige" and continue their work for racial change in the state.[47]

Spearman did not find sympathy among the majority of South Carolina UCW members, who preferred the status quo. United Church Women of South Carolina resisted national efforts to promote a civil rights agenda even when a South Carolinian was appointed to direct a major UCW initiative. In 1961, United Church Women received a three-year grant of sixty-six thousand dollars from the Field Foundation to conduct "Assignment: *Race.*" This project was designed to launch a nationwide, interdenominational attack on racial discrimination in churches, housing, schools, and employment. The grant specified that UCW would recruit and train women in race relations work at the local level.[48] Carrie E. Meares of Fountain Inn, South Carolina, a former YWCA director and a graduate of Winthrop University in Rock Hill, headed the project.

In preparation for "Assignment: *Race,*" the national office called for state UCW officials to submit reports on the response of local councils to sponsoring workshops on racism. UCW-Columbia was the only South Carolina branch to report any participation in the program at all.[49] In October 1966 the group co-sponsored an interdenominational statewide conference in Columbia called "The Racial Revolution in Christian Perspective." According to the conference program, very few women were included on the official planning committee, although it appears that UCW-Columbia members did most of the organizing work. And although UCW-Columbia itself was not mentioned as a sponsor, the program did list the names of such individual UCW members as Mrs. M. H. Baxley, a Methodist; Mrs. Theodore J. Ledeen, a Presbyterian; and Mrs. Jules Haley, an Episcopalian and the chair of the arrangements committee for the conference.[50]

The conference was regarded as a resounding success by Mrs. Jules Haley, who reported 310 reservations for the conference dinner. As she thanked UCW-Columbia for its participation, she also invoked the Christian convictions on which the organization was founded by noting that she "had many expressions that the Holy Spirit was moving upon the conference in helping witness to the reconciling group."[51] This conference appears to have been the limit of overt racial activism for UCW-Columbia in the 1960s as the group increasingly shifted its focus away from integration and onto one of the most visible consequences of racism, the grinding poverty pervading much of the state.

United Church Women and Antipoverty Work in South Carolina

After President Lyndon Johnson announced his nationwide War on Poverty in 1964, business, civic, and religious organizations formed coalitions to attack the multiple problems associated with poverty.[52] The national UCW, along with the National Council of Catholic Women, the National Council of Jewish Women, the National Council of Negro Women, and the National Board of the Young Women's Christian Association, created Women in Community Service (WICS) in 1964. WICS, which was affiliated with the federal government's Women's Job Corps, recruited young people, young women in particular, to work in its various antipoverty programs. It also relied on volunteers to work in poverty, illiteracy, unemployment, and malnutrition programs across the nation. Integration was absolutely essential not only to WIC's strategy, but also to its success.[53]

The national UCW worked to establish chapters of WICS in South Carolina. At the WICS organizational meeting in Charleston, women discussed ways to improve the situations of impoverished young women. Mrs. Paul Pfeutze of the WICS national office in Washington, D.C., outlined the ways in which Job Corps participation encouraged young women to seek opportunities for advancement beyond their impoverished communities. UCW-Columbia and the South Carolina Council on Human Relations joined forces to co-sponsor Head Start programs in twenty-five South Carolina counties. Project Head Start operated for eight weeks during the summer and provided skills and training for underprivileged children who were entering first grade in the next academic year.[54]

The formation of WICS in South Carolina made it possible for black women to enter the mainstream of UCW activities and to design far-reaching social programs for the state.[55] In 1965, Mrs. Calvin R. Greene, a librarian at Charles A. Brown High School and a graduate of South Carolina State University with a master's degree in library science from Indiana University, was installed as project director of WIC in Charleston. Greene had also been a Job Corps volunteer and a social welfare worker at Saint Catherine's Auxiliary of the Blessed Sacrament Roman Catholic Church in Charleston. Her education and experience fitted her for the demands of the WICS program. Other women who volunteered as assistant directors of WICS in Charleston came from the local Council of Jewish Women, Council of Negro Women, and United Church Women.[56] Thus, the WIC program provided women from different racial and religious backgrounds with an opportunity to work together to improve conditions in South Carolina.

In 1966, UCW members held a worship service with the theme "Poverty and Affluence," which they turned into a study course and an annual worship event. The following year they invited Latitia Anderson of the Division of General Studies at the University of South Carolina, the head of the South Carolina Head Start Program, to address members on "Affluence and Poverty." Clearly recognizing the impact that an organization such as United Church Women could have on race-based poverty, Anderson urged members to volunteer in community Head Start programs and provide financial assistance for supplies and food for day-care centers. She challenged white women to use United Church Women's resources to "become active in this service to the community."[57]

Although UCW members' efforts improved living and health conditions among poor rural blacks, many of whom were migrant workers, the women were not pioneers in such efforts. Black women's organizations had been doing similar work since the early decades of the twentieth century; indeed, they had had ongoing projects to bring health care and education to African Americans on South Carolina's Sea Islands for some time. When Septima P. Clark, a member of United Church Women in Charleston and a well-known activist, was a young teacher on Johns Island in the 1920s, she secured funds from the Gamma Xi Omega chapter of Alpha Kappa Alpha Sorority, Inc., to help blacks obtain ringworm treatment and diphtheria immunization. She also enlisted the help of a white Presbyterian women's group and of Mrs. Ashley Halsey, a white Charlestonian who used her influence to improve the island's water system, help families upgrade their diets, and convince landowners to inspect tenant homes.[58]

By the late 1960s when the national UCW Board had reestablished the organization as Church Women United (CWU), the councils in South Carolina began to focus almost solely on migrant poverty. In 1968, CWU-Columbia member Mrs. F. E. Reinartz suggested taking a trip to Charleston for a "Go-See" tour of migrant camps because members were concerned about living and health conditions.[59] Serving African Americans in rural pockets of poverty remained much less threatening to the status quo than pursuing integration and calling for political equality and first-class citizenship. To this end, churchwomen developed day-care activities and provided clothes and health kits for families through their May Fellowship Day offering. They also sponsored African American minister Willis Goodwin as a chaplain in the migrant camps as part of Rural Mission, Inc., on Johns Island.[60] Church Women United of Charleston helped secure funds from the Office of Economic Opportunity in the mid-1960s to create the South Carolina Commission of Farm Workers to help expand the services available to migrant workers.

CWU members participated in South Carolina's Adult Basic Education (ABE) program in the late 1960s and 1970s. ABE was designed to "eliminate the inability of adults in need of basic education to read and write English." According to the 1960 Census, twenty-three million Americans over twenty-five years of age had completed less than eight years of schooling.[61] In Columbia, churchwomen supported the Greater Columbia Literacy Council, which trained volunteers to tutor those who could not read.[62] Unlike the Voter Education Project sponsored by the biracial Student Nonviolent Coordinating Committee (SNCC) in the 1960s, which educated African Americans to register, vote, run for office, and understand their rights as citizens, ABE concentrated simply on adult literacy.[63] Its goal was to raise educational levels, thus creating better-qualified job applicants and perhaps reducing welfare roles. ABE presented less of a challenge to white supremacy than the Voter Education Project, which called for equal access for African American voters, but it provided considerable access to managerial positions for black women. With the help of Alice Leppert of the CWU national staff, South Carolina's ABE program, which included such black members as Johnetta Edwards and Ada Campbell in Charleston County, developed workshops for Charleston ABE volunteers under the leadership of professors from the University of South

Carolina. Septima P. Clark, a co-chair of the local unit of basic education volunteers in Charleston, helped to plan area workshops in cooperation with local and state adult education leaders.[64]

Black Women's Membership in United Church Women

Nationally, UCW membership had been integrated since the 1940s, and officers expected local UCW chapters to be integrated as well. Black women certainly must have been interested in UCW programs, and may even have sought membership. Prior to the 1960s, however, there was little visible black participation in UCW-SC with the exception of Anna Reuben, wife of the president of the historically black Morris College in Sumter, South Carolina, who became the first African American woman elected to a position in UCW-SC in the early 1950s.[65]

An exception to the exclusion of black members from local councils seems to have been the Aiken council. A UCW-Columbia member admitted in 1967 that her council had been "playing at being a part of the national group for many years," but only the Aiken council had been fully integrated from the beginning.[66] Although there is little extant documentation, United Church Women in Aiken had proudly maintained integrated membership since 1953: "Entering our tenth year of existence as an 'integrated' council, we have indeed felt the sustaining arm of our Lord. . . . Our bi-racial aspect has been a unique experience for us all and we truly believe our work, though done quietly, has been blessed."[67] The United Church Women in Aiken seem also to have actively sought out predominantly African American women's clubs throughout South Carolina and offered them membership in the Aiken branch of UCW.[68]

In Orangeburg County, where there was a large population of educated African Americans and two African American institutions of higher learning, a predominantly black chapter of United Church Women operated. In 1965, the Episcopal Church Women of Saint Paul's Episcopal Church (black) sponsored a community forum entitled "Knowing the Time," which local African American churchwomen in Orangeburg used to create an interdenominational organization through which women of all faiths could convene to discuss social problems. Other community churchwomen responded overwhelmingly to these efforts, and they too were later invited to attend the community forums. They officially affiliated as United Church Women of Orangeburg in 1965.

Although the Aiken and Orangeburg chapters of United Church Women provide examples of the possibilities of integrated racial activism, UCW-Columbia was clearly not integrated until the late 1960s. Prior to that, black women members of UCW-Columbia were few and possibly only tokens. However, one black woman stands out as an active member of UCW-Columbia: Myrtle Ruff Witherspoon. Although her name does not appear in UCW-Columbia records until 1967, she clearly used her membership to promote changes for African Americans in Columbia and throughout Richland County. Witherspoon was most active in South Carolina's Office of Economic Opportunity, and she served on a similar committee in UCW-Columbia, requesting donations and volunteers from among its members. She assumed a more prominent position in CWU-Columbia in the early 1970s, and served as its president from 1970 to 1971.[69]

This also was the case at the state level. In 1971, Alice Waltena Josie became president of Church Women United in South Carolina. Josie, a former high school teacher, was also the first president of Church Women United of Orangeburg from 1966 to 1969 and an active member of the Episcopal church. After she organized and became the first president of Church Women United in Orangeburg, Josie was elected state president of Church Women United and also served as a member of the national board of managers.[70]

Although it is not clear what their relationship was to the UCW before the 1960s, both Myrtle Witherspoon and Waltena Josie became leaders in the organization and actively involved themselves in UCW programs that served African American communities. Further, the fact of integrated membership in UCW by the 1960s illustrates how far white women members had come as they adopted national mandates for integrated councils and actively participated in the national agenda for combating racial injustice.

Conclusion

United Church Women in Columbia took small steps toward racial justice in South Carolina despite deep-seated racial attitudes that limited any activism deemed controversial. Exemplified by the national UCCW in the 1940s, religion proved a powerful incentive for women to examine their own racial attitudes and to analyze their communities' practices in order to recognize that Christianity was incompatible with racial prejudice and discrimination. The *Brown* v. *Board of Education* decision was an important watershed for UCW-Columbia and UCW-SC, as members further acknowledged racial problems in South Carolina and realized the implications of ending segregation. Although some UCW members shied away from overt racial activism after the

Brown decision, others pushed the organization to live up to the program of the national UCW, which forcefully called for churchwomen to fight racial and social injustices.

United Church Women in Columbia and in South Carolina as a whole also struggled with admitting black women to membership in the organization, although they supported separate organizations for them. Some branches, however, like the United Church Women in Aiken, had proudly maintained integrated membership since the 1950s. In Orangeburg, black churchwomen created a predominantly African American branch of United Church Women. By the late 1960s, black women were token members of UCW-SC and UCW-Columbia, but the leadership positions held by at least two women, Myrtle Witherspoon and Waltena Josie, attest to the raised consciousness of white members over that of earlier decades.

Even so, black and white women largely continued to work separately in mostly segregated organizations for racial and social change. Unfortunately, many white women were unable to translate Christian ideals into daily practice. Because they feared the risks involved with racial activism, they found it easier to retreat to the safety of white privilege. Other white women supported such programs as Women in Community Service or Adult Basic Education, aimed at alleviating poverty among migrant workers in the South Carolina low country and preparing poorly educated African Americans for jobs. The fact of white women working closely with black women in these organizations was more socially acceptable than civil rights activism per se. An analysis of UCW ventures in South Carolina reveals that despite tremendous obstacles to interracial activism, United Church Women throughout the state worked consistently to educate and inspire members to implement small but important steps toward racial and social justice.

Notes

1. "Echos from the Atlanta Conference," *Church Woman* (October 1954): 36–37, General Commission on Archives and History of the United Methodist Church, Drew University, Madison, N.J. [hereinafter GCAHUMC].

2. Ibid.

3. Harvard Sitkoff, "Racial Militancy and Interracial Violence in the Second World War," *Journal of American History* 57 (December 1971): 661; Susan Lynn, *Progressive Women in Conservative Times: Racial Justice, Peace, and Feminism, 1945 to the 1960s* (New Brunswick: Rutgers University Press, 1992), 2.

4. Gladys Culkin, *Follow Those Women* (New York: Office of Publication and Distribution, 1961), 58.

5. Susan Hill Lindley, *"You Have Stept out of Your Place": A History of Women and Religion in America* (Louisville: Westminster John Knox Press, 1996), 307. To remain historically accurate, this essay uses United Council of Church Women (UCCW) in reference to the 1940s organization and United Church Women-Columbia (UCW-Columbia) and United Church Women of South Carolina (UCW-SC) for the 1950s and 1960s. In the late 1960s the group became Church Women United.

6. Jacquelyn Dowd Hall, *Revolt against Chivalry: Jessie Daniel Ames and the Women's Campaign against Lynching* (New York: Columbia University Press, 1993), 59, 66.

7. Ibid., 88, 180.

8. "New Race Problems," *Church Woman* (February 1943): 35, GCAHUMC.

9. Lindley, *Out of Your Place,* 307.

10. Culkin, *Follow Those Women,* 65.

11. Lindley, *Out of Your Place,* 307.

12. Ibid., 391. Observed annually on the first Friday of Lent, World Day of Prayer began in 1887 to unite Christians in prayer and for offerings for Christian missions at home and abroad.

13. "New Race Problems," 35.

14. *New South* 1.1 (1946): 7; *Church Woman* (January 1944): 9–10; (June 1944): 23–27, GCAHMC.

15. "History of the Women's Interdenominational Missionary Unions, South Carolina, 1915–1940," Dacus Library Special Collections and Archives, Winthrop University, Rock Hill, S.C. [hereinafter Winthrop University Archives], box 1, folders 1–2.

16. Ernest McPherson Lander Jr., *A History of South Carolina* (Chapel Hill: University of North Carolina Press, 1960), 137.

17. "History of the Woman's Interdenominational Missionary Unions, South Carolina, 1915–1940," Winthrop University Archives, box 1, folders 1–2; Paula Giddings, *When and Where I Enter: The Impact of Black Women on Race and Sex in America* (New York: William Morrow, 1984), 172.

18. Minutes of meeting, Church Women United in Columbia Records, January 11 and 21, 1944, March 21, 1944, Winthrop University Archives, box 1, folder 2; Nancy Woloch, *Women and the American Experience: A Concise History,* 2nd ed. (Boston: McGraw-Hill Higher Education, 2002), 324; "Juvenile Delinquency in Wartime," *Church Woman* (June 1944): 27; "Race Relations," *Church Woman* (June 1944): 23, GCAHUMC.

19. Minutes of meeting, Church Women United, May 4, 1945, May 2, 1947, November 1947, and March 21, 1944, History of the Woman's Interdenominational Missionary Unions, South Carolina, 1915–1940, Winthrop University Archives, box 1, folders 1–2.

20. Minutes of meeting, CWU-Columbia, November 15, 1946. This minister's race is not clear in the minutes.

21. South Carolina Council for Human Relations Records [hereinafter SCCHR], South Caroliniana Library, University of South Carolina, Columbia, box 24, folder 637.

22. *Church Woman* (April 1950): 36, GCAHUMC.

23. Minutes, Board of the Columbia Council of Church Women, December 15, 1951, United Church Women in Columbia Records, Winthrop University Archives, box 1, folder 1.

24. Walter Edgar, *South Carolina: A History* (Columbia: University of South Carolina Press, 1998), 522. The other was from Virginia.

25. Correspondence from Edith M. Dabbs, Chairman, Public Relations, South Carolina Council of Church Women, SCCHR, box 24, folder 637. Unfortunately, no extant records reveal the outcome of this meeting.

26. "A Check List for Your Local Schools," *New South* 8.9 (1953): 1–8.

27. SCCHR, box 24, folder 637, January 30, 1954.

28. Ibid.

29. David R. Goldfield, *Black, White, and Southern: Race Relations and Southern Culture, 1940 to the Present* (Baton Rouge: Louisiana State University Press, 1990), 78, 87.

30. Edgar, *South Carolina,* 524.

31. Howard H. Quint, *Profile in Black and White: A Frank Portrait of South Carolina* (Washington, D.C.: Public Affairs Press, 1958), 28.

32. Ibid., 170–71; "Southern Leaders Confer," *Church Woman* (March 1954): 30–31.

33. Edgar, *South Carolina,* 525.

34. "Southern Leaders Confer," *Church Woman* (August–September 1954): 30–31, GCAHUMC.

35. "Echos from the Atlanta Conference," *Church Woman* (October 1954): 36–37, GCAHUMC.

36. Minutes of meeting, UCW,-Columbia, March 6, 1956, SCCHR, box 24, folder 652c.

37. Minutes of meeting, UCW-Columbia, March 6, 1956, SCCHR, box 24, folder 642c.

38. Ibid.

39. Ibid.

40. Correspondence dated January 21, 1960, SCCHR, box 24, folder 652.

41. Minutes of meeting, UCW-Columbia, November 26, 1956.

42. Ibid., January 3, 1957.

43. "Report on Localities Approached for United Church Women Workshops," March 29, 1957, 1224-4-2:03, Racism Program, 1225-2-3:03, Summaries of Reports from CWU State and Local Council, 1957–1959, GCAHUMC. The reports do not specify which council it was.

44. "Church Woman's Head Quits," *New York Times,* March 16, 1958, 38:7.

45. Alice N. Spearman to Sarah Daniels, January 21, 1960, SCCHR, box 24, folder 652. For more information on Spearman, see the essay by Marcia Synnott in this volume.

46. Alice N. Spearman to Sarah Daniels, January 21, 1960, SCCHR, box 24, folder 637. Spearman also requested that the letter be destroyed.

47. Correspondence, January 20, 1960, SCCHR, box 24, folder 652.

48. Dorothy S. Macleod, "United Church Women Receives $66,000 Grant," *Church Woman* (November 1961): 23, GCAHUMC.

49. Ibid.

50. "A Conference on the Racial Revolution in Christian Perspective," Tuesday, October 19, 1966, United Church Women Records, Winthrop University Archives.

51. Minutes of meeting, UCW-Columbia, October 24, 1966.

52. Margaret Shannon, *Just Because: The Story of the National Movement of Church Women United in the U.S.A., 1941 through 1975* (Corte Madera, Calif.: Omega Books, 1977), 138.

53. Helen Turnbull, CWU/WIC Staff Liaison to CWU State and Local Presidents in South Carolina, July 26, 1968, UCW-Columbia Records, Winthrop University Archives, 3–12.

54. "WICS Organize Local Chapter," *Charleston News and Courier*, May 21, 1965, C10.

55. Alice N. Spearman to Mrs. Herbert McAbee, May 26, 1965, Church Women United in South Carolina, Winthrop University Archives, box 1, folder 3.

56. "Mrs. Greene Installed as WICS Director," *Charleston News and Courier*, June 19, 1965, B12.

57. Minutes of meeting, UCW-Columbia, February 2, 1967.

58. Edward H. Beardsley, *A History of Neglect: Healthcare for Blacks and Mill Workers* (Knoxville: University of Tennessee Press, 1987), 103.

59. UCW-Columbia, Representatives' Meeting, September 27, 1968.

60. "Godwin to Speak on Rural Missions," *Columbia (S.C.) State*, Legislative Report, January 29, 1971, A16.

61. *South Carolina Church Woman* 1.2 (1971): 2.

62. Barbara H. Stoops, "Church Women Observe World Day of Prayer," *State and Columbia Record*, March 2, 1969.

63. "Introduction—Purpose of Conference," Johnetta Edwards Papers, Winthrop University Archives, box 15, folder 67.

64. "Volunteers in Adult Basic Education: A Report on Action in Ten Cities in Eight Southern States by Church Women United, during the Months of April–June 1970," Johnetta Edwards Papers, Winthrop University Archives.

65. UCW-Columbia Records, approximately 1952, newspaper name unknown. It is not clear, however, exactly what her position was within the organization. The December 1963 issue of the *Church Woman* listed Mrs. James W. Watson of Fayetteville, North Carolina, as the new president of the Woman's Home and Foreign Missionary Society of the AME Church. Watson had also served on the state and national boards of managers of UCW and on the board of UCW-SC. A teacher in the Fayetteville public schools

for fourteen years, Watson had also been an instructor of literature and music at Clinton Junior College in Rock Hill, South Carolina, for four years.

66. Mrs. G. M. Howe to Mrs. Casper Jones, December 11, 1967, Church Women United Records, Winthrop University Archives.

67. Newsletter, February 1963, United Church Women in Aiken, box 1, folder 1.

68. "Dickie" to Waltena Josie, April 8, 1971, UCW-Aiken Records, box 1, folder 3, Winthrop University Archives.

69. "Church Women United in Columbia, Triennial Report (1971, 1972, 1973)," Church Women United Records, Winthrop University Archives, box 2, folder 2.

70. "In Celebration: The 25th Anniversary Celebration: Church Women United in Orangeburg, Orangeburg, South Carolina, May 24–25, 1991," Miller F. Whitaker Library, South Carolina State University, Orangeburg, S.C.

chapter 6

Challenging the Segregationist Power Structure in Little Rock

The Women's Emergency Committee to Open Our Schools

LAURA A. MILLER

For the first time, women in significant numbers are running political campaigns,
winning elections and making their organized power felt in a commanding way.
—Arkansas Gazette, January 7, 1962

Women's Emergency Committee meeting, September 1958, Little Rock, Arkansas. WEC leaders, seated left to right: Vivion Brewer, Ada May Smith, Adolphine Fletcher Terry, and Dottie Morris. Courtesy of the *Arkansas Democrat-Gazette.*

∞

THE WOMEN'S EMERGENCY COMMITTEE to Open Our Schools (WEC) was formed in the fall of 1958 following the dramatic events of the 1957–58 school year when the Little Rock, Arkansas, School Board admitted nine African American students to previously all-white Central High School. Tensions were so high that Governor Orval Faubus implemented a recently passed state law and closed Little Rock's public high schools in September 1958 to prevent further desegregation. Faubus labeled the women of the WEC "integration-ists" for being part of the only Little Rock organization publicly speaking in favor of moderation and reopening the schools. The women, and in particular the organization's leaders, often endured harassment at the hands of segrega-tionists. WEC members received hate mail and threatening telephone calls and were subjected to state police surveillance. In spite of this, or perhaps because of it, the WEC grew into an effective grassroots political organization. Collec-tively, this group of white, largely middle- and upper-middle-class women led the fight against massive resistance to school desegregation in Little Rock and defined the school-closing issue for white moderates as one of saving public education rather than supporting integration.

Many women who otherwise favored maintaining segregation joined the WEC because they saw it as their civic duty to preserve public education and Little Rock's reputation. For others, however, the organization provided an outlet for developing and honing political skills while supporting racial justice. The women who succeeded in developing a high degree of political sophisti-cation were the ones who became comfortable dealing with male political lead-ers. Through its actions in helping bring an end to the school crisis and its continued support for women's and minority issues, the WEC served as a training ground for a new generation of female political activists.

The WEC was unusual among women's organizations, particularly south-ern ones. While many members entered the fight because they saw preserving education as an appropriate arena for mothers, they did not rely solely on be-nevolence or "moral superiority" to sway public opinion.[1] Instead, they edu-cated themselves on the political process and worked within the existing politi-cal system to effect change by such activities as organizing campaigns, securing candidates for office, and educating voters. That their actions coalesced into what the *Arkansas Gazette* would later term a "female political force" is re-markable.[2]

Members came to the WEC through their contacts with each other in the Parent-Teacher Association, the League of Women Voters, the American Association of University Women, the Council of Jewish Women, and other church and civic organizations. A membership survey undertaken by the WEC in 1960 found that the average member was between thirty-seven and fifty years old, married with two or more children, and had lived in the South for more than twenty years. Many of the women, however, had either spent their formative years outside the South or cited college or work experience outside Arkansas as an influence on their views of race relations. Eighty percent of the members surveyed had attended college, and 21 percent had more than four years of college. Forty-four percent reported annual family incomes between $8,500 and $15,000 ($51,829 and $91,463, respectively, in 2002 dollars), and more than one-third reported incomes under $8,500. Census figures for Arkansas in 1960 show that the median family income for families headed by a professional male (as most of the husbands of WEC members were) was nearly $6,000 ($36,585 in 2002 dollars), indicating that the majority of WEC members were financially better off than many families in Little Rock but were not necessarily among the city's wealthiest families.

WEC executive secretary Irene Samuel observed that many women she considered "elite" did not join the WEC for fear of economic reprisals against their husbands and loss of standing in the community.[3] The majority of WEC members were the wives of younger professional men in Little Rock who had access to the city's civic and business leaders and were young enough to rebuild their careers if they suffered reprisals.

Historian Lorraine Gates argues that WEC members were motivated less by concerns of racial equality than by their desire to protect their families and their community. In addition, she states that the WEC's main goal became to convince the city's male leaders to take action to resolve the crisis because WEC members were in no position to assume leadership in their own right. As women, their responsibility remained in the home. Although the members' gender protected them from the reprisals that silenced the men and allowed them to publicly challenge Faubus, it also limited the WEC's effectiveness as a true political organization.[4] Conversely, historian Karen Anderson notes that many WEC members, particularly the leaders, because of their religious beliefs and educational experiences outside the South, had developed more egalitarian notions with regard to race relations and transformed their vast prior experience in civic organizations to work toward political goals. Although the WEC led the charge against resistance to school desegregation in Little Rock, their compromises with moderate male leaders helped replace that resistance with the "politics of tokenism," and in the end their organizational power could not completely redefine gender or race relations in the community.[5]

While both arguments raise important points about the WEC's accomplishments and effectiveness, neither fully captures the experiences or achievements of its members. The women did not set out to redefine gender or race relations—at least not in the short term; nor did they hesitate to step outside their homes and exert their influence to preserve public education. What they did do was to convince large numbers of women to work for school desegregation (even if they referred to it as "saving education") and educate themselves on the political process. Over the nearly five years of the WEC's existence, many of the women assumed leadership positions and learned how to build power and support for social change. Certainly, the women of the WEC were the products of southern patriarchy and noblesse oblige, and many of them retained these attitudes. Just as female abolitionists in the nineteenth century and women's rights activists in the early twentieth century learned to define highly charged issues in single-issue terms to deflect criticism, so too did the WEC, which used the traditional arguments that, as mothers, they were interested only in preserving education for their children.[6]

The WEC remained a segregated organization in an effort to divert controversy, and its members used their positions as white, middle- and upper-middle-class women to garner public support, just as the Association of Southern Women for the Prevention of Lynching had done before them.[7] Initially, they focused entirely on reopening the schools, even though they understood that desegregation would continue when that happened. This allowed them to step in and "save" public education without addressing the more politically charged issue of racial equality. Although politics has long been defined in masculine terms, the WEC built on the experiences of women's reform activism. Its members repositioned themselves inside Arkansas politics by supporting social change, educating the public, and mobilizing large numbers of women to work for social justice. As the *Arkansas Gazette* stated, the WEC made "political" and "female" compatible in the same sentence.[8]

The Crisis

Following the Supreme Court's 1954 ruling in *Brown v. Board of Education of Topeka,* which declared racial segregation in public education unconstitutional, the Little Rock School Board issued a statement that it would comply with the decision once the court had outlined its method for implementation (which it did in the *Brown II* decision the following year). In May 1955 the school board adopted a plan of gradual desegregation known as the "Blossom Plan," after Superintendent Virgil Blossom.[9] The plan originally called for desegregation to begin at the elementary level because Superintendent Blossom felt that younger children would not necessarily come to school with the ingrained prejudices that older students might have developed. When Blossom presented his plan at PTA meetings, however, the parents of children in elementary schools appeared to him to be more outspoken against the *Brown* decision than the parents of older children. The school board thus decided to change the plan to affect only Central High School in the first year. In addition, with the construction of a new all-white high school, Hall, and a new all-black high school, Horace Mann, desegregation could proceed at a slower pace at the high school level because three new attendance zones could be drawn to ensure that black students did not outnumber their white counterparts except in the Horace Mann zone. Since transfers to the schools would be voluntary, white students in the Horace Mann attendance zone could simply attend a high school where their race was in the majority.[10] This action drew criticism from the city's working-class white citizens because it appeared to favor the wealthier residents of Pulaski Heights, whose children would attend Hall High School, scheduled to open in the fall of 1957.[11] To working-class whites, the decision appeared designed to insulate Little Rock's elite white citizens from involving their own children in the steps toward integration.

In 1956, attorneys for the National Association for the Advancement of Colored People (NAACP) filed suit on behalf of thirty-three African American children who attempted to register in white Little Rock schools (at all levels) but were denied admittance.[12] As the summer of 1957 progressed, the NAACP pursued the matter through the courts as white opposition to desegregation escalated. Segregationists argued that the Supreme Court lacked the authority to compel local school districts to integrate because the *Brown* decision affected only the litigants. Not until Congress passed a new law affirming *Brown,* if it ever did, would the decision be applicable nationwide.[13] Segregationists also maintained that the governor could "interpose" the state's sovereign power between the federal government and its citizens to prevent implementation of the *Brown* decision. Although the interposition doctrine lacked authority under constitutional law, it seemed to many to be a way to negate or delay the Supreme Court's ruling.[14]

The Mothers' League of Central High School, formed on August 22, 1957, announced its intention to prevent integration at Central. In the words of its first president, Nadine Aaron, the group organized because, "this is a matter for the mothers to settle. It is time for the mothers to take over."[15] Closely aligned with the Capital Citizens' Council (itself a branch of the White Citizens' Council), the Mothers' League served as a vehicle through which segregationists could align their cause with the respectability of motherhood.[16] Although members initially denied this close connection, council leader Wesley Pruden later admitted that the league arose out of male segregationists' attempts to create a "more palatable" message to appeal to moderate citizens.[17] They used the ideals of motherhood and femininity to soften their otherwise extremist position. The council had approximately 381 members in 1957, and Mothers' League members were often council members themselves or the wives of members. Nearly 50 percent of the council's membership came from the southwestern part of Little Rock and consisted primarily of individuals from the middle and lower economic classes. Although an additional 15 percent of their members came from a more affluent area of the city, neither the council members nor the Mothers' League members were part of the city's business and civic elite.[18]

On August 27, the league's recording secretary, Mary Thomason, filed a petition seeking a temporary injunction against school desegregation. Although it was initially granted by the county chancellor, the injunction was subsequently nullified by Federal District Judge Ronald Davies, who ordered the school board to proceed with its integration plans.[19] The conflict reached crisis proportions when Governor Faubus, citing the potential for violence, called on the Arkansas National Guard to prevent the desegregation of Central. Many residents were astounded by Faubus's action. Although most opposed integration, they had resigned themselves to comply with the court's decision.

Faubus's actions, and President Dwight D. Eisenhower's subsequent involvement, brought national attention to the crisis. On September 20, Judge Davies ordered Faubus to remove the guardsmen. The following Monday, nine African American students entered Central High through a side door.[20] The Little Rock police could not control the unruly crowd and had to remove the nine shortly before noon. The next day, under orders from the president, members of the U.S. Army's 101st Airborne Division and a federalized Arkansas National Guard force surrounded the school and escorted the nine students inside.[21] The National Guard troops stayed for the remainder of the school year.

In addition to giving up their extracurricular activities and normal social lives, the "Little Rock Nine," as they would come to be known, endured severe mistreatment at the hands of many of their fellow students. An organized group of white students persisted in tormenting them throughout the year, pushing, hitting, and spitting on them; breaking into their lockers; throwing rocks at them; and committing various other forms of harassment. Their actions prevented other students from treating the nine in a normal way, thus isolating them within the school.[22] Unable to use military force against unarmed teenagers, the troops did not intervene to stop the harassment; they could only record it.[23]

Outside the school, the situation remained equally volatile. The white leadership of Little Rock remained silent; while the governor erected barricades to the advancement of civil rights, the voice of reasonable and responsible leadership in the white community was nowhere to be found. With the exception of the editorial tone of the *Arkansas Gazette* and a few local ministers' ineffective calls for order, local moderates had no organization to counter the segregationists.[24]

By December 1957, local businessmen had begun receiving anonymous letters warning of massive boycotts against them if they continued advertising in the "pro-integration" *Gazette*.[25] The newspaper itself lost millions of dollars in revenue as a result of this intimidation campaign.[26] Business and civic leaders were thus silenced by a combination of fear of economic reprisals and the desire of many for continued segregation.

Ernest Green became the first African American to graduate from Central High School on May 25, 1958, but this event hardly signaled the end of the conflict in Little Rock.[27] In fact, it was just the beginning of a major battle for control of the Little Rock School Board and public education in the state as a whole. While African American leaders continued their assault on segregation through the federal courts, Little Rock's white citizens entered a struggle of their own. As the summer of 1958 progressed, segregationist whites and moderate whites, who generally favored maintaining segregation but would not openly violate the law, squared off over the issue of continued desegregation.

On July 29 of that same year, Orval Faubus was elected to a third term by an impressive majority of almost two to one.[28] Taking this overwhelming victory as a sign of popular support for his continued opposition to integration, Faubus called a special session of the Arkansas legislature to consider a package of "segregation bills." During the session, legislators approved several bills, including Act 4, which authorized the governor to close any or all public schools in any district, pending a public referendum either for or against the racial integration of all the schools in the district; and Act 9, which authorized the removal by recall of any or all members of a local school board.[29] The latter bill, intended to allow citizens to remove pro-integration school board members, would backfire on its supporters in the Little Rock School District within a year.

During the summer the school board asked the court to delay the gradual desegregation plan, citing problems from the previous year such as repeated bomb threats at the school, discipline problems among the student body, and threats against school staff and district board members. U.S. District Court Judge Harry Lemley granted the school board's request, but his decision was overturned by the Eighth Circuit Court of Appeals, which also granted a thirty-day stay in its decision to allow the school board time to appeal to the U.S. Supreme Court. The Supreme Court issued its ruling on September 12: the school board must proceed with its desegregation plan.[30] In response, Faubus signed Act 4 into law and promptly ordered all four of Little Rock's public high schools closed.[31]

The Rise of the WEC

Infuriated by business and community leaders' failure to respond to the school closings, a few white women met on September 16, 1958, to form the Women's Emergency Committee to Open Our Schools. They were led by Adolphine Fletcher Terry, a member of one of the city's most influential families.[32] Terry had long been active in community organizations, including interracial ones, and she felt strongly that city leaders—meaning the white, male leadership— had remained silent too long.[33] She met with Velma Powell, a member of the Arkansas Council on Human Relations, an interracial organization dedicated to the implementation of equal opportunity, and Vivion Brewer, a graduate of Smith College whose father was a former mayor of Little Rock and whose husband was a nephew of and former aide to Arkansas senator Joe T. Robinson, to discuss what they could do about the continuing school crisis.

Forty-eight women attended the first meeting of the WEC. Brewer recalled that when she began to discuss plans for contacting African American women with similar views, several women in the audience quietly left. The WEC members then decided that the only way for them to be effective was to remain a segregated group. The women believed that no one in the white community would listen to them if the organization were interracial, and also that they would become targets for the segregationists—which they soon became any-way.[34] In addition, regardless of the more egalitarian views of many of the organization's leaders, many women (especially mothers of high school students) had joined simply to help save public education, not because they favored integration. While limiting the WEC's membership to whites ensured the growth of the organization, it lost the WEC support among the African American community. The WEC had received many of its initial contributions from prominent African American citizens. After the women decided to remain segregated, these donations declined sharply.[35]

Immediately, the members agreed to help organize an effort to "get out the vote" for the public referendum and reopen the schools. One week later, nearly 170 members met and established a plan for the upcoming election. Members volunteered to take pages from the poll tax book and contact eligible voters to try and determine the level of support for reopening the schools. They agreed to host parties to provide legal information for interested citizens to let them know that Governor Faubus's plan to lease public school buildings for private, segregated schools was not legal and to explain the wording of the ballot to them. They also agreed to use their vehicles to take voters to the polls and to serve as poll watchers to keep an eye on the election process and results.[36]

The WEC had little time to prepare for the election. Faubus had set the date for September 27, which gave the organization a mere eleven days to organize its campaign. In addition, the ballot's wording favored segregation because it required Little Rock's voters to vote either in favor of the immediate integration of all the schools in the district or against it. The ballot did not offer voters the choice of continuing with the current desegregation plan.[37] The WEC became the only organization to publicly support an affirmative vote on the issue.[38] In spite of the committee's efforts, Little Rock's white citizens voted almost three to one against the measure. As a result, the city's public high schools remained closed for the duration of the 1958–59 school year.[39]

After this loss, although the WEC focused its efforts solely on reopening the public schools, its members quickly became the targets of outspoken segregationists, who labeled them "integrationists."[40] This climate of intimidation, with its attendant fear of economic reprisals, prevented white and African American leaders from meeting openly to try to resolve the crisis. Nevertheless, after some initial setbacks, the WEC members gradually were able to mobilize support for the schools. As women, they were somewhat insulated from the threat of economic reprisals that had effectively silenced the male leaders.[41] In addition, because of their class, they were able to use their access to the power structure of Little Rock—as well as their time, money, and organizational resources—to garner support for the schools. In doing so, they were able to shift the focus of the crisis from integration to keeping the schools open.[42] Understanding that they needed to define the school closing as a single-issue cause, they announced that the WEC stood "neither for integration nor for segregation, but for education," and they prepared a "Policy and Purpose" statement to reflect their goals for the school district, which included opening the schools, retaining the teachers, and regaining accreditation.[43]

For their part, school board members felt trapped between a court order mandating desegregation and four schools closed by a state law of undetermined constitutionality. In response to what they described as a situation of "utter hopelessness, helplessness, and frustration," five of the six board members voted to buy out the remainder of Superintendent Blossom's contract and then resigned their own positions.[44] Their timing allowed only three days before the filing deadline for board positions.

Adolphine Terry single-handedly recruited three moderate candidates for the school board, including WEC member Margaret Stephens. Hoping to prevent public backlash against the moderates, the WEC did not take an official stand in the school board elections. Privately, Vivion Brewer met with one of the moderate candidates, Ted Lamb, prior to the election and agreed to provide WEC backing. In return, Lamb, head of a local public relations firm, agreed not to portray the moderate candidates as supporting segregation.[45] The moderate candidates knew that while many local business and civic leaders still favored segregation, they also understood the economic consequences of not having functioning public high schools; in the end, the moderates appropriated the WEC's single-issue stance. Working behind the scenes, Terry encouraged WEC members to support the "business men's slate" and asked for volunteers for the campaign. Members rushed to secure signatures for the petitions endorsing the moderate candidates.[46]

With the advice of local attorney Henry Woods (who later was appointed a federal district court judge), executive secretary Irene Samuel developed the WEC's campaign strategy. Samuel had been recruited to join the WEC because of her work as legislative chair of the Council of Jewish Women. Samuel's experiences outside Arkansas in personnel administration for the U.S. Housing Authority during the Roosevelt administration had broadened her views of race relations. During World War II, her job had been to recruit clerical workers for the department. Because of the shortage of available workers, Samuel took to heart the provisions of, as she termed it, "Mrs. Roosevelt's" Fair Employment Practices Commission and recruited African American as well as white workers. She felt that this was not only morally right, but also the only sensible thing to do given the general dearth of available employees.[47]

During the school board election campaign, Samuel divided the WEC members into groups representing each of the city's five voting wards. Each ward captain delivered postcards and flyers to precinct workers, who in turn addressed and mailed them or placed them on voters' doorsteps. Precinct workers also called voters listed in the poll tax book and set up carpools for election day.[48] Voters partially rewarded the WEC's efforts and elected three moderate candidates to the board; however, they also elected three segregationist candidates, which meant that the six-member board was evenly divided on the desegregation issue.[49]

The WEC continued its public relations campaign throughout the year. The organization mass-produced flyers and newspaper advertisements in an ongoing effort to change public sentiment about the need to reopen the public schools. In just over two months, the WEC sent out more than three thousand flyers in support of public education.[50]

Members routinely received hate mail, often written on the back of their own flyers and advertisements. One such note read: "Rape, murder and all types of indecency will be the price because of your capitulation to the NAACP." Another respondent lashed out at the fact that the WEC was a women's organization, saying, "go home and tend to your own knitting and let our Governor take care of our school system."[51] WEC leaders received telephone calls from anonymous segregationists every fifteen minutes between eight and twelve o'clock on two evenings per week, and they often were followed to WEC meetings by the Arkansas State Police, who reported their activities to the governor.[52]

In December 1958, members composed a letter to send to friends and families with their Christmas greetings. This "Letter from Little Rock" announced to the rest of the nation the efforts of the WEC: "We know it will be a long time before the State of Arkansas can live down the shame and disgrace with which it is now viewed by the entire world. We thought you might like to learn that there is one group here dedicated to the principle of good public education with liberty and justice for all."[53]

The WEC addressed statewide education issues as well. During the 1959 legislative session, members lobbied for pro-education legislation and formed a watchdog committee looking for segregationist bills. Irene Samuel recruited and trained the WEC members who took this duty. She began by selecting the best-informed women, but she soon discovered that the male legislators disliked the fact that many of the women were better informed than they were. Never afraid of compromise if it would help to achieve her goals, Samuel decided that the best way to ensure that the men would listen was to select young, attractive members to lead the lobbying effort and gain initial entrance into the halls of the legislature. While Samuel never doubted the abilities of any of the women she chose for the lobbying effort, she understood the prevailing views of women's traditional roles and did not hesitate to use this form of sexism to the WEC's advantage.

WEC members worked with others from the PTA, the League of Women Voters, and the American Association of University Women in these lobbying efforts. Despite their hard work, however, the state legislature approved several anti-education bills, including one to place an amendment on the 1960 ballot that would eliminate the state's requirement to provide free public education for all children.[54] WEC members also lobbied vehemently against Faubus's proposed "school-board packing bill," which would have allowed the governor to appoint three additional members to the Little Rock School Board and thus break the three-to-three deadlock on decisions. State Senator Ellis Fagan finally succeeded in tabling the bill in the Senate after much lobbying by the WEC.[55]

While the WEC used publicity very effectively to achieve its goals, many WEC supporters insisted on anonymity because their friends, family, and even husbands supported segregation and would shun them if they knew of their involvement with the committee. The organization itself did not keep a membership roster, relying instead on individual cards that could be moved to different locations for protection. When a new segregationist member of the Little Rock City Board of Directors, L. L. Langford, attempted to invoke the "Bennett ordinance" (a 1957 ordinance named after state Attorney General Bruce Bennett designed to harass the NAACP) and force the WEC to reveal its membership, the organization could honestly say that it had no membership list to reveal.[56] In a rather heated exchange of letters, the WEC did provide information about its officers, its net income, and a statement of its policy and purpose.[57] Edwin Dunaway, a local attorney, suggested that some members should offer to be arrested to publicize Langford's harassment. Although some of the women might have been willing, WEC recording secretary Dottie Morris—the recipient of Langford's letters—was horrified by the idea, as was her husband.[58]

As the year progressed, attitudes among Little Rock parents, particularly those with teenage children, began to shift in favor of desegregation, if only to reopen the schools. Likewise, business and professional leaders faced the fact that no new major industries had located in Little Rock since September 1957; nor would they without an acceptable public education system.

The Recall Election

Soon after the school board elections in December, the WEC, recognizing that successfully reopening the schools meant maintaining a cohesive faculty and staff, passed a resolution asking the board immediately to renew the contracts of all the district's teachers and administrators. In opposition were segregationist leaders who wanted to remove teachers and administrators who had taken moderate or integrationist stances during the prior year. Some segregationist students and their parents felt that by disciplining the white students who repeatedly harassed and abused the nine African American students, these teachers and principals displayed favoritism toward the Little Rock Nine.[59]

When the school board convened its regular meeting on May 5, 1959, one of the items on the agenda was the renewal of teacher contracts. The board reached a three-to-three stalemate on each issue they considered that morning. The moderate members refused to consider the renewal of any one teacher, or of the teachers in any one school, because they wanted to reinstate all the teachers in the district. When the board reconvened after lunch, the moderate members read a statement supporting the reemployment of all personnel and then withdrew from the meeting in an attempt to prevent a quorum and any further action by the board. The remaining members, however, decided that they could continue because a quorum had existed at the beginning of the meeting. They subsequently voted not to renew the contracts of forty-four teachers and administrators whom they accused of being "integrationists."[60] Billie Wilson, who was monitoring the school board meeting for the WEC, interrupted the WEC's final meeting of the school year to advise members of the situation. After talking with Wilson, Vivion Brewer announced to the other WEC members that the school board was "firing our teachers left and right."[61]

The WEC, not surprisingly, was the first group formally to condemn the actions of the school board. The PTA quickly followed suit, as did the Arkansas Education Association and the League of Women Voters, among others.[62] In fact, this outrageous move finally motivated many of Little Rock's business leaders to take action. The businessmen formed a group called Stop This Outrageous Purge (STOP) and vowed to fight for a recall of the three segregationist board members under the auspices of Act 9. Volunteers drawn mainly from the ranks of the WEC (whose husbands formed the core of STOP) circulated recall petitions to obtain the necessary signatures to put the measure on the ballot. They collected more than nine thousand signatures in less than seven days. Segregationist supporters, meanwhile, formed their own group, the Committee to Retain Our Segregated Schools, or CROSS, and likewise filed petitions demanding the recall of the moderate board members. Members of the Mothers' League of Central High, the Capital Citizens' Council, and the States' Rights Council collected more than seven thousand signatures in support of their recall petition.[63]

The WEC was able to put into action the political expertise its members had gained in the previous elections. Irene Samuel again divided campaign workers into five ward groups. Block workers received voter cards containing the names of eligible voters within a particular block. They then contacted voters and identified those who supported the moderates and STOP. Samuel compiled this information and recorded it in her copy of the Master List of Electors for Pulaski County, more commonly known as the poll tax book. Her copy reveals an elaborate system of recording individuals' affiliations and views, such as WEC member, STOP member, Friend, Signed STOP petition, Signed CROSS petition, and Citizens' Council member.[64] The campaign workers used their own shorthand symbols. They named voters who supported STOP "saints"; segregationist supporters they labeled "sinners"; and those who seemed inclined toward the moderate stance were "savables." The cards were then compiled and redistributed to the block workers, who did not contact the "sinners" lest they inadvertently remind them to vote. Workers contacted only the "saints" and "savables" and urged them to vote to recall the segregationist board members and retain the moderate ones.[65] WEC members made nearly twenty-three thousand calls, mostly door-to-door, to elicit support for their cause.[66] CROSS workers and Mothers' League members, who lacked the WEC's ward and precinct organization, made no formal effort to contact voters.[67]

The WEC, with the assistance of the League of Women Voters, secured the appointments of a few election officials and had supporters on hand on election day to serve as "stand-in" judges in case the appointed ones failed to show at a particular polling place.[68] They also succeeded in getting members named to seventy out of seventy-eight poll-watcher positions.[69] Members closely monitored the election returns from WEC headquarters. They knew, for example, that the results from the Westover Hills Presbyterian Church precinct, in the Fifth Ward, would favor the moderate board members. The WEC poll watchers deliberately withheld reporting the count from this ballot box until the results came in from the Adcock Lighting and Supply precinct, a largely working-class area that their voter identification efforts had revealed heavily supported the segregationists. Samuel later joked that if they had been losing the election, they could have "found" surplus favorable absentee ballots to add to the Westover Hills count to offset the returns from Adcock. Fortunately, such drastic—and fraudulent—action was unnecessary.[70]

When the results came in, Little Rock's citizens had voted to retain the three moderate board members and to remove the three segregationist ones. On June 11, 1959, the County Board of Election Commissioners named three moderates to the board vacancies.[71] In a letter to Samuel, school board member Everett Tucker Jr. noted: "I do not believe that the schools would be operating today had it not been for the foresight and determination of you ladies and it is perfectly obvious to me that we who withstood the recall election . . . would not now be in office without your dedicated work in our behalf."[72] Tucker added, "[D]on't go into hiding now; we may be needing your help again somewhere down the line."[73] He could not have known the tremendous impact the WEC would continue to have on Arkansas politics in the years ahead.

The Little Rock public high schools reopened on August 12, 1959, and continued with the court-approved desegregation plan, or "Blossom Plan." Segregationists rallied at the state capitol and then marched toward Central High School, where they were turned away by police and firefighters.[74] Although integration involving substantial numbers of students did not occur until the 1970s, the reopening of the schools in the fall of 1959 closed an important chapter in the history of public education as Little Rock's citizens opted not to destroy free public education for the sake of maintaining traditional patterns of segregation.

Far from going into hiding after they had achieved their goal, the members of the WEC remained vigilant to threats against public education in the city and the state. They continued their public education, lobbying, and campaigning activities into the next decade. Of her involvement in the WEC, Sara Murphy noted: "All of us have learned more about court procedure, legislative action, election laws and the like than we would have bothered to learn in a lifetime otherwise and we will be better citizens in the future because of it."[75]

The WEC's Continuing Efforts

Despite their success in the May recall election, WEC members knew that segregationists would continue their efforts to prevent further desegregation. They understood that the WEC needed to continue its publicity and education campaign to gain more members and convince citizens that the threat to Little Rock and the state had not vanished. They organized workshops on women's political activism and spoke to similar groups in other states in an effort to share the lessons they had learned in the recall election. In addition, they maintained their watch on the state legislature's activities.

Recognizing that businessmen considered the economy to be the important issue rather than integration, the WEC undertook an ambitious project to survey Little Rock businesses on the effects of the integration crisis of the previous two years. Eleven WEC members served on the advisory board for the study. The "Little Rock Report: The City, Its People, Its Business, 1957–1959" is an impressive record of the economic devastation wrought by the city's school problems. Directed and edited by Anne Helvenston and Grace Malakoff, the survey revealed that no new industries had located in Little Rock since the fall of 1957; in addition, retail and residential sales had fallen and new construction was down 10 percent.[76]

Samuel and other WEC leaders strongly supported the study's completion, even though the schools had reopened before they published the results, because they felt that they needed to demonstrate to the public, in concrete terms, exactly how devastating the events of the past two years had been. Some WEC members opposed releasing the report after the fact because they feared offending Little Rock's leaders and worried about the effect this might have on the WEC's future.[77] Ultimately, however, the "Little Rock Report" was well received, in the state and in other states as well. The WEC sent copies to the New York Public Library, Harvard University, the Southern Regional Council, and many organizations.[78] They also sent free copies to all Arkansas state senators and representatives and to the Arkansas congressional delegation. Tremendous interest in the report led the WEC to produce second and third printings.[79]

In 1960, WEC members worked to defeat Amendment 52, a bill passed by the legislature in the previous session that would have allowed citizens to hold local elections to determine how local and state educational funds should be used in their districts—in other words, to allow segregationists to use state funds for private, segregated schools. WEC members served with forty-five others on the statewide Committee against Amendment 52 to educate the public on the dangers associated with the proposed amendment. The WEC held fifty-five study groups to educate its own members on the possible effects of this legislation and encouraged them to relay their message to others in the community and state. Voters defeated Amendment 52 by a three-to-one margin in the general election in spite of Governor Faubus's televised appeal for the amendment's adoption.[80]

The WEC's success in 1960 also signaled the beginning of dissent within the organization. In September, Vivion Brewer resigned as WEC chair, in part because she did not favor the WEC becoming a purely political group, which, in her opinion, was where Samuel and Pat House, another WEC member, were taking the organization.[81] Samuel and House would later work together in seeking to rouse the African American vote against Orval Faubus. Brewer also disapproved of the WEC's support for Tommy Russell for the state senate. Brewer became upset when she entered local attorney Henry Woods's office and found Samuel, Adolphine Terry, and House discussing the candidate with Woods, Jim Youngdahl, and Sheriff Marlin Hawkins from Conway County.[82] Hawkins was an extremely powerful political organizer in his own right, and a sometime ally of Faubus. The WEC leaders agreed to support Hawkins's associate in return for the sheriff's support in defeating Amendment 52 in his county. House later recalled that Hawkins told her in advance how many votes he would be able to produce to defeat the amendment. On election night, he called her and gave her the actual total, which was just slightly more than he had promised.[83] Upset by the WEC's involvement with controversial candidates and the political machine in Conway County, Brewer resigned from the WEC. The organization then elected House as its new chair.[84]

In late 1960 and early 1961, Irene Samuel formed a business with fellow WEC members Josephine Menkus and Dottie Morris. Truly born out of necessity, Jet Letter Service provided public relations, direct mail, and advertising services. During the STOP campaign, the WEC had had difficulty finding a company that would agree to copy informational flyers and pamphlets for them. A local minister allowed the WEC to use the church's mimeograph machine, and after the election donated it to the organization. Menkus added five hundred dollars of her own to purchase a typewriter and supplies, and the women were in business. Although it was not necessarily a tremendous money-making operation, at least initially, the women used the business's resources to provide necessary services for the WEC's various, and controversial, projects, such as information on integrating public housing and pamphlets informing members of civil rights protests.[85] By creating their own business, the women bypassed printing firms that were reluctant to print activist material because they feared that segregationists would boycott their businesses.[86]

In addition to their political activities, WEC members supported the Conference on Community Unity, a race relations forum organized by the American Friends Service Committee. Several WEC members attended the first conference at Camp Aldersgate, a Methodist church camp, in September 1959. The conference called for whites and African Americans to come together, learn from each other, and discuss the problems facing Little Rock. By meeting with African Americans—and for many of the women this was a new experience—and listening to their concerns about social justice in subsequent conferences, WEC members added to their awareness of race relations.[87] In later years, WEC members provided information on developing support for integrated education to similar groups around the country, including Help Our Public Education (HOPE) in Atlanta and Alabamians Behind Local Education (ABLE) in Mobile.[88]

In 1963, the WEC sponsored a statewide workshop on public education entitled "What Can Women Do?" at which Samuel and House discussed the WEC's campaign strategy, including the effectiveness of organized telephone chains, voter card files, voter registration, and working with elected officials.[89] Later that year, the WEC held a workshop entitled "Women in Action" that encouraged women to become more active in the political process. In announcing the workshop, the WEC stated:

> Women can be the state's most dynamic political force—this institute will tell you how. Next year will be a crucial election year; there are significant stirrings of dissatisfaction with the "Old Guard" and machine politics. Many legislative seats last summer were won by narrow margins—a little more effort on the part of women might be a deciding factor next year.[90]

Clearly, members of the WEC knew they had become a significant force in Arkansas politics. Several members, Samuel and House in particular, worked to convert more women to become politically active and to work for social justice.

In early 1963, in an effort to broaden its base of support, the WEC elected to integrate and welcomed its first African American member.[91] Even though the initial crisis had ended in 1959, Little Rock's racial climate remained volatile. Earlier in 1963, the WEC had agreed to continue to concentrate on public education and related issues, particularly electing candidates who would support education.[92] Before the year was out, however, the organization voted itself out of existence. Many members believed that Samuel and House had taken the group much further into political activism than they wanted to go. In addition, they believed that through those two, the WEC had supported several "questionable" candidates for various local and state positions. The single-issue school-reopening campaign had appealed to many members when the organization was formed, but these women were not interested in increasing their political activity. According to Sara Murphy, they "were unwilling to get down into the rough and tumble part of politics to support candidates who were not so pure in order to get other things done."[93]

Thus, the very activities that made the WEC such an effective organization within the larger, male-dominated political world also hastened its demise. While several members remained immersed in Arkansas politics, others felt that their level of involvement in political activities and their support for certain candidates and issues took them beyond their traditional female roles. In reporting on the organization's demise, the *Arkansas Gazette* lauded the WEC's "feline sharpness" and added that in addition to the group's success in saving public education it had "served the important function of developing some women leaders."[94]

One group of former WEC members, for example, continued their work for social change by attacking problems at their source. While the WEC had concerned itself with opening Little Rock's high schools and preserving public education, the organization neither directly addressed race relations nor openly advocated integration. Realizing the need for open discussion in order to change public attitudes about race and prejudice, Sara Murphy organized the Little Rock Panel of American Women in 1963. Based on the national Panel of American Women (PAW) founded in Kansas City by Esther Brown in 1956, the Little Rock panel offered participants and audience members alike the opportunity to learn about the experiences of women of different races, religions, and cultures.[95]

The first panels consisted of five or six women panelists—Jewish, Catholic, African American, white Protestant, and occasionally Asian—and a moderator who were recruited for their "commitment to diversity, both religious and racial, and for their ability and willingness to articulate that commitment effectively."[96] During the hour-long presentations, each panelist spoke for three to five minutes about her own experiences with prejudice. The moderator then opened the remainder of the presentation to questions from the audience. According to former moderator Brownie Ledbetter's notes, "by discussing these things with you today," the panelists hoped "to satisfy some of your curiosity about our differences and possibly clear up a few misunderstandings, and we hope to learn something from your ideas on human relations."[97] The talks were personal and anecdotal, and their main goal was to provide a "structured forum in which open discussion about . . . religious and racial differences was acceptable."[98] For example, African American panelist Gwen Riley talked about being excluded from such places as the city park and the library when she was a child. She would then ask the audience if she should tell her small daughter that there were people who would look down on her because she was African American.[99] Other panelists fielded questions like, "Do Catholics really believe theirs is the only church?" or, "Do members of the Jewish race believe in an after-life?"[100] Panelists answered all of the questions in a non-threatening (and often humorous) manner and encouraged audience members to continue communicating with others.

While the idea behind the panel presentations may seem simple, in the early 1960s, particularly in the South, these presentations provided the only opportunity for many to see intelligent, articulate, nonthreatening people of other races and religions and to hear about the effects of prejudice in their lives. The PAW presentations helped lessen the anxiety some people, mainly whites, felt over continued integration. As one former panel member, Martha Bass recalled, "the Panel has given many parents a chance to see and hear a competent, attractive Negro teacher. . . . It has eased some of the fears they otherwise would have had [about school faculty desegregation]."[101] The women of the PAW understood that the panels were somewhat contrived, but they were quick to point out that the social barriers that separated people of different backgrounds were equally artificial.[102] In an editorial about the organization, the *Arkansas Gazette* stated: "[T]he testimony of these courageous women offers a revealing commentary on the universality of prejudice—and on its nuances. . . . [I]n handing out credits to people who are working on remedies, Little Rock's 'Panel of Americans' must be high on anybody's list."[103]

Perhaps those most affected by the panel's presentations were the panelists themselves. In traveling the state together and presenting hundreds of panel discussions to sometimes friendly, sometimes hostile audiences, the women formed strong friendships across racial and religious lines—some for perhaps the first time in their lives. As Katherine Lambright said, "I had never known a Negro on a really personal level, other than as a servant in the home."[104] Another member, Joan Chowning, said: "I have developed deeper relationships with people on the Panel than with some people I have known all my life. Everyone here is trying to be honest with each other, to get at the truth, to reach beyond racial and religious barriers to the point where we can meet as human beings."[105]

Emboldened by their success in public speaking, some of the women became involved in political campaigns and voter education efforts, as several members of the WEC had done before them. Panelist Gwen Riley headed up a successful voter education project in the African American community, recruiting volunteers and demonstrating how the new voting machines worked in Pulaski County.[106] Several other panelists worked on statewide campaigns and talked with voters about relevant issues. As panelist Helen Littleton remarked, "[The panel] has given me more concern for all people and made me more aware of the importance of electing officials who share that concern."[107]

With the advent of court-ordered busing to achieve racial balance, integration once again focused on the public schools. In 1971, PAW shifted its emphasis to the schools as places to continue its work in changing attitudes. The organization received a federal grant from the Department of Health, Education, and Welfare (HEW) to work in eight Arkansas school districts. They hired a small staff and incorporated as a nonprofit organization to "devise, develop and promote programs of youth and adult education to counteract prejudice and discrimination based on racial, religious, nationality or ethnic group membership."[108] The next year, PAW joined forces with three other organizations and applied for an HEW Emergency School Aid Act grant to work in the Little Rock School District.[109] As part of their work, members developed and presented human relations activities for students, including the Green Circle Program, a flannel-board presentation developed by an African American teacher and presented at the National Panel of American Women Conference. In addition, PAW provided human relations in-service training for teachers and a newsletter informing district parents about the programs. Through the 1970s, the organization grew to more than one hundred members and a staff of eight.[110]

In 1980, the organization changed its name to the Little Rock Panel, Inc., and focused on issues of economic and social justice. In the mid-1980s, the panel merged with the Arkansas Public Policy Project and formed the Arkansas Public Policy Panel, Inc. The organization continues to this day, providing research on environmental issues, tax reform, and rural economic development issues as well as grassroots training for individuals and community organizations to participate in shaping the state and local policies that affect their lives.[111]

Unlike the WEC's activities, the PAW presentations provided an opportunity for the state's citizens, still reeling from the school crisis and the social upheaval of the growing civil rights movement, to begin to address the debilitating effects of racial, ethnic, and religious prejudice. Like the WEC members, the women of the PAW found in the organization an opportunity to make a difference in their own lives and in their communities and to continue working for social justice.

Conclusion

In the late 1950s, the WEC directed its appeals to male leaders simply because they *were* the leaders at the time. The women felt that men had abdicated their duty to lead by allowing the school situation to escalate uncontrollably.[112] Certainly, they did not envision themselves as replacing all of the men in elective office; but even then, some members could conceive of themselves holding office in their own right, as WEC member Margaret Stephens clearly did when she ran for a Little Rock School Board position in the midst of the crisis. In addition, the women understood that the immediate crisis lay in reopening the schools rather than in redefining gender or race relations in Little Rock. What the WEC accomplished was to force Little Rock's leadership to take a stand in favor of at least gradual desegregation to preserve the community's public school system. Along the way, the organization's leaders mobilized large numbers of women, many of whom were unprepared to lead the charge for desegregation, and educated them about politics, creating many future female leaders in the process. During an era when women supposedly did not know much about politics, the WEC became an integral force in organizing wards and precincts, getting out voters who supported their cause, lobbying legislators, and convincing business and civic leaders to effect positive changes in Little Rock. Although many former WEC members retained their traditional roles as nurturers of home and family, some found their political calling within the organization and clearly understood the power that organized women could wield. The women of the WEC did not hide behind their privileged status to help maintain segregation and the "traditional southern way of life." Instead, they used their access to the power structure of Little Rock to work for social change. Far from being limited as an effective political organization, in the years after the 1959 recall election the WEC, and later the PAW, trained their own political leaders and provided a venue though which women could develop power in their own right.

Notes

1. For additional information on women's activism, see Lori D. Ginzberg, *Women and the Work of Benevolence: Morality, Politics, and Class in the Nineteenth-Century United States* (New Haven: Yale University Press, 1990); Nancy Hewitt, *Women's Activism and Social Change: Rochester, New York, 1822–1872* (Ithaca: Cornell University Press, 1984); Alma Lutz, *Crusade for Freedom: Women in the Antislavery Movement* (Boston: Beacon Press, 1968); Sara Hunter Graham, "The Suffrage Renaissance: A New Image for a New Century, 1896–1910," in *One Woman, One Vote: Rediscovering the Woman Suffrage Movement*, ed. Marjorie Spruill Wheeler (Troutdale, Ore.: New Sage Press, 1995); and Glenna Matthews, *The Rise of Public Woman: Women's Power and Women's Place in the United States, 1630–1970* (New York: Oxford University Press, 1992).

2. *Arkansas Gazette,* January 7, 1962.

3. *1969 Census of Population,* vol. 1: *Characteristics of the Population,* part 5, *Arkansas* (Washington, D.C.: U.S. Department of Commerce, Bureau of the Census); Irene Samuel, interview with the author, October 24, 1996, Little Rock, Arkansas; and the Papers of the Women's Emergency Committee to Open Our Schools, Arkansas History Commission, Little Rock, box 1, folder 6.

4. Lorraine Gates, "Power from the Pedestal: The Women's Emergency Committee and the Little Rock School Crisis," *Arkansas Historical Quarterly* 55 (spring 1996): 39, 57.

5. Karen Anderson, "Women and the Politics of Race: The Little Rock School Integration Crisis, 1957–1964" (paper presented at the Tenth Berkshire Conference on the History of Women, June 8, 1996, Chapel Hill, North Carolina), 8, 17.

6. Kathleen Barry, *Susan B. Anthony: A Biography of a Singular Feminist* (New York: New York University Press, 1988), 288–96; Henry Alexander, *The Little Rock Recall Election* (New York: McGraw-Hill, 1960), 7.

7. Jacquelyn Dowd Hall, *Revolt against Chivalry: Jessie Daniel Ames and the Women's Campaign against Lynching* (New York: Columbia University Press, 1972), 181; and Vivion Brewer, *The Embattled Ladies of Little Rock, 1958–1963: The Struggle to Save Public Education at Central High* (Fort Bragg, Colo.: Lost Coast Press, 1998), 8.

8. *Arkansas Gazette,* January 7, 1962.

9. For further information on the Little Rock school crisis, see Numan Bartley, *The Rise of Massive Resistance: Race and Politics in the South during the 1950's* (Baton Rouge: Louisiana State University Press, 1969); Virgil Blossom, *It HAS Happened Here* (New York: Harper Brothers, 1959); Richard Kluger, *Simple Justice: The History of* Brown v. Board of Education *and Black America's Struggle for Equality* (New York: Knopf, 1976); Roy Reed, *Faubus: The Life and Times of an American Prodigal* (Fayetteville: University of Arkansas Press, 1997); Daisy Bates, *The Long Shadow of Little Rock* (New York: David McKay, 1962); and Elizabeth Jacoway and C. Fred Williams,

eds., *Understanding the Little Rock Crisis: An Exercise in Remembrance and Reconciliation* (Fayetteville: University of Arkansas Press, 1999).

10. Blossom, *It HAS Happened Here*, 16–17.

11. Tony Allen Freyer, *The Little Rock Crisis: A Constitutional Interpretation* (Westport, Conn.: Greenwood Press, 1984), 16–17.

12. *Arkansas Gazette*, February 9, 1956.

13. Tony Allen Freyer, "Politics and the Law in the Little Rock Crisis, 1954–1957," *Arkansas Historical Quarterly* 40.3 (1981): 197. The doctrine of interposition had held no legal basis in constitutional law since the end of the Civil War, but the idea appealed to white southerners seeking to delay integration.

14. Freyer, *The Little Rock Crisis*, 205.

15. *Arkansas Gazette*, August 23, 1957, as quoted in Graeme Cope, "A Thorn in the Side"? The Mothers' League of Central High School and the Little Rock Desegregation Crisis of 1957," *Arkansas Historical Quarterly* 57 (summer 1998): 163.

16. Pete Daniel, "Bayonets and Bibles: The 1957 Little Rock Crisis" (paper presented at the annual meeting of the Southern Historical Association, October 31, 1996, Little Rock, Arkansas, 3); Neil R. McMillen, "The White Citizens Council and Resistance to School Desegregation in Arkansas," *Arkansas Historical Quarterly* 30 (summer 1971): 107.

17. Graeme Cope, "'Honest White People of the Middle and Lower Classes'? A Profile of the Capital Citizens' Council during the Little Rock Crisis of 1957," *Arkansas Historical Quarterly* (spring 2002): 45.

18. Ibid., 45, 50–56.

19. *Arkansas Gazette*, August 28, 30, and 31, 1957.

20. Superintendent Blossom originally asked the principals of the black junior high and high schools for the names of students interested in transferring to Central. Approximately eighty students signed up, but Blossom screened the applicants for those with the best academic and behavioral records and ultimately reduced the number to seventeen students. As tensions began to mount prior to September 1957, eight of the seventeen students changed their minds, leaving nine to desegregate Central High. See Blossom, *It HAS Happened Here*, 19–21.

21. *Arkansas Gazette*, September 25, 1957.

22. Melba Pattillo Beals, *Warriors Don't Cry: A Searing Memoir of the Battle to Integrate Little Rock's Central High School* (New York: Pocket Books, 1994), 2.

23. "Operation Arkansas," Histories Division, Office of the Chief of Military History, U.S. Department of the Army, 227.

24. Alexander, *The Little Rock Recall Election*, 5; Sara Alderman Murphy, *Breaking the Silence: Little Rock's Women's Emergency Committee to Open Our Schools, 1958–1963* (Fayetteville: University of Arkansas Press, 1997), 82–83.

25. *Arkansas Gazette*, December 13, 1957.

26. Harry Ashmore, *Civil Rights and Wrongs: A Memoir of Race and Politics, 1944–1994* (New York: Pantheon, 1994), 132.

27. *Arkansas Gazette,* May 26, 1958.

28. Reed, *Faubus,* 243.

29. Alexander, *The Little Rock Recall Election,* 4.

30. *Arkansas Gazette,* June 22, August 19, August 29, and September 13, 1958.

31. Alexander, *The Little Rock Recall Election,* 6. The four high schools were Central, Hall, Horace Mann, and Metropolitan Technical High. Under the Blossom Plan, they were the only schools affected by the desegregation for that year and thus were the only schools in the district to close.

32. Ibid.; Adolphine Fletcher Terry as told to Carolyn Auge, "Life Is My Song, Also," unpublished autobiography, University of Arkansas at Little Rock Archives and Special Collections, Ottenheimer Library, University of Arkansas at Little Rock [hereinafter UALR].

33. Gates, "Power from the Pedestal," 31; Diary of Mrs. D. D. Terry, September 1958, Fletcher-Terry Family Papers, UALR.

34. Murphy, *Breaking the Silence,* 74–75.

35. Brewer, *The Embattled Ladies of Little Rock,* 8; Murphy, *Breaking the Silence,* 73; and WEC List of Contributions, personal collection of Irene Samuel.

36. Minutes of the Women's Emergency Committee, September 16 and 23, 1958, personal collection of Irene Samuel.

37. Murphy, *Breaking the Silence,* 76, 79; and *Garrett* v. *Faubus,* Brief for Women's Emergency Committee to Open Our Schools, Thomas Downie, 1959, proclamation depicting sample ballot, appendix 2, personal collection of Irene Samuel. The ballot's wording was the work of segregationist Attorney General Bruce Bennett, who phrased the ballot so that a vote against integration also meant a vote in favor of keeping the schools closed.

38. Murphy, *Breaking the Silence,* 88. Although a few local ministers and lawyers opposed the governor's school-closing policy, among Little Rock's white population, no other organization publicly spoke in favor of voting "for" integration.

39. *Arkansas Gazette,* September 18, 1958. The actual vote was 19,470 to 7,561. In response to the school closing, segregationist supporters opened a private, segregated high school, T. J. Raney High School, which remained in operation for the 1958–59 school year but then closed due to lack of funding. Some students attended schools outside Little Rock, moving in with relatives or friends in other parts of the state or other states to attend classes.

40. Alexander, *The Little Rock Recall Election,* 7.

41. Gates, "Power from the Pedestal," 36.

42. Anderson, *The Little Rock Recall Election,* 6.

43. WEC Policy and Purpose Statement, personal collection of Irene Samuel.

44. Alexander, *The Little Rock Recall Election,* 8; and *Arkansas Gazette,* November 13, 1958.

45. Murphy, *Breaking the Silence,* 105-7.

46. WEC Minutes, December 2, 1958.

47. Irene Samuel, interview with the author, October 17, 1996, Little Rock, Arkansas.

48. Murphy, *Breaking the Silence,* 107; and Samuel interview, October 24, 1996.

49. Alexander, *The Little Rock Recall Election,* 9.

50. WEC Minutes, December 2, 1958.

51. Women's Emergency Committee Papers.

52. Samuel interview, October 24, 1996; and Arkansas State Police surveillance report to Governor Faubus, May 10, 1960, Orval E. Faubus Papers, series 15, subseries 3, box 540, folder 5, University of Arkansas Special Collections, Mullins Library, University of Arkansas at Fayetteville.

53. "Letter from Little Rock," December 1958, personal collection of Irene Samuel.

54. Murphy, *Breaking the Silence,* 117, 122-23.

55. *Arkansas Gazette,* March 3, 1959.

56. Murphy, *Breaking the Silence,* 129.

57. WEC Minutes, March 3, 1959.

58. Dottie Morris, interview with the author, April 19, 1999, Little Rock, Arkansas.

59. Alexander, *The Little Rock Recall Election,* 10.

60. *Arkansas Gazette,* May 6 and 10, 1959.

61. WEC Minutes, May 5, 1959.

62. Alexander, *The Little Rock Recall Election,* 14-15.

63. *Arkansas Gazette,* May 13, 1959.

64. 1958 Master List of Electors, Pulaski County, Central High Museum Historical Collections, UALR.

65. Alexander, *The Little Rock Recall Election,* 24-25.

66. WEC Papers.

67. Alexander, *The Little Rock Recall Election,* 26.

68. Samuel interview, October 24, 1996.

69. Alexander, *The Little Rock Recall Election,* 29; WEC Papers, box 1, folder 1.

70. Samuel interview, October 24, 1996.

71. *Arkansas Gazette,* May 26 and June 19, 1959.

72. Everett Tucker Jr. to Irene Samuel, December 4, 1959, Little Rock, Arkansas, personal collection of Irene Samuel.

73. Ibid.

74. *Arkansas Gazette,* August 13, 1959.

75. WEC Papers.

76. "Little Rock Report: The City, Its People, Its Business, 1957-1959," WEC Papers.

77. Murphy, *Breaking the Silence,* 200.

78. WEC List of Contributions, 1958–62, personal collection of Irene Samuel.

79. WEC Papers; Murphy, *Breaking the Silence*, 200.

80. Murphy, *Breaking the Silence*, 210–11; and "Letter from Little Rock," December 1960, personal collection of Irene Samuel.

81. Born in Pangburn, Arkansas, House was no political novice. Her mother had been active in civic organizations and her father was deeply involved in local politics. Pat House, interview with the author, April 15, 1999, Little Rock, Arkansas.

82. Brewer, *The Embattled Ladies of Little Rock*, 257.

83. House interview, April 15, 1999.

84. Murphy, *Breaking the Silence*, 213.

85. WEC List of Expenditures, 1958–62, personal collection of Irene Samuel; Irene Samuel, interview with the author, March 11, 1997, Little Rock, Arkansas; and Morris interview, April 19, 1999. Morris actually became Jet Letter's first employee; later, she bought into the business and became a partner. Under different ownership, the business remains in operation.

86. Samuel interview, October 24, 1996.

87. Murphy, *Breaking the Silence*, 215, 217–18.

88. WEC Papers, box 5, folder 9; and Murphy, *Breaking the Silence*, 219.

89. WEC Papers.

90. Ibid.

91. WEC List of Board Members, 1963, personal collection of Irene Samuel.

92. WEC Minutes, May 8, 1963.

93. Murphy, *Breaking the Silence*, 232.

94. *Arkansas Gazette,* November 3, 1963.

95. Murphy, *Breaking the Silence*, 236. The national Panel of American Women's founder, Esther Brown, had also been involved in the fight to desegregate Kansas City schools, which culminated in the Supreme Court's *Brown* v. *Board of Education of Topeka* decision. For more information, see Milton S. Katz and Susan B. Tucker, "A Pioneer in Civil Rights: Esther Brown and the South Park Desegregation Case of 1948," *Kansas History* 18 (winter 1995–96): 234–47.

96. "The Panel of American Women—A Review, 1963, 1975," Panel of American Women Papers, Butler Center for Arkansas Studies, Central Arkansas Library System, Little Rock, Arkansas [hereinafter PAW Papers].

97. Notes for speech by Brownie Ledbetter, PAW Papers.

98. "The Panel of American Women—A Review, 1963–1975," PAW Papers.

99. Murphy, *Breaking the Silence*, 241.

100. *Arkansas Democrat,* December 7, 1969.

101. Martha Bass as quoted in *Arkansas Gazette,* May 7, 1967.

102. *Arkansas Gazette,* May 7, 1967.

103. *Arkansas Gazette,* October 10, 1963.

104. *Arkansas Gazette,* May 7, 1967.

105. Ibid.

106. Ibid.

107. Ibid.

108. Little Rock Panel of American Women, Inc., Articles of Incorporation, April 1971, PAW Papers.

109. "The Panel of American Women, A Review, 1963–1975," PAW Papers. The other three organizations were the YWCA, the Urban League of Greater Little Rock, and the Arkansas Council on Human Relations. The purpose of the grant was to assist school districts in eliminating minority group segregation in public schools.

110. Ibid.; "There's Got to Be a Way!" flyer for the Panel of American Women, n.d., PAW Papers.

111. Arkansas Public Policy Panel informational brochure, n.d., PAW papers.

112. Diary of Mrs. D. D. Terry, September 1958.

chapter 7

Elite White Female Activism and Civil Rights in New Orleans

SHANNON L. FRYSTAK

What I learned in my early life was that there has to be justice. That if there can't be justice, a civilization is barbarous. And I wanted to make it as just as I could.
—Betty Wisdom, 1988[1]

Rosa Freeman Keller, activist with the New Orleans League of Women Voters, the Urban League, and the Save Our Schools Committee. Courtesy of the Amistad Research Center at Tulane University.

❦

NEW ORLEANS, with its colonial French and Spanish architecture, the Spanish moss that hangs from ancient oaks, and the numerous bayous that wind through small neighborhoods, is a beautiful city rich in history. Equally famous for its two-week-long Mardi Gras celebration and the eccentric, if not infamous, political characters it has produced, the Crescent City is also known for a deadening humidity tempered only by a culinary culture that rivals the French and a music culture that rivals any in the world. Indeed, New Orleans makes a fascinating subject for historical study for all of these reasons and more. Calling Louisiana the "most diverse and unique" of all the southern states, historian Adam Fairclough notes, "the Crescent City was in many ways a world unto itself, and its lazy, hedonistic culture *seemed* to discourage racism."[2] However, Jim Crow ruled as powerfully in New Orleans as in any other Deep South city. While it is not as prominent in the civil rights literature as Selma or Montgomery, New Orleans was instrumental to the success of the modern civil rights movement.

In her study of women and politics in New Orleans, Pamela Tyler argues that elite white women broke out of their "appropriate spheres" to accomplish "an astonishing amount of beneficial community work." These "club women" indeed became a highly influential political force with which the established powers were forced to reckon. Although Tyler's work is a significant addition to the history of elite white women's involvement in local politics, her focus on one woman's efforts to challenge the dominant racial paradigm in the Crescent City omits the numerous other white women of community standing who bravely challenged the racial status quo.[3] Similarly, in his work on the struggle for racial equality in Louisiana, Adam Fairclough pays scant attention to the significant role played by Save Our Schools and its elite female constituency.[4] This essay expands on Tyler's and Fairclough's research by including and highlighting the elite white women who eschewed their privileged, segregated upbringing to work toward establishing racial justice in a city that embraced Jim Crow. It addresses the significance of the organizations founded by these privileged women, organizations dedicated to altering the segregated patterns most New Orleanians hoped to preserve.

In the immediate post–World War II years, biracial organizations such as the Young Women's Christian Association (YWCA), the National Association for the Advancement of Colored People (NAACP), and the National Urban

League (NUL) attracted a few privileged white women who developed racial sensitivities well before the implementation of the *Brown* decision. The YWCA was among the first predominantly white organizations not only to include African Americans in its membership, but also to provide them with opportunities for leadership. As early as 1916, the national board created an interracial committee for the "avowed purpose of laying the foundation for more Black participation." By year's end, there were sixty-five "colored branches" with the "same status as other branches" in existence across the country.[5] In 1935, the New Orleans YWCA established a segregated black branch in which members had full participatory status within the organization. Although the two branches did not merge until 1944, their joint planning and goals gave white members solid experience in interracial dialogue.

Historian Jacqueline Jones cites the YWCA as one of the first women's clubs to solicit middle-class black women as members, thus creating personal interactions between black and white women that "held special significance in a society that held up the housewife–domestic servant relationship as the only legitimate model of interracial contact for women."[6] African American women used such membership to their advantage. As one black woman stated, "We have in New Orleans . . . such fine outstanding Negroes and many of the white people do not get an opportunity to know them intimately. The YWCA is a medium through which the right kind of contacts can be made as well as interpretation to other groups within the community."[7]

The YWCA of New Orleans did, in fact, provide such a medium. Many of the white women who worked in the New Orleans chapter were from well-to-do families. As Tyler notes, such women "shared ties to the planter-business elite that had long dominated New Orleans and Louisiana politics; they were well-educated, married, and economically secure."[8] And thus they had the time needed to work within volunteer associations of varying types. Many of New Orleans's white female civil rights activists attributed their emergent interest in racial issues to their involvement with the local YWCA. For example, Rosa Freeman Keller, Anne Dlugos, and Mathilde Dreyfous, who worked diligently on integration issues in the Crescent City, claimed membership in the YWCA during the 1940s and 1950s.[9]

While many New Orleans neighborhoods had black and white families living in close proximity, if not next door to one another, the white women not involved with the YWCA or Urban League often had little intimate contact with black women outside the employer-employee relationship. Jacqueline Jones describes the "separate spheres" inhabited by middle- and upper-class white women as a world that "had little relevance to black women whose status was defined first and foremost by the labor they performed."[10] Because of this limited and unequal contact, most privileged white women saw black women merely as domestics and thus concluded that they were apolitical. Rosa Keller, who replaced her mother on the YWCA Board of Directors after her mother died, soon came to value the importance of interracial organizational work. "As one of an interracial group who met, deliberated, and worked together," Keller recalled, "I met for the first time Negro women who were self-respecting and well educated, women who could and should have been welcome anywhere."[11] Keller also recalled that she

> had grown up in this New Orleans community and never before had known the existence of such people. They were not acceptable in white hotels, stores, restaurants, or even public places such as parks or libraries. We never discussed these issues, but these were my friends, and I began to see things as I imagined they must surely have viewed them. It was bad enough that they were kept out of privately owned facilities, but worse was my perception that "public" meant "public for whites only." These were wrongs, inconsistent with the professed beliefs of our nation and it was high time we set about correcting them.[12]

The YWCA of New Orleans was one of only a few organizations in the city that not only strove to promote interracial practices in the South prior to the *Brown* decision of 1954 but was also itself interracial, a rare and oftentimes dangerous situation in the segregated South. Rosa Keller recalled, "There were so few places where blacks . . . and the rest of us could even begin to know each other. The YWCA—not the YMCA—was one."[13] According to historian Susan Lynn, the real significance of the YWCA was in the organization's willingness to embrace radical issues such as racial inclusiveness as well as fostering leadership by black women. Because the YWCA "endorsed virtually every item on the agenda of major civil rights organizations," it unwittingly became midwife to the predominantly female-led organizations that were formed as a result of the desegregation crises in the South.[14] These attributes contributed to the revolutionary nature of elite white women's dissent from racial injustice, particularly during the school desegregation crisis, with the creation of Save Our Schools, the Community Relations Council, and the Panel of Women.

In addition to her work in the YWCA, Keller also ascribed her racial awareness and subsequent activism to the consciousness-raising of the Urban League. She learned about the organization through a friend in the Jewish community, Gladys Cahn, who was president of the league's board of directors at the time. Keller also joined the board of directors, and her real education in racial issues began.

> I did not realize it at the time, but the Urban League had never involved anyone of my type. There were Rabbis, priests, social workers, educators, and a few Jewish people whose sensitivities were much keener about discrimination than those of most of the rest of us. I was a gentile, a member of a prominent New Orleans family, and had wealth and a secure social position. We were the kind of people who usually did not develop sensitivities to the terribly underprivileged. We had no concept of how it felt to be Negro in a society not ready to accept these people except in menial capacities.[15]

Organizations such as the National Urban League and the YWCA provided a venue where black and white women could interact on a level playing field. Commitments developed through the YWCA and the Urban League later transferred to women's work in other similarly progressive organizations such as the League of Women Voters and the National Council of Jewish Women. Many of these women formed organizations that were dedicated to what would become the most important and divisive issue in the city: the school desegregation crisis of 1960.

Little Rock Comes to New Orleans:
The School Desegregation Crisis, 1960–1962

The YWCA and the National Urban League worked on issues of racial justice in a variety of ways during the post–World War II years, yet, arguably, the most trying time for integrationists anywhere in the South arose after the Supreme Court's 1954 *Brown v. Board of Education* decision. While cosmopolitan New Orleans might have seemed more diverse than other urban areas of the Deep South, the Crescent City practiced Jim Crow segregation, discrimination, and disenfranchisement as thoroughly as the rest of the South. White New Orleanians lived under false assumptions regarding race relations in their city; particularly erroneous was the assumption that "blacks and whites had long enjoyed good relations and that contentment characterized blacks' emotional landscape."[16] The *Brown* decision, which rendered null one of Louisiana's most notorious court cases, *Plessy v. Ferguson,* ended any moderation on issues of race and threw the state into an uproar.

In the wake of the *Brown* decision, the Louisiana legislature passed a spate of laws to counter attempts to desegregate the state's public schools. Staunch segregationist and proud member of the Louisiana Citizens' Council William

"Willie" Rainach, of Claiborne Parish, organized the Joint Legislative Committee to Maintain Segregation. Aided by his counterpart from Plaquemine Parish, Leander Perez, the two created what Fairclough calls "obstructionist laws" and devised "a broad strategy to forestall integration."[17] In response, African American parents and the NAACP in Louisiana fought through the courts to get black children admitted to previously all-white schools, to no avail. Despite Federal District Judge J. Skelly Wright's 1956 warning to the Orleans Parish School System to prepare for integration, the statewide Louisiana School Board succeeded in delaying any desegregation activity. Finally, in May 1960, Judge Wright imposed an integration plan requiring that all first-grade students be admitted to the nearest neighborhood school, whether it had previously been for whites only or for African Americans. In response, the Orleans Parish School Board asked segregationist Governor Jimmie "You Are My Sunshine" Davis to block integration. Governor Davis toyed with the idea of closing the public schools that year, as Governor Orval Faubus had done in Little Rock in 1958.[18]

A moderate, urban, middle-class "save-the-schools movement" was mobilizing and gaining strength across the South in the late 1950s to oppose the extremist tactics of some southern state legislatures. At an Urban League of Greater New Orleans function in 1959, the principal guest, Miss Roberta Church, minority groups consultant for the Department of Labor, spoke eloquently and presciently on the role of women in times of crisis. She stated that women have the power to "exert great influence both as individuals and through their organizations by taking the initiative in the community to stand for high moral principles in all areas, and by moulding [sic] public opinion to support this stand." Church continued, "It is important that women accept this responsibility for it is they who should see to it and insist the proper moral tone prevails in the home, the community, and the nation."[19] In attendance at this meeting were a number of female members of the Urban League who took her advice to heart. Other respectable and progressive organizations such as the national Parent-Teacher Association (PTA) and the League of Women Voters (LWV) also became more vocal in their criticism of southern ultrasegregationist factions.[20]

In New Orleans, a group of elite white clubwomen began collecting and sharing information from across the South regarding public school integration.[21] In 1959, Gladys Cahn and Rosa Keller, who had been working on racial issues for a number of years, organized Save Our Schools (SOS), arguably the most important of the organizations formed during the New Orleans school desegregation crisis. The nonprofit organization sought "to further, by all proper and legitimate means, the continuation of a state-wide system of free public education."[22] From its inception, SOS downplayed integration and emphasized uninterrupted free public education for all.

Cahn and Keller had fought for racial justice for years, both together in the Urban League of Greater New Orleans and the YWCA and separately—Cahn with the National Council of Jewish Women and Keller in the League of Women Voters. As one member of SOS recalled, Gladys Cahn "was already ahead of her time in terms of integration."[23] Rosa Keller became what Tyler labels an "informal liaison officer linking the black community and the white power structure."[24] Her dedication to the rights of African American New Orleanians was noteworthy. Beginning in the 1940s, Keller worked on voter registration and education in the predominantly black sections of the city. Appointed to the city board after the election of Mayor DeLesseps "Chep" Morrison in 1954, she successfully fought for and won desegregation of the public library system. Keller also aided in the integration of the League of Women Voters and the city's public transportation system. Along with the legal aid of white attorneys John P. Nelson and Katherine Wright, she almost solely financed the lawsuit that eventually desegregated Tulane University in 1962. She was instrumental in the creation of Pontchartrain Park, an affordable African American housing community built through her husband's contracting business and the financial backing of her socialite friends Edith and Edgar Stern, philanthropists and heirs to the Sears, Roebuck fortune.[25] Thus her work with Save Our Schools represented simply one of her many efforts toward creating a more just and democratic society.

While many prominent men also supported Save Our Schools, it was women who organized and spearheaded this particular battle. When former Urban League president Helen Mervis heard that some white women were forming a pro-integration organization, she was immediately interested. As she later stated, "I knew all the people that put it together"—women like Rosa Keller, Gladys Cahn, Mary Sand, Betty Wisdom, and Anne Dlugos. Mervis joined the board of SOS that first year, taking charge of organizational fundraising. In addition to raising money, she had to "devise strategies on how to influence people on [our] behalf ... [and] defuse the opposition." She continued her association with the Urban League at the same time, although her efforts frequently put a strain on her and her family. The Mervis's home, like the Kellers,' was a meeting place for her white and black friends. "[W]henever anyone was ever concerned about having a meeting that was mixed," she recalled, it was held at her house. Subsequently, like many other women in the organization, she received harassing phone calls and threats.[26]

Also at the fore of the new organization were Anne Dlugos, Peggy Murison, Mary Sand, civil rights attorney Katherine Wright, and Betty Wisdom (who was the niece of both Rosa Keller and the liberal judge John Minor Wisdom).[27] All of these women were also active in one or more of the city's progressive organizations—the local YWCA, the Urban League of Greater New Orleans, the National Council of Jewish Women (NCJW), the NAACP, the LWV, or the American Civil Liberties Union (ACLU).[28] In fact, as early as 1959, Dlugos and Wisdom, in concert with the ACLU, organized local support for keeping the public schools operational, the early beginnings of the Save Our Schools movement. Dlugos recalled that SOS provided "an organization through which I could work . . . to bring about change. [It was] the intensest [sic] experience, second only to childbirth that I ever had." Betty Wisdom joined the SOS board as public relations chair. Wisdom, Dlugos, and Peggy Murison "ferried" the children to the newly integrated schools, held meetings in their homes, and organized educational materials to change community opinion. "I really do think that SOS was the only decent thing in the community for a time," Dlugos later said. "The churches had their tail tucked between their legs."[29]

Wisdom, who was often harassed by anti-integrationists in the city, joined the Urban League and the ACLU, as well as the LWV—but only *after* it integrated in 1963. In the 1960s, Wisdom became a member of the ACLU Board of Directors and then sat on the New Orleans Park Commission, where she worked successfully to integrate the New Orleans Park Board of Directors. All of this made her see that "change was possible. I had always gone on the theory that it was . . . but there were times I got discouraged. As changes started happening, it was very exciting."[30]

Peggy Murison, a northerner and recent transplant to New Orleans, became involved in SOS when fellow Urban Leaguers Keller and Cahn approached her about serving on the board of directors. Murison later recalled that she thought the "whole democratic system was at stake" in the desegregation controversy. Although SOS leaders asked her to act as president in 1961, she accepted only the vice presidency, believing that a less visible role would be safer for her children. In her stead, Mary Sand accepted the presidency that first year, and many of the women remember her bravery as she became the focus of the ultrasegregationist faction in the city. Anne Dlugos remembered Sand as "one of the greatest unsung heroines in New Orleans. She's the one who had to endure threats . . . to her five year old daughter who just started school."[31]

Murison also suffered the wrath of the anti-integrationist demonstrators, who threw rocks and eggs at her car, breaking windows and side mirrors. She experienced threatening and harassing phone calls and a cross was burned on her front lawn. Murison recalled that her work with SOS was "the only time I was really heroic. You have heard men talk about when they were in the war; it was the same thing."[32] The relentless dedication of its members made SOS one of the most important and influential organizations during the school desegregation crisis in New Orleans.

As New Orleans faced mandatory desegregation, Cahn and Keller met with the school board to suggest that integration begin in the Uptown area of the city because it contained a large percentage of Tulane professors who would likely support sending their children to integrated schools. The board, however, was intent on starting integration at two other schools, McDonogh 19 and Frantz. Both schools were in the Ninth Ward, an impoverished working-class neighborhood already fraught with racial tensions. Rosa Keller later recalled that the schools chosen for integration were "the worst two schools in the city to desegregate."[33] Nevertheless, if the state legislature would not facilitate peaceful desegregation, these women determined they would work locally to that end.

Save Our Schools held its first organizational meeting in February 1960, during heightened fears that the governor would close the public schools. The membership comprised mainly women and a handful of men from the elite, liberal segment of New Orleans's white community. Members quickly found themselves mired in planning strategy, stuffing envelopes with educational brochures, and knocking on doors seeking support. In addition, Keller, Dlugos, Mervis, and Wisdom traveled to Baton Rouge to testify before the state legislature on the necessity of peaceful desegregation, seemingly to no avail.

Because of continued strong anti-integrationist sentiment throughout the state, and particularly in New Orleans, SOS decided not to invite blacks to join the organization. It was a strategic decision based on the extreme political climate of the time. Board members felt they could accomplish more if they did not include black women, and hence were not seen as "integrationist" or "extremist." Keller met with her contacts in the black community, and they agreed with the decision.[34] Paul Rilling, field director for the Southern Regional Conference, wrote Keller that African Americans had *not* participated in the save-the-schools movement in the South, and that

> the general thinking of Negro leadership is that they could not with integrity
> participate in a movement with the limited goal of keeping schools open. It
> has also been felt by white as well as Negro leaders that a movement aimed at
> bringing pressure on political figures and public opinion would be more

effective strategically if it represented primarily white constituency. It is assumed that the attitude of Negro leadership is on record, that white persons
will have more success with white legislators, and that it needs to be demonstrated that *white* people are interested in keeping the schools open regardless of the segregation-desegregation issue.[35]

The school board also contacted SOS and requested that they not include
"too many Jews or too many known liberals."[36] Within a few months SOS
claimed more than five hundred members, and by year's end had close to
twelve hundred, many of them members of the Tulane University community.
Much to the dismay of the school board, numerous SOS members were, in
fact, Jewish and liberal.[37]

Throughout the spring of 1960, SOS members met frequently to discuss
integration efforts in other southern communities, problems of community
power structures, and how to prevent the schools from closing.[38] The organization made no excuses regarding its stance on the public schools; members
refused to argue the merits of segregation versus desegregation or to debate
states' rights issues or the 1954 *Brown* decision. The organization's official purpose was to keep the public schools open. "People didn't want to give the im-
pression that this was an extreme liberal assault on the community," recalled
Peggy Murison. "They wanted it to look like we were just keeping the schools
open, although in the back of our hearts a lot of us were assaulting the bastions
of segregation."[39] Although most of the organizers were pro-integration, the
board realized that some SOS members "differed widely as to the wisdom
and timing of the court order." Consequently, the organization's official statement was that "the [*Brown*] decision was an accomplished fact and that the
only realistic course was to support any reasonable plan, acceptable to the
courts, which would keep the public schools open." Indeed, "the question
was no longer segregation or desegregation, but open schools versus closed
schools."[40]

Anti-integrationist sentiment remained very strong throughout Louisiana.
The public generally associated membership in SOS with being a "liberal integrationist," an extremist, and oftentimes a "Nigger-loving Communist."[41] The
organization's only defense was a good offense. Before the schools opened in
September 1960, the SOS publication committee, headed by Wisdom, prepared several newsletters about gradual integration to be distributed to parents, local businessmen, and the media. They also published weekly statements in the local newspapers detailing the disastrous effects that closing the

public schools would create and tried to inform the public about how well integration had worked in other areas of the South. They responded to inaccuracies and falsehoods presented by their opposition, the segregationist faction in the city. Through local television and radio spots, as well as mass distribution of newsletters, SOS members made sure that the New Orleans community remained informed about the school desegregation crisis. SOS also created a legal committee headed by attorneys John P. Nelson and Katherine Wright, who prepared summaries and legal analyses of twenty-one bills that the legislature had labeled "emergency legislation" and passed immediately after Judge Wright's desegregation order. They were prepared to challenge any attempts to close the schools.[42] When Judge Wright finally set "desegregation day" for November 14, 1960, the state superintendent of schools reacted by declaring that day a holiday for public schools throughout the state. The Orleans Parish School Board, however, voted to keep their schools open. Three African American girls integrated the McDonogh 19 school, and one girl integrated the Frantz school.

The SOS board detailed members to escort the four African American girls—Tessie Provost, Leona Tate, Gail Etienne, and Ruby Bridges—through the mobs and into their respective schools. The women escorting the children suffered at the hands of the rioting mobs; they found their car tires slashed and car windows broken. Betty Wisdom recalled an incident that occurred when she was escorting the black girls home from school and an angry mob formed around them, brandishing clubs, tire irons, and other weapons. She remembered fearing for their lives. Peggy Murison escorted Yolanda Gabrielle, one of the few white children who remained at the newly integrated school. When the White Citizens' Council published the names, telephone numbers, and license plate numbers of the female escorts, harassing phone calls and even death threats followed. "They could say things like, 'We're outside waiting for you. Don't go out of your house.' And it could get really scary," recalled Wisdom. A cross was burned on Peggy Murison's front lawn, and at one point members of the mob tried to get into her car.[43] Many white parents refused to allow their children to attend the two integrated schools, and some of the white students who did attend were harassed for not withdrawing. Undeterred by the dangers, Murison and Wisdom escorted the children to school for a few weeks at the beginning of each school year, "until the problems eventually died down."[44] Indeed, as one SOS pamphlet states, the "whole back to school movement in New Orleans rested solely on the SOS ferry service, and most of the white parents sent their children to Frantz because they trusted SOS."[45]

Save Our Schools also tried to assist families who had suffered property damage or who had lost jobs because they kept their children in a desegregated school. Members of SOS found themselves raising funds not only for their own organization, but also on behalf of these parents. When James Gabrielle lost his job for keeping his daughter at Frantz, the women of SOS formed a Back-to-School Committee to raise money for those who needed help with living expenses.[46] For a time, the women of SOS also collected funds to pay the teachers at McDonogh and Frantz schools, who were illegally denied their salaries by an act of the state legislature. The Orleans Parish School Board, unable to secure monies from the state legislature, was denied loans (borrowed against property taxes) by local banks as well.[47] Rosa Keller even used her personal Coca-Cola endowment to pay the salaries of some of the Franz and McDonogh teachers.[48]

Working in SOS became a full-time job for many of its leaders. When the school year finally ended, SOS members turned their attention to issuing press releases, mailing desegregation information, and educating New Orleans community members about the social, economic, and psychological effects of segregation and the impact on those individuals directly involved. In addition, SOS prepared a comprehensive study of how desegregation had been accomplished in other areas of the South and the social and moral benefits it had brought to cities similar to New Orleans.[49] Members also worked vigorously to convince white parents to end the boycotts of the two schools, conducting a telephone campaign to solicit support and funds toward this effort.[50] Betty Wisdom noted that by December, more than a few mothers "frantic to get their kids back to school" had contacted the group but feared reprisals. When CBS news came to New Orleans to film an episode of *Eyewitness to History,* members of SOS appeared on-camera and spoke eloquently and articulately on the legal interference by the governor and state legislature and on the necessity of retaining a public school system. Although by now much of the New Orleans community regarded SOS members as liberal integrationists, the organization remained firmly committed to avoiding a debate on integration. In fact, when Charles Kurault asked if SOS contained both integrationists and segregationists, President Mary Sand responded that "it contained all shades of opinion."[51]

Members of Save Our Schools, in concert with the League of Women Voters and other similarly progressive organizations, also turned to the New Orleans business community seeking support for their efforts. The women believed that a strong statement from local businessmen on behalf of open schools would be an effective counter to the opposition. This task proved to be quite daunting. Prior to the integration of the schools, the New Orleans Young Men's Business Club and a number of other influential civic organizations had refused to endorse an open-schools resolution.[52] In fact, throughout the initial desegregation fiasco, businessmen in the city had remained conspicuously silent on the issue. Even the seemingly moderate mayor, Chep Morrison, contemplating a run for governor that year, refused to take a stand in support of SOS or open schools. "Either the men felt that they had too much to lose," Wisdom remembered, "or they didn't have the courage of their convictions, *or* they just didn't have any convictions." Richard Freeman, Wisdom's uncle and Rosa Keller's brother, complained that every time Rosa made a speech, members of the community would call him up and say, "Get your goddamned red [Coca Cola] machines out of my business." At one point, Leander Perez led a boycott of Freeman's Coca Cola business as a result of Rosa Keller's actions in the school desegregation crisis. Even Keller's husband, an influential community leader in his own right, complained about her activities; but Keller held firm. When her husband ordered her to end her civil rights activities and barred the subject from the house, Keller responded: "If you are serious about this, you are going to have to bar me too because I have come to this place where I cannot walk out. You fought your war and I was very helpful to you. I took care of your children and did everything like that. You were gone for two years and I took care of them. This is my war and it's gotta be done. Somebody's got to do it."[53] As Betty Wisdom later reported to the Southern Regional Council (SRC), "If I had to choose one characteristic of New Orleans men which, more than any other, had caused all our troubles, I think I'd choose conceited pigheadedness."[54]

Certainly, business leaders in the New Orleans community were "reluctant to make any attempt to resolve the problem apparently out of fear that this might bring economic sanctions from the [White] Citizens' Councils," as it had for the Freemans' businesses.[55] Betty Wisdom noted the apathy demonstrated by business leaders in the city: "Here we have *panis and circenses* once a year at Mardi Gras and that, apparently, is the extent of the *noblesse oblige* and civic pride."[56] Yet, the city's business leaders could no longer ignore the damage that was being done to the local economy and the city's tourism and trade industries. As a number of historians have noted, when the chaos began to affect the city economically, the New Orleans business elite finally rallied "in defense of order and stability."[57] Yet SOS must be given some credit for its intense lobbying campaign. The members' efforts attracted national attention

to the New Orleans crisis, attention that contributed to the eventual conciliation of the New Orleans business community. In a letter to the *Nation*, Betty
Wisdom addressed the apathy of the New Orleans business community:

> I was there, day after day, escorting children to school past the howling har-
> ridans. The screamers shouted obscenities (Nigger-Jew bitch, dirty Jew, and
> others too filthy to record) and then raced home to telephone the returning
> families and their escorts with threats of arson, acid-throwing, kidnapping,
> beatings and murder. Until we began reading the stories and editorials in the
> outside press, we felt cut off from the world. In a crisis like ours, there are few
> things worse than this feeling of isolation. It induces the racists to commit
> ever more terrible outrages, secure in the knowledge that no one but approv-
> ing fellow citizens will ever see their actions. It induces the moderates and
> integrationists the feeling that there is a Sisyphean task which no one ap-
> proves or understands.[58]

By the end of December, the publicity and the assiduous lobbying by the
women of SOS and other organizations was showing results. More than one
hundred business and professional men from the city ran a three-quarter-page
advertisement in the local newspaper that was distributed to newspapers
throughout the country "appealing for an end to threats and street demonstrations and for support of the school board." SOS members jumped on the
bandwagon and secured the signatures of 196 local parents in support of this
statement and of a future statement by local clergymen, who had similarly refused to take a stand.[59] Ironically, as local newspapers "lauded the efforts of the
New Orleans men," the group of "liberal to moderate women" who for more
than a year had incessantly "prodded the city's leadership" and other local
organizations into "taking public stands on the necessity of keeping the public
schools open" received no recognition.[60] As Pamela Tyler so eloquently notes,
"the women themselves seemed to understand that in the social climate of
1960, their signatures on a public statement would command insufficient respect to effect a significant alteration in the public mood."[61]

The following year, when Judge Wright broadened the public school desegregation order to include middle schools and high schools, the state legislature
again responded by enacting "emergency legislation" to hinder these efforts.
State legislators called for New Orleans to operate under a two-school system—one public and one private.[62] Anti-integrationists raised the specter of
miscegenation by questioning the wisdom of operating coeducational schools,
particularly at the high school level. Their arguments harkened back to the
obsessive fears of race mixing that had dominated southern discourse since the

seventeenth century. Fears of black male teenagers mingling with white female teenagers aroused the furor of ultrasegregationists. As one person stated in a letter to the editor of the local paper, "We are all equal under God, but there are a very great physical and mental differences between certain races. The desire today seems to be not so much for equal education but intermingling of the races."[63]

Although the women who founded Save Our Schools initially did so with the intention merely of keeping the Orleans Parish public school system in operation, their struggle ultimately involved much more. The beginning of the 1961–62 school year was much like the previous one. Following Judge Wright's order, the number of desegregated schools in New Orleans expanded, and white and black students integrating schools, as well as members of SOS, contended with the usual harassment. The school year, however, ended with pupil attendance up among both black and white students. The white student enrollment in Louisiana at the end of 1961 totaled 10,266,673, and black student enrollment was 3,210,724, up from 10,173,399 and 3,088,261, respectively.[64] The number of children attending integrated schools continued to climb and by 1962, 190 black children were even attending thirty-four formerly white parochial schools. Thanks in large part to the efforts of SOS and its elite white female constituency, the expanded desegregation efforts in the city continued with little fanfare.[65]

Their Work Was Not Yet Done

Although the school crisis itself abated, the work of the white activists did not. Gladys Cahn and Helen Mervis invited people from other progressive organizations in the city to discuss civil rights, labor conditions, and integration in other areas of the city. Out of these meetings, "a group of progressive-minded citizens . . . [working] to ameliorate racial tensions and promote community relations among all members of the New Orleans community regardless of race, color, ethnicity, or religion" came together in 1962 to form the Community Relations Council (CRC).[66] Unlike SOS, the CRC had both black and white members; like SOS, the members came from all faiths and most were women.[67] One member described the CRC as "a group of people who sort of found each other . . . who had this dream about a beautifully integrated society which didn't recognize color."[68]

With the immediate school crisis behind them, many former members of SOS actively participated in CRC activities. They included Mathilde Dreyfous, whose husband, attorney George Dreyfous, working with the ACLU had contributed much to school integration; Rosa Keller; Betty Wisdom; and Peggy Murison. The CRC continued to work on civil rights issues in New Orleans; however, the council also included local, regional, and national agencies that expressed interest in finding economic, social, and political solutions to the seemingly endless racial crises in the city. Gladys Cahn, a cofounder of SOS, served as the CRC's first president.

The CRC addressed a number of racial justice issues. Its members conducted a study of the city's hospital system to find out if the hospitals were, in fact, complying with the provisions of the Civil Rights Act of 1964. Jane Buchsbaum, a latecomer to SOS and an activist for CRC, remembered "[sneaking] around corridors, [trying] to see if there was anybody black who was not in anything but a janitorial capacity."[69] After that, the CRC tackled the segregated city park system. In partnership with the New Orleans Park Commission, on whose board Betty Wisdom sat, CRC successfully integrated the city's Recreation Department as well as the New Orleans Science Fair. In 1964 the CRC held a conference at Xavier University entitled "A Look at New Orleans and Race Relations." The meeting included progressive members of the city's white and black communities, all seeking to take inventory of where the city of New Orleans stood "in relationship to progress in race relations with the rest of the nation" as well as to discuss the effects of the Civil Rights Act, barriers to voter registration in the city, and Louisiana public accommodation laws.[70] "There were little things that we did all the time," recalled Buchsbaum.

> This may sound very idealistic . . . but I think it's important. Those of us who really cared a lot, we tried to live out our lives that way. We entertained on an integrated basis in our homes, we associated with black people publicly, that was just a tremendously big step at certain points . . . just belonging to the Community Relations Council was just a really communist thing to do. It wasn't necessarily the particular project, although there were some, it was just the constant involvement with black people nobody else had.[71]

Throughout the 1960s and well into the 1970s, the CRC continued its commitment to end discrimination, conducting investigations of police brutality, equal employment, community relations, housing, and education.[72]

Concurrent with the founding of the CRC, Helen Mervis assembled an interracial group and founded the Panel of Women in New Orleans.[73] Much like the national Panel of American Women that was formed in Kansas City in the 1950s, Mervis gathered women willing to talk openly about their experiences of discrimination. Each panel consisted of four women, each speaking from a particular racial or ethnic perspective. Jane Buchsbaum, for instance, described prejudice she had encountered as a Jewish women, and Blanche Francis, the wife of the president of Xavier University, detailed experiences in segregated New Orleans. The panel spoke before citywide groups and organizations to "as many people as they could," recalled Mervis. They revealed painful personal experiences with prejudice and discrimination and spoke "particularly in churches, which were hotbeds of racial animosity. It took a lot of courage for those women to [tell] their stories . . . and to bare themselves in front of audiences. But the feedback was so rewarding."[74] Buchsbaum recalled that Blanche Francis was such an effective speaker that "even before she got [to] the microphone, she would start to cry. She would talk about her kids integrating school. It was marvelous and the whole audience would break down."[75] Out of this group emerged a younger generation of elite white female activists who continued the tradition begun in the 1940s and 1950s by the YWCA, the Urban League, and the NAACP.

Conclusion

Some may wonder whether the case of New Orleans, where members of privileged groups took up the cause of civil rights, was unique in the Deep South. Sociologists Gary Marx and Michael Useem think not; they suggest that "rarely have oppressed minorities been entirely responsible for their own liberation." They cite the ending of slavery in Greece and Rome as well as the French and Russian Revolutions as illustrating a tendency for "some among the privileged to defect and take up the cause of the oppressed."[76] Much like the actors in those movements, the women examined here did not personally suffer from segregation. All of them, however, came from backgrounds that included a penchant for social activism, whether it was their family; their religious background; their college experiences; or their prior involvement with liberal, humanist, integrated organizations. Each was able to draw on something inside herself that allowed her to risk social ostracism in order to speak out for racial justice. Together they formed a strong network of female support able to sustain them in their dissent against an undemocratic system. While the story of these privileged white female activists committed to racial justice is not unique, it is a story rarely told. Women like Rosa Keller, Gladys Cahn, Betty Wisdom, and Jane Buchsbaum appear only in the margins of the numerous works on the civil rights movement published to date although their contributions to race relations are notable.

One of the unintended consequences of World War II was the political activism it generated among women who believed it was their civic duty to work with such groups as the Red Cross and the League of Women Voters.[77] In the postwar political climate, when many of the older generation of elite white women in New Orleans became concerned about issues of justice and democracy, they did so by walking a fine line between maintaining their status in the community as proper southern women and standing for the democratic process and human rights. Furthermore, middle- and upper-class women brought to their community efforts what historian Joanne Meyerowitz calls a decidedly female ethic, "specifically to build bridges across racial lines."[78] Indeed, although they were forced to work within the constraints of both their gender and their race, the progression of their activism—working for justice through issues of social welfare to working on issues of race to promote greater justice— seems natural.

Second, their lives as elite southern white women ironically aided them in their efforts at racial conciliation. While they might have experienced some gender- and race-related barriers in organizations like the NAACP, which were traditionally male dominated, they strategically chose to work within organizations that afforded them unusual opportunities because of their gender, race, and class. Moreover, the tactics they employed to achieve their ends—lobbying, education, fund-raising, and publicity—fell well within the confines of traditional and acceptable forms of social activism supported by women and men of their class. They worked within the system, not outside it. As Marx and Useem argue, these privileged women came to social movements "with more of the skills and experience which are important for the success of the movement, such as writing, internal organizing, strategy planning, and fund raising."[79] Indeed, in some instances it may have been easier for white women of privilege and social standing to use the system and their connections to their advantage. Middle- and upper-class women were somewhat insulated, not only because of their gender but also because of their social position. Though not exempt from harassment and violence at the hands of anti-integrationists, their elite status and female gender provided safety and brought pressure to bear on the white establishment.

Finally, these elite white women should be seen as somewhat revolutionary for their class as well as for the era. Working on issues of racial justice in the early postwar era, as Meyerowitz notes, was a "watershed in women's social reform activism, one that would ultimately lead to more general challenges to discrimination based on race and gender," particularly for women with community standing. In working in the area of civil rights, they basically created within organizations such as SOS and the CRC what one historian deems a "community of subversives."[80] Ostracized not only by the larger New Orleans community for their work on behalf of African Americans but also by members of their own class, the women recall being labeled "reds," "scalawags," and "Nigger lovers." They lost numerous friends in their own social circles, although not one of the women interviewed suggested that it hindered their activities in any way. Indeed, they created for themselves a new community based on interracial cooperation, a "beloved community" similar to that which defined the Student Nonviolent Coordinating Committee of the 1960s. These New Orleans women eventually brought black and white to work together, and that, in and of itself, was a revolutionary act for this privileged group.

Notes

I wish to thank Leslie Berman, Sarah Duncan, Denise Maruna, Elizabeth Palumbo, Jonathan Sarnoff, Natasha Whitton, Mary Williams, Newcomb College Center for Research on Women, the outside readers for this press, series editors Stanley Harrold and Randall M. Miller, and especially this volume's editor, Gail Murray, for their invaluable comments and suggestions. I am also extremely grateful to those women who allowed me to interview them through the years about their participation in the New Orleans movement, and to Kim Lacey Rogers, who had the foresight to interview the heroic New Orleans activists before their stories were lost.

1. Kim Lacey Rogers interview with Betty Wisdom, June 14, 1988, Kim Lacey Rogers-Glenda Stevens Collection, Amistad Research Center, New Orleans, Louisiana [hereinafter Rogers-Stevens Collection, ARC].

2. Adam Fairclough, *Race and Democracy: The Civil Rights Struggle in Louisiana, 1915–1972* (Athens: University of Georgia Press, 1995), xix, 139; emphasis mine.

3. Pamela Tyler, *Silk Stockings and Ballot Boxes: Women and Politics in New Orleans, 1920–1963* (Athens: University of Georgia Press, 1996), 3. Tyler does acknowledge the difficulties surrounding biracial organizational development in a chapter that concentrates on Rosa Keller and the League of Women Voters ("In Two Worlds: Rosa Freeman Keller, Race and Reform"). For an extended discussion of the issues surrounding the New Orleans League of Women Voters, see Shannon L. Frystak, "With All Deliberate Speed: The Integration of the New Orleans League of Women Voters, 1953–1963," in *Searching for Their Places: Southern Women across Four Centuries*, ed. Thomas H. Appleton Jr. and Angela Boswell (Columbia: University of Missouri Press, 2003).

4. See Fairclough, *Race and Democracy*, chap. 9, particularly 236–37.

5. Paula Giddings, *When and Where I Enter: The Impact of Black Women on Race and Sex in America* (New York: Bantam Books, 1984), 155; and Eva D. Bowles, "The YWCA among Colored Girls and Women," January 1924, YWCA New Orleans Papers, Special Collections, Tulane University, New Orleans, Louisiana [hereinafter YWCA-NO Papers].

6. Jacqueline Jones, "The Political Implications of Black and White Women's Work

in the South, 1890–1965," in *Women, Politics, and Change,* ed. Louise A. Tilly and Patricia Gurin (New York: Russell Sage Foundation, 1990), 114.

7. Mrs. Cordella Winn to Mrs. Elizabeth S. Thompson, May 20, 1935, YWCA-NO Papers, box 41, folder 4.

8. Tyler, *Silk Stockings,* 5.

9. See also Sarah Mitchell Parsons, *From Southern Wrongs to Civil Rights: The Memoir of a White Civil Rights Activist* (Tuscaloosa: University of Alabama Press, 2000).

10. Jones, "Political Implications," 111.

11. Rosa Freeman Keller, "Autobiography," unpublished manuscript, 1977, section 37, copy in possession of the author.

12. Ibid.

13. Ibid.

14. Susan Lynn, *Progressive Women in Conservative Times: Racial Justice, Peace and Feminism, 1945 to the 1960s* (New York: Oxford University Press, 1991), 64.

15. Keller, "Autobiography," section 37.

16. Tyler, *Silk Stockings,* 204.

17. Fairclough, *Race and Democracy,* 169–70.

18. Ibid., 234–35.

19. "Women Should Accept Responsibility—Miss Church," *Louisiana Weekly,* June 20, 1959, Amistad Research Center, New Orleans, Louisiana [hereinafter ARC].

20. Bartley, *The Rise of Massive Resistance: Race and Politics in the South during the 1950s* (Baton Rouge: Louisiana State University Press, 1969), 320–21.

21. See Save Our Schools Papers, ARC, folders 17–20 [hereinafter SOS Papers, ARC].

22. Save Our Schools Pamphlet, 1961, SOS Papers, ARC, box 1, folder 11.

23. Kim Lacey Rogers interview with Jane Buchsbaum, November 28, 1978, Rogers-Stevens Collection, ARC.

24. Tyler, *Silk Stockings,* 205.

25. Keller, "Autobiography," sections 43–51. Ponchartrain Park was so successful that baseball player Jackie Robinson, who integrated the Brooklyn Dodgers in 1947, used it as a model when he created a similar housing project in New York.

26. Kim Lacey Rogers interviews with Helen Mervis, November 11, 1978, and July 1, 1988, Rogers-Stevens Collection, ARC.

27. Interviews with the white women suggest that the black community was in agreement with the decision to keep SOS an all-white organization because it would prevent the conservative anti-integrationist faction in the city from labeling the organization communist or extremist. Discussion of all of the participants is beyond the scope of this essay; however, the women discussed here are representative of other women members of the organization.

28. Minutes of Board Meeting, May 9, 1960, SOS Papers, box 1, folder 6. A discussion of the role of Jewish women in the civil rights movement in New Orleans deserves

further attention but is beyond the scope of this essay. For more information on the role of Jewish women in the civil rights movement, see Debra Schultz, *Going South: Jewish Women in the Civil Rights Movement* (New York: New York University Press, 2001); and Clive Webb, *Fight against Fear: Southern Jews and Black Civil Rights* (Athens: University of Georgia Press, 2002).

29. Kim Lacey Rogers interview with Anne Dlugos, June 30, 1988, Rogers-Stevens Collection, ARC.

30. Kim Lacey Rogers interview with Betty Wisdom, June 14, 1988, Rogers-Stevens Collection, ARC.

31. Kim Lacey Rogers interview with Peggy Murison, May 14, 1979; and Dlugos interview, June 30, 1988, Rogers-Stevens Collection, ARC.

32. Murison interviews, May 14, 1979, and July 13, 1988, Rogers-Stevens Collection, ARC.

33. Interview with Rosa Keller by the author, March 13, 1996.

34. Keller interview, April 8, 1988, Rogers-Stevens Collection, ARC. Interviews with black members of the New Orleans community corroborate this statement. Author interviews with Sybil Morial, December 4, 2001; and Madelon Cochrane, December 11, 2001.

35. Paul Rilling to Rosa Keller, December 23, 1959, Southern Regional Council Papers, Library of Congress [hereinafter SRC Papers, LOC], series IV, reel 144.

36. Murison interview, May 14, 1979, Rogers-Stevens Collection, ARC.

37. Gladys Cahn to Paul Rilling, n.d., SRC Papers, LOC, series IV, reel 144.

38. Save Our Schools Board Minutes, March 23, April 6, April 25, April 28, and May 9, 1960, SOS Papers, ARC.

39. Murison interview, May 14, 1979, Rogers-Stevens Collection, ARC.

40. "Save Our Schools, Inc., 1960," SOS Papers, ARC.

41. Rosa Keller, "The League of Women Voters of New Orleans History, 1942–1985," manuscript dated 1985, copy in possession of the author.

42. "Plans and Program for Save Our Schools," July 1, 1961–December 31, 1961, SOS Papers, ARC, box 1, folder 12.

43. Betty Wisdom interview with the author, November 29, 2001; and Murison interview, May 14, 1979, Rogers-Stevens Collection, ARC.

44. Murison interview, May 14, 1979, Rogers-Stevens Collection, ARC.

45. "SOS, Inc.," 1961, SOS Papers, ARC, box 1, folder 11.

46. Murison interview, May 14, 1979, Rogers-Stevens Collection, ARC; "Cite Pair Who Bucked New Orleans Race Mob," *Louisiana Weekly*, March 4, 1961; and "Save Our Schools, Inc.," n.d., SOS Papers, ARC, box 1, folder 11.

47. The state legislature was later enjoined by the Justice Department to release funds to pay the Orleans Parish schoolteachers, which it reluctantly did; see Fairclough, *Race and Democracy*, 246–47.

48. Segregationist Leander Perez led a boycott of Coca-Cola in New Orleans as a result of Rosa Keller's civil rights activism.

49. "Fact Sheet for SOS Discussion Leaders—Confidential," 1961, SOS Papers, ARC, box 1, folder 13.

50. Paul Rilling to SOS, December 6, 1960, SRC Papers, LOC, series IV, reel 143.

51. Betty Wisdom to Paul Rilling, November 30, 1960, SRC Papers, LOC, series IV, reel 143.

52. In fact, the Young Men's Business Club actually "commended the actions of state officials to maintain segregated schools"; cited in J. H. Foster, "Race Relations in the South, 1960," *Journal of Negro Education* 30 (spring 1961): 146.

53. Keller interview, April 8, 1988, Rogers-Stevens Collection, ARC.

54. Betty Wisdom to Paul Rilling, April 6, 1961, SRC Papers, LOC, series IV, reel 143.

55. *New York Times* article, December 6, 1960, as cited in Morton Inger, "The New Orleans School Crisis of 1960," in *Southern Businessmen and School Desegregation,* ed. Elizabeth Jacoway and David R. Colburn (Baton Rouge: Louisiana State University Press, 1982), 94.

56. Betty Wisdom to Paul Rilling, December 23, 1960, SRC Papers, LOC, series IV, reel 143.

57. Fairclough, *Race and Democracy,* 253–54; Inger, "The New Orleans School Crisis," 94–95.

58. Wisdom, "Letter from a New Orleans Mother," *Nation,* November 4, 1961, Howard University Libraries. Note: Betty Wisdom had no children.

59. Inger, "The New Orleans School Crisis," 94; and "Plans and Programs from SOS," July 1, 1961–December 31, 1961, SOS Papers, ARC, box 1, folder 12.

60. Other organizations in the city that issued statements at the behest of SOS were the Tulane Faculty Senate, the Central Trades Council, the American Association of University Women, the American Association of University Professors, the Independent Women's Organization, local PTAs, and various church groups, cited in "Plans and Programs for SOS," SOS Papers, ARC, box 1, folder 12.

61. Tyler, *Silk Stockings,* 228–29.

62. *States-Item,* June 26, 1962, and April 6, 1962, respectively, SOS Papers, ARC, box 2, folders 17 and 8, respectively.

63. *States-Item,* June 26, 1962, and June 28, 1962, SOS Papers, ARC, box 2, folder 17, and box 1, folder 18, respectively.

64. *New Orleans Times-Picayune,* December 12, 1961, SOS Papers, ARC, box 3, folder 2.

65. See *States-Item,* September 4, 7, and 8, 1962, SOS Papers, ARC, box 3, folders, 5, 6, and 10, respectively.

66. "History," Community Relations Council Papers, collection 97, Amistad Research Center, New Orleans, Louisiana [hereinafter CRC Papers, ARC].

67. Helen Mervis recalled that there were "2 or 3 women to every man"; Mervis interview, November 18, 1978, Rogers-Stevens Collection, ARC.

68. Kim Lacey Rogers interview with Jane Buchsbaum, November 28, 1979, Rogers-Stevens Collection, ARC.

69. Ibid.

70. CRC newsletter, April 24, 1964, CRC Papers, ARC, box 2.

71. Buchsbaum interview, November 28, 1978, Rogers-Stevens Collection, ARC.

72. "History," CRC Papers, ARC, collection 97.

73. For additional information on the Panel of American Women, see Laura Miller, "Challenging the Segregationist Power Structure in Little Rock"; and Gail Murray, "White Privilege, Racial Justice," in this volume. The New Orleans women did not adopt the full title, Panel of American Women, and thus may not have been affiliated with the national movement.

74. Mervis interview, November 18, 1978, Rogers-Stevens Collection, ARC.

75. Buchsbaum interview, November 28, 1978, Rogers-Stevens Collection, ARC.

76. Gary T. Marx and Michael Useem, "Majority Involvement in Minority Movements: Civil Rights, Abolition, Untouchability," *Journal of Social Issues* 27 (1971): 97.

77. Susan Lynn, "Gender and Progressive Politics: A Bridge to Social Activism of the 1960s," in *Not June Cleaver: Women and Gender in Postwar American, 1945–1960,* ed. Joanne Meyerowitz (Philadelphia: Temple University Press, 1994); see also Susan Hartmann, *The Home Front and Beyond: American Women in the 1940s* (Boston: Twayne, 1982), specifically chaps. 2, 9, and 11.

78. Joanne Meyerowitz, "Introduction: Women and Gender in Postwar America, 1945–1960," in Meyerowitz, ed., *Not June Cleaver,* 106.

79. Marx and Useem, "Majority Involvement," 85; see also Susan Ostrander, *Women of the Upper Class* (Philadelphia: Temple University Press, 1984).

80. See Catherine Fosl, "There Was No Middle Ground: Anne Braden and the Southern Social Justice Movement," *National Women's Studies Association Journal* 11 (1999): 17.

chapter 8

White Privilege, Racial Justice

Women Activists in Memphis

GAIL S. MURRAY

When the women get together to do something, the average man snickers and shakes his head, but he's nervous when he does it. For he recognizes, and even fears, their sometimes amazing capacity for dedication and accomplishment.
—*Memphis Commercial Appeal*, June 19, 1969[1]

The newly organized Concerned Women of Memphis and Shelby County vote to urge the City Council to meet with representatives of the city Sanitation Workers' Union (AFSCME) to avert another strike in 1969. CWMSC adopted an ambitious agenda for economic and social reform. Courtesy of Jocelyn Dan Wurzburg, Wurzburg Papers, Scrapbook, Mississippi Valley Special Collections, McWherter Library, University of Memphis.

THE SLIGHTLY BEMUSED COMMENT by Memphis editor Gordon Hanna that introduces this essay suggests that women's activism was making significant inroads into the lazy paternalism of this Mississippi River town. By 1970, scores of southern-born, middle-class and elite Memphis women had become actively committed to equal opportunity, impartial justice, and expanded social services for African Americans. While some took up racial justice work because of religious convictions about human equality, others developed empathy for the civil rights struggle gradually through the friendship and influence of African American women in the city's few biracial women's organizations. Yet others found their voices because a single consciousness-raising event or confrontation forced them to question the white privilege and race discrimination endemic to Memphis culture. A few mobilized only after the shocking assassination in their city of Dr. Martin Luther King Jr. Many volunteers began with a limited understanding of racial discrimination, trusting that good intentions could eliminate inequality.

If they sometimes overlooked the entrenched institutional racism of their community and instead focused their attention on cultivating personal friendships with women of color, even that was a radical idea in 1960s Memphis. Unlike white male liberals, their vision of race relations centered more on personal relationships and child-centered reforms than on legislative change. Volunteerism propelled white women into hands-on grassroots organizing that enabled many of them to appropriate and internalize much broader concepts of social justice and racial equality than did many of their friends and neighbors. Because they concentrated on personal transformation rather than on securing legislative mandates, on providing social services rather than waiting for government to provide them, they modeled a successful biracial community life even as much of America was resegregating in the wake of black nationalism. For their time and place, these little-heralded women brought compassion, energy, and vision to a struggling city and showed again the power of women's networks.

This essay examines the twentieth-century history of some white Memphis women's efforts to enter the local and national civil rights movement. It argues that traditional female concerns for clean and safe neighborhoods, high-quality pediatric care, and excellent schools, along with the influence of articulate African American women, propelled a few Memphis white women into outspoken civil rights activity. This study adds the stories, the expectations, and the successes of white women activists to the history of those African Americans who inspired the civil rights struggle in Memphis as elsewhere.[2]

Early Female Biracialism

The story of Memphis women's experience with biracial organizing began well before the traditionally defined civil rights movement of the 1950s and 1960s. It was rooted in the Young Women's Christian Association (YWCA), which was established in Memphis in 1918, and in the United Council of Church Women (UCCW), which was formed in 1941. The Memphis YWCA pioneered a biracial Public Affairs Forum as early as 1935 to discuss international affairs and race relations; however, it met not at the YWCA headquarters, but at all-black LeMoyne College.[3] In 1942, the YWCA's Interracial Committee established a segregated Negro branch and launched a summer camp program for African American girls. Although the national YWCA adopted an interracial charter in 1946 calling for the "full inclusion of Negro women and girls," the Memphis branch, like most in the South, continued to maintain separate facilities while integrating its committee work and fund-raising activities. Many prominent women in the African American and white communities established relationships of trust and mutual respect through their common efforts at the YWCA.[4]

From its inception, the UCCW sought members from all local Protestant churches, thus providing an opportunity to plan benevolent projects and to socialize across racial lines.[5] The group began an integrated ministry to incarcerated women, held "sew-ins" to produce Easter clothing for poor children, and organized literacy tutoring and job placement for newly released female prisoners. Their Second Chance Fund assisted women trying to rebuild their lives after incarceration. Early national UCCW policy statements supported full desegregation of schools and churches, thus beginning the education on racial justice of its white membership. Local members took public criticism for even studying these issues, as well as for housing national civil rights consultants who visited Memphis in the early 1960s. Known as Church Women United after 1966, the UCCW had members who served on the boards of the YWCA, the Peace and Justice Center, and the Economic Justice for Women Coalition. They were instrumental in the creation of the Woman of Achievement Awards that honored black and white women for outstanding civic contributions. Because of the input of African American members, Church Women United donated money for striking sanitation workers in 1968.[6] When

Presbyterian Julia Wellford Allen returned to live in Memphis in the early 1960s, she found more women committed to racial justice in Church Women United than in any other organization in the city. It was "the best place to work for better race relations," she later recalled, and was very active "on behalf of the poor and disenfranchised."[7]

Biracial groups such as the YWCA and the UCCW allowed women to develop connections based on "shared roles as mothers and homemakers" and to draw from these biracial experiences renewed energy to work in their separate communities. According to historian Mary Frederickson, while white women depended on black women "for help in developing reform agendas," black women used their white connections for "resources to be used in their own communities."[8] Biracialism was mutually beneficial as women set about various social housekeeping chores. It was also suspect, especially in the white community, and women active in the YWCA or UCCW seldom found allies in their denominational women's groups or among their neighbors.

Early Civil Rights Activism

Most Memphis civic leaders hoped to preserve the social and economic status quo by gradually making limited opportunities available for "deserving" blacks while maintaining a segregated society. Although the local chapter of the National Association for the Advancement of Colored People (NAACP) brought suit against the city school system shortly after the Supreme Court's *Brown* v. *Board of Education of Topeka* decision, desegregation was stalled in the courts throughout the late 1950s and 1960s. African American and white civic leaders founded the Greater Memphis Race Relations Committee in 1954, but several of the white members refused even to hold integrated meetings. The group attempted to work by having an integrated committee discuss proposals from the larger, segregated committee. Public criticism of even such half-hearted measures forced the committee's dissolution within less than three years.[9]

A somewhat more "liberal" group of businessmen formed the Memphis Committee on Community Relations (MCCR) in 1959 to encourage "voluntary progress toward equal treatment of all Memphis citizens." Membership included clergy from all denominations, many prominent businessmen, newspaper editors, and one woman (Frances Coe, the lone woman on the Memphis City School Board). This group hoped to promote gradual desegregation and thus head off both black direct action campaigns and court-mandated desegregation. Seeking to deflect the public criticism that had brought about the demise of its predecessor, the MCCR tried to avoid publicity and only occasionally issued statements to the press. The group engaged in serious biracial dialogue and included more than token representation from the African American community; however, the majority supported only gradual and partial desegregation.[10] The MCCR's appeal to white business owners emphasized the "unpleasant publicity" and possible violence and disruption to business if sit-ins and marches occurred in Memphis. Lawsuits filed by O. Z. Evers against the city bus company in 1956, by Jessie Turner against the city's segregated libraries in 1958, and by the local NAACP against the city's parks and zoo in 1959 were followed by sit-ins at lunch counters, libraries, and the Brooks Art Museum in 1960. According to researcher Laurie Green, the minimal coverage of the sit-ins by the white press led "many white Memphians to believe . . . that the city had largely escaped the southern sit-in movement." Thus, the white community heralded the gradualist approach of the MCCR and believed Memphis to be a model southern city when it came to race relations.[11]

Early in 1963 the MCCR began to work toward voluntary desegregation of private facilities like movie theaters and restaurants. Meanwhile, local NAACP leaders applied pressure on downtown merchants, not only to desegregate but also to hire people of color for more than manual labor. Members organized picket lines and staged sit-ins at local banks, department stores, and restaurants. The MCCR tried to negotiate between the NAACP leadership and the downtown businessmen, proposing that if businesses agreed to voluntary desegregation, the NAACP would call off its demonstrations. While department store owners were agreeable, many restaurateurs were not, and the MCCR mediation failed. Some individual businesses desegregated or hired minorities while denying any credit to the NAACP. Green notes that the failure of the media to cover the downtown protests "promoted a historical memory in which white moderates, not Black students, were the primary force ushering in desegregation."[12] The city's "historical memory" not only failed to acknowledge the influence of black activism, it ignored the efforts of white women and of biracial women's clubs to influence racial justice as well.

As restaurants gradually desegregated, a handful of Memphis women decided to "test" restaurants on their racial seating policies. Such an organized effort was possible only because these women had already formed bonds of friendship and trust through their work with the YWCA or Church Women United or within the two local political parties. Marjorie Cherry, who moved to Memphis is 1958 and had been active in the Unitarian Fellowship and the League of Women Voters, told her friend Ann Johnston that she missed the African American friends she had known as a young activist in Charlottesville,

Virginia. Johnston introduced her to a teacher from the historically black Owens College one afternoon over lunch. That led to several biracial luncheons in private homes until Johnston suggested they "go public." Six black and six white women gathered at the private Wolf River Club in 1963 and plotted to visit restaurants as small, integrated groups and see if they were courteously seated and served. From this beginning came the Saturday Luncheon Club. The group grew by word of mouth, for there were no formal announcements of meetings, no officers, and no dues. A white member always called for a reservation to ensure that the integrated party would not be turned away "for lack of space." Participants encountered few problems in being served.[13] One of them later remarked, "You didn't talk about it, and you didn't say to the kooks, 'Come on! Look! We're integrating.' You just went ahead and did it very quietly."[14]

Most of the Euro-Americans in the group were middle- and upper-class homemakers; African American members included teachers, a labor organizer, wives of black professionals, and retirees. After the passage of the 1964 Civil Rights Act making segregated facilities illegal, the purpose of the Saturday Luncheon Club shifted from testing integration to providing a regular place for biracial conversations. Upward of seventy-five women would meet monthly for a catered lunch, with no set agenda or program. An integrated committee planned each luncheon and sent out announcements courtesy of the YWCA's bulk mailing permit. Instead of hearing invited speakers, the group used its time in this biracial setting simply to converse about neighborhood, city, or personal issues. One woman reported, "You just sat down beside somebody you didn't know." These friendships proved particularly important later in the tense days following the assassination in Memphis of Dr. Martin Luther King Jr.[15]

The contrasting goals of black and white Memphis activist women could not be more evident than in this strictly social organization. African American women added the monthly luncheon to an already busy schedule of community involvement because they believed prejudice could be eradicated through personal contacts. They claimed desegregated space while at the same time using their conversations with white friends to suggest programs needed in the black community. To others, the luncheons were simply enjoyable. One woman who worked full time at a restaurant and cared for a large family as well reported that what she liked best about the Saturday Luncheon Club was getting dressed up and being waited on, something white members took for granted.[16] While African American women were keenly aware of continuing discrimination in employment, housing, and educational opportunities, many

white women understood race relations only in terms of establishing friendships across the color line. To them, biracial meetings were themselves radical
statements. Some were surprised to encounter longtime friends or neighbors
at the luncheon group because genteel southern white women rarely discussed
their racial attitudes among themselves.[17]

Such "practice" at integration spurred the desegregation of a long-standing
local institution, the Memphis City Beautiful Commission (MCBC). The commission had been established in the 1930s after the prestigious all-white Nineteenth Century Club sought the mayor's help in beautifying the city's unattrac-
tive riverfront; he established the MCBC as a voluntary agency under the
Commissioner of Public Works. About ten years later, chair Margaret Fowler
created a "Negro Division" within the MCBC, drawing its members from
some of the city's most prominent black families. Although white and black
volunteers worked in separate neighborhoods, they occasionally met together
to plan the city's annual cleanup campaigns. The volunteers had to meet in the
carriage house behind the Nineteenth Century Club mansion, as both it and all
public facilities were segregated. Volunteers implemented programs developed by the City Beautiful Commission to encourage well-kept lawns, clean
parks, and safe streets, and to investigate reports of unsightly areas. Although
the membership of the commission itself remained entirely white, both African
American and white women served as paid inspectors for citizen complaints.
When the commission's offices and staff moved into City Hall around 1950,
these women inhabited segregated spaces.[18]

A new chair, Anne Shafer, changed all that in 1964 when she brought the
two African American inspectors out of their cloakroom office and integrated
the MCBC office. She also prompted the appointment of the first African
Americans to the commission board, integrated the annual "Clean Up, Fix Up
Parade," and held integrated luncheons for black and white neighborhood
captains. When she attempted to get the "Miss City Beautiful" contest to admit
black contestants, however, the men's club, which had long financed the pag-
eant, refused. With the election of segregationist Henry Loeb to the mayor's
office in 1968, the racially integrated programs of the City Beautiful Commission came to a halt.[19]

Shafer's work at the MCBC typifies the way white female activists in Memphis used memberships in multiple organizations to reach a wider audience for
their racial justice projects. Shafer had some experience with conditions outside the South. Born in 1923 into a working-class Memphis family, she grew up
in Memphis but later lived in California with her engineer husband where they
experienced multicultural neighborhoods. After returning to Memphis in

1951, she rejected segregation whenever she could. She remembers the hostile looks she got after inviting an African American woman to sit with her at a luncheon following a church retreat, for although Catholic women might worship in a biracial setting, they did not eat in one. She worked diligently to create and energize the local Catholic Human Relations Council and was a regular member of the Saturday Luncheon Club. Shafer exemplifies the southern activist who brought her humanistic values, organizational skills, and political savvy into a static Delta mentality and made a difference. From then on, she worked steadily for racial justice and open, participatory government.[20]

The MCBC provided white Memphis women of various economic levels the opportunity to meet women with similar interests in the black community. In addition, as the City Beautiful volunteers worked closely with neighborhood civic clubs, they served as the major link to politics and municipal government for many African Americans. Particularly in black neighborhoods, civic clubs—like those in Binghamton and Klondike—were major bases for political organizing and rallying points for desegregation activities.[21] In this sense, the race relations work of the MCBC touched more lives than did that of the middle-class YWCA or Church Women United.

Influence of Women's Networks

Another avenue whereby African Americans and Euro-Americans joined forces to combat racial discrimination was the Fund for Needy School Children. Despite its Dickensian name, the fund was a dynamic, multipurpose, biracial, voluntary organization that provided school supplies, clothing, enrichment activities, and free lunches to thousands of Memphis school children. Equally important, it placed privileged white women in inner-city schools where they experienced firsthand the multiple effects of institutional racism: underemployed parents, undernourished children, and underfunded schools. The need for volunteer assistance in the public schools became apparent to activist Myra Dreifus after she heard local social workers talking about the virulent poverty in Memphis—something she had never encountered in her many civic activities. Through her friendship with school board member Frances Coe, Dreifus arranged to visit an all-black elementary school and talk with its principal, Herbert Robinson, about the children and the neighborhood. At lunchtime, she was shocked to see scores of children who had neither a home-packed lunch nor money to buy a cafeteria meal; they sat in the lunchroom with their heads resting on the table as the other students around them ate.[22]

Like generations of reform-minded women before her, Dreifus set out to find a way to feed those children and help their families. She established a steering committee to investigate the federal free-lunch program and find out why the Memphis city schools were not participating fully in it. She made sure her task force included African American volunteers, women she had met through Saturday Luncheon Club and other civic activities. Her committee discovered that fewer than 700 children (out of 120,000 in the system) received subsidized lunches, although many more were eligible for them. Dreifus learned that the school board reviewed all free-lunch applications forwarded by school principals and rejected many of them. She found censorious notations on applications such as "father smokes and mother drinks" or "mother writes well enough, she ought to have a job." The board also turned down applications if the parents owned a car or TV, although the federal guidelines for free lunches contained no such screening provisions. Dreifus's committee also learned that Memphis city schools turned back free commodities for both breakfasts and lunches rather than participate in the federal program.[23] Since the schools with the most poor children were also all-black schools, it was impossible not to draw racial conclusions from the board's resistance to the federal meal programs.

Dreifus badgered the Memphis Board of Education to survey the entire school district to find out exactly how many families might actually qualify for the school lunch program. When the superintendent insisted such a task was too time-consuming for his staff, Dreifus took matters into her own hands. She recruited friends from the National Council of Jewish Women, the Saturday Luncheon Club, the Symphony Guild, and anyone else she had volunteered with over the years, including a number of prominent African American women, to conduct the survey. The volunteers' report concluded that at least forty thousand children qualified for federal free-lunch support (compared with the seven hundred who were currently receiving it). Superintendent of Schools E. C. Stimbert argued that nutrition was not part of the school's mission; Dreifus retorted that "you cannot teach a hungry child." Through persistent lobbying she persuaded the superintendent and the principals of four inner-city schools to let her volunteers handle the registration process necessary to enroll eligible students and hence expand Memphis's free-lunch program.[24]

This volunteer foray into the public schools in 1963–64 accomplished several things. Many—if not all—of the white volunteers traveled into neighborhoods they had never before visited and saw clearly the inequity of the de facto segregated school system: overcrowded facilities, no playgrounds, broken equipment and bathrooms, nonexistent libraries. They saw the effect poor nutrition had on children. One volunteer "had [her] conscience pricked and became involved" in trying to secure not only better schools but better economic opportunities for people of color. Another reported, "The thing I learned was that poverty is a very lonely thing. . . . This was a revelation to me."[25] Dreifus and her chief associate, Selma Lewis, learned how to lobby city and county officials for funds, because an expanded free-lunch program required additional cafeteria and management personnel. Lewis once entertained one of the county commissioners, who was quite a gourmand, at a dinner party just before a critical tax vote. After serving him a fine meal, she took him aside and reminded him, "You know if you don't vote for the tax for this lunch program, there will be hungry children, and it will be your fault." He voted for the tax.[26]

Word of these unusual volunteers quickly spread through the school system, and other principals wanted their schools to be included in the Fund for Needy School Children's efforts. In the fund's second year, about thirty-five volunteers worked at fourteen schools with the permission of their principals. They not only interviewed families and helped them complete their free-lunch applications but also assisted in the lunch distribution. One of their essential concerns was ensuring that students who received subsidized lunches remained anonymous to the staff and other students. Dreifus lobbied to get the same kind of lunch tickets for subsidized students and paying students. Dreifus and Lewis appealed to various women's organizations in Memphis churches and synagogues, most of them all-white, urging them to "adopt" a particular school. For example, Idlewild Church, Memphis's most prestigious all-white Presbyterian congregation, adopted Porter Elementary School in a segregated neighborhood of north Memphis. Members handled the entire free-breakfast program, provided tutoring, bought school supplies, and built a playground.[27]

Within a few years, 98 percent of the students in some schools were in the free-lunch program. By early 1969 the fund had placed 140 volunteers into fifty-seven elementary schools and assisted seventeen junior high schools in enrolling students in the school lunch program. Fund members became vital volunteers at their adopted schools, planning enrichment programs, starting parents' groups, and taking children on field trips. Such hands-on work by the Fund for Needy School Children brought privileged women without full-time employment into daily contact with African American teachers and students.[28] With so many volunteers involved, members chose a steering committee to develop new projects: a free used-clothing closet, a "shoes fund" for children in Head Start, and parents' meetings at the schools that did not have official PTAs. Many volunteers began to see the connection between malnourished children and a caste system that consigned blacks to menial, low-paying jobs. Of course, noblesse oblige pervaded some of their efforts, and volunteers later reflected on how much they had to learn about what it was like to grow up poor and black in Memphis. "We gave the mothers sewing patterns, and later learned [that] some of them couldn't read.... And many couldn't even come to our daytime [parent] meetings because they worked as domestics."[29]

The Fund for Needy School Children brought media attention to the problems of poverty in Memphis. Some of the fund's volunteers supported striking black sanitation workers in 1968 because they had seen the consequences of substandard wages. Others worked on community action projects or lobbied for summer recreation programs, job training, and race-blind hiring practices. A reporter evaluating the work of Myra Dreifus in 1969 argued that the fund "had broken to the surface as an organization able to sway politicians, school officials," and the public. Dreifus herself summed up the work of many hard-nosed female activists when she said that friends had warned her that if "I did not learn to play cards and do the 'social bit,' someday I would be old and lonely. I do not have time to be either!" However, neither did she "want to be the president of some structured group where you . . . bang gavels. I want to work with a raw thing that doesn't know exactly what it's supposed to do or where it's going to go."[30] Volunteers also gained valuable political experience as Dreifus took them to city council, city and county school board, and county quorum court meetings to secure funding and space for their projects. The fund went on to work with the U.S. Department of Agriculture to get funding for new infant care programs, and its volunteers were instrumental in establishing a day-care center in a downtown housing development.[31]

Maternal concern for children's well-being also underlay the biracial "Rearing Children of Good Will Workshops" sponsored by the National Conference of Christians and Jews (NCCJ). Based on the NCCJ's founding principles of brotherhood and humanitarianism, the workshops brought together mothers from various ethnic groups to share common interests in parenting and world peace while encouraging color-blindness across racial and ethnic lines. Although the first successful workshop was held at Vassar College in 1945, the Memphis affiliate of NCCJ did not introduce the project until local journalist and teacher Joan Beifuss formed a steering committee with representatives from NCCJ, Church Women United (CWU), the Catholic Human Relations Council, and the Jewish Anti-defamation League. The letters of invitation that went out to local churches and synagogues in February 1968 were headed "We Cannot Afford Another Generation of Prejudice." About sixty women, including fifteen African Americans, met once a week for several hours to hear professional presentations on the psychology of prejudice, the impact of prejudice on children, and the difficulties women who worked outside the home encountered in finding adequate day care. Afternoon sessions featured biracial small-group discussions. Although the bulk of the participants came because of their commitment to racial justice, some were new to biracial dialogue and integrated lunches.[32]

Just as the first of the five workshops began, Dr. Martin Luther King Jr. made his first visit in support of the striking sanitation workers. Local racial tensions escalated when the march turned violent, through no fault of the strikers; King left, vowing to return and lead another peaceful demonstration. The city responded to this incident by stationing National Guard troops throughout the downtown area as the daily marches continued. Fearful of escalating racial tensions (the city officials were white, and all of the striking sanitation workers were African American), the Rearing Children Workshop organizers postponed their weekly meeting and instead sent a delegation to Mayor Henry Loeb's office to ask him to settle the strike before more violence occurred. Although he received them graciously, if paternalistically, Loeb took little notice of their suggestions. He pointedly dismissed them as outside agitators because he could not detect a southern accent as some of them spoke.[33]

White Women and the Sanitation Strike

The Memphis Sanitation Workers' strike (February–April 1968) is known worldwide as the event that brought Dr. Martin Luther King Jr. to Memphis and resulted in his death at the hands of an assassin the night before he was to lead his second Memphis demonstration. In traditional civil rights historiography, the strike has become the penultimate action of the civil rights movement (the final being the Poor People's March on Washington in the summer of 1968). The major local media, however, portrayed the strike only as the mayor and city council saw it: as an unlawful labor dispute financed by East Coast–based national unions. Most white citizens did not interpret the poor working conditions and poverty wages paid to city employees as racially determined at all, but simply as what unskilled laborers could expect in a tax-poor city.

The leaders in the African American community, the three black city councilmen, and African American clergy from large congregations were not among the working poor. Within two weeks of the walkout, however, these middle-class black leaders and national labor organizers had formed an organization to give the strikers financial support and keep the daily demonstrations staffed. The Community on the Move for Equality (COME) joined with the NAACP in portraying the strike as a racial issue and a struggle for human dignity.[34] Few in the white community believed the strike was really about racial discrimination, however, and the loose network of white Memphis women committed to biracialism in the YWCA, Church Women United, the Saturday Luncheon Club, and the Fund for Needy School Children was thus strangely inactive during the first month of the strike. Initially, even they stood behind the mayor's refusal to negotiate with the strikers until they went back to work; they supported strike-breakers and volunteer garbage collection.

Not until several weeks into the strike did the organizers of the Rearing Children Workshops meet with the mayor, as mentioned above, and Church Women United send a delegation to talk with the mayor about compromise. Some Presbyterian women urged presbytery support of the strike, and some Roman Catholic women worked through the Catholic Human Relations Council to bring the influence of the bishop to bear on the city's position. Julia Allen was instrumental in helping the Tennessee Council on Human Relations set up meetings of middle-class whites to hear the strikers' perspective. A few white sympathizers organized Save Our City and took out a newspaper ad declaring support for the strikers' boycott of downtown businesses, urged citizens to contact the mayor in support of the worker grievances, and joined strikers at their daily rallies. Few among even the "liberal" Memphians, however, understood the connection between race, underemployment, and collective bargaining. One African American member of the Saturday Luncheon Club said to a white friend, "It's time for sympathetic whites to get off the fence."[35] However, for most white citizens of Memphis, it took the horror of King's assassination to expose the relationship between poverty and racial discrimination. Later, one white activist would remember, "We believed we had a good start on integration here—that race relations were good. . . . And then when Dr. King was shot, many of us realized for the first time that the only black person we really knew was a servant. Reality hit us then."[36] Until that consciousness-raising event, many white women had failed to make the connection between southern society, poverty, and race.

In the wake of the assassination and the subsequent nationwide condemnation of Memphis, white businessman John T. Fisher set out to organize the "Memphis Cares" rally, a biracial service to honor King's memory. The difficulties in convincing citizens even to attend such a public rally pointed to the deep rift between the city's black and white communities. Several of the white women interviewed indicated that only their friendship with, and respect for, black female friends gave them the courage to attend the rally.[37]

Biracial Organizations' Responses

Dr. King's assassination, the attempt to unite the city at the Memphis Cares rally, and the too-late settlement of the strike produced a crisis of conscience for many Memphis women. When Jocelyn Wurzburg, a young mother from a prominent Jewish family, attended the Rearing Children of Good Will Workshops that resumed after the strike, she recognized the similarity between their panel presentations and those of the Little Rock Panel of American Women whom she had recently heard at Temple Israel. The national Panel of American Women (PAW) was founded by white activist Esther Brown, who had worked with the Kansas City NAACP on school integration even before the *Brown* decision in 1954. The panel was so named "because it looked like America," with Jewish, African American, white Protestant, Asian, and Catholic women participants. Their purpose was to share personal experiences of discrimination and remind white Protestants of their majority-based privilege, and thus seek to pave the way for improved ethnic and race relations.[38]

Working with the local NCCJ and the Little Rock PAW, Wurzburg set about establishing a similar panel in Memphis. She initially gathered about twenty volunteers, seeking a balance of African American, Catholic, Protestant, and Jewish members. Using her contacts from the Saturday Luncheon Club, the Rearing Children Workshops, and the Republican Party, she made contacts with women in the NAACP, YWCA, and CWU as well. Her recruits spent the summer and fall of 1968 participating in sensitivity training, preparing their individual five-minute presentations, and reviewing each other's speeches. In mock question-and-answer sessions, panelists who firmly opposed segregation and considered themselves "unprejudiced" often discovered deep racial and ethnic biases. Frank discussions followed. Eventually, "if you did not get the answers right, you were not invited to stay in the group," said one former member.[39] Panelists developed a deep trust in one another and knew how fellow panelists would respond to questions. One African American panelist later reflected that she often felt that what she said had little impact on the white audience, yet she also felt "the time was right" to open biracial dialogues. Her participation on the panel, though often frustrating, was "a calling" and part of her contribution to "the freedom struggle."[40]

Panel members accepted invitations to speak before church auxiliaries, civic groups, and neighborhood associations (usually exclusively white groups). Wurzburg served as the volunteer coordinator for six years and often served as moderator when the four panel members presented a program. She learned whose chemistry worked well together and often used the same combinations of four panelists. When participants presented a program, they played up the fact that they were "just housewives" speaking only for themselves. They "dressed up" as if going to a business meeting. They avoided telling the audience members what they "should" do or believe, and appealed instead to their common experiences as wives, mothers, and concerned citizens. They told personal stories of overcoming their own prejudices and stressed what all of them had in common as wives and mothers, regardless of religion or race. All were volunteers who relied on husbands and child-care workers in order to participate in as many as three panels a week. In 1974, when the court ordered the Memphis city school system to achieve at least 20/80 percent faculty integration in all its schools, the panel members made seventeen presentations in three days of in-service training.[41]

Former PAW members talk freely about their transformative experiences as panel members and their development of a sense of sisterhood and a firm belief that people *could* learn to forgo prejudice and discrimination. They began to socialize as families, holding interracial parties as "models" of the kind of community they wished to promote. Their actions represent small statements about living in an integrated city, but in the highly polarized atmosphere of Memphis at that time, they were significant indeed. One participant later commented, "That experience—I'll tell you—it made me a human being."[42]

Also in response to the King assassination, Berniece Sells, whose husband was a scientist at St. Jude Children's Research Hospital, founded another women's interracial, cross-cultural organization. Faculty Women and Wives (FWW) brought together women associated with the University of Tennessee Medical Schools, St. Jude Children's Research Hospital, LeBonheur Children's Hospital, LeMoyne-Owen College, the University of Memphis, Christian Brothers University, and Southwestern College at Memphis. The women began socializing at monthly potlucks just to bring this multicultural group together, but soon they took up a series of social causes centered on problems associated with poverty. Members worked with the local War on Poverty committee to open preschool classes in low-income areas, lobbying the Memphis Board of Education to provide space and furniture for the preschools while they provided the volunteer staff. They applied for a federal grant to open a kindergarten program in an African American neighborhood but were told they could get federal money only if the class was integrated. Two white FWW members enrolled their children in the program, and Caldwell Elementary Kindergarten became a reality. Members also arranged for businesses to "adopt" inner-city schools and provide resources and enrichment programs. Seeking to improve the restricted employment opportunities for African Americans, the women started a tutoring program to prepare high school dropouts to pass the GED exam, staffing classes three afternoons a week at a local church and an elementary school. During the summers of 1969 and 1970 they organized and ran reading enrichment programs for "underachievers," hiring African American high school students as coaches and aides.[43] The strength and success of these efforts resulted from the solid working relationship FWW members established among themselves, the medical community, and several inner-city principals.

When the city sanitation workers' union (Local 1733 of the American Federation of State, County, and Municipal Employees, or AFSCME) could make no headway on its 1969 contract negotiations with the city, it sought to capitalize on white sympathies that had developed after King's assassination. The union and the city had signed a one-year contract granting a five-cent-an-hour wage increase, merit-based promotions, and a union dues check-off procedure that would ensure the union's viability.[44] The contract had to be renegotiated by July 1969, and workers expected the city to stall further wage increases and benefits. Lester Rosen, chair of the newly formed Memphis Human Relations Commission, and AFSCME official Jessie Epps contacted Wurzburg and asked for PAW's assistance in swaying public opinion. Rosen and Epps believed they stood a better chance of bringing a women's network to their side than the white male business establishment. National PAW regulations prohibited the organization from taking sides in any political or labor dispute, but nothing barred *individual* women from cooperating with the union. Rosen and Epps then planned a "home tour" whereby elite and middle-class suburban women could see the living conditions of some of the city workers and thus understand the need for support of the requested wage increases.

Using her extensive network of activist friends, Wurzburg telephoned women whom she thought might participate in this media event/information tour. Members of PAW, the Fund for Needy School Children, the Saturday Luncheon Club, and church and synagogue groups continued the telephoning, reaching neighbors and friends from the Junior League, bridge clubs, and PTAs. Organizers rejoiced when more than one hundred women turned up the following Saturday to board buses for the inner-city tour. (All of the participants were white; African Americans already knew about the living conditions in the inner city.) En route, union officials provided fact sheets about city employees' salaries and benefits. The union selected the homes to be visited and prepared the residents for the type of questions they might get from the visitors. They told the workers and their wives to be prepared to discuss salaries, heating bills, car payments, and other personal matters with the "tourists."[45] When asked why city employees would allow their homes and families to be put on display, one of the former strikers answered, "Sure, we didn't want them lookin' at us, but we was desperate. They had to see the conditions we lived under."[46]

The "home tour" brought the reality of poverty to a wider range of women than had been involved in any of the previously described organizations. Most were shocked to find that men who worked full time could afford no better housing. After visiting the uninsulated, shotgun-style wooden homes, one visitor noted, "[They] pay the same utility bills as I do and I've got five tons of air-conditioning." Others were embarrassed to have supported a mayor who condoned "starvation wages" for city employees. The tour had not been undertaken with the idea that the women would formally organize, but the plight of the workers compelled them to act. Immediately following the bus tour they reconvened at nearby Sienna College and chose a steering committee composed of women active in both Republican and Democratic circles and representing Episcopal, Catholic, and Jewish faiths. The committee drafted a statement to present to a City Council committee that was meeting the next day. They took pains neither to criticize the city's low wages nor to support a strike by city employees; rather, they insisted they were simply "anti-poverty, anti-hunger, and anti-racism."[47]

Dorothy "Happy" Jones, Diana Crump, and Anne Stokes, all wives of prominent businessmen, were chosen to speak to the City Council committee. After listening to the women's thoughtfully prepared statement, however, the councilmen belittled them with hostility and sarcasm. Noting that two of the women on the steering committee were Catholic, one councilman suggested that the Catholic church could give up its tax-exempt status to provide the city with more income to pay the sanitation workers. Another councilman suggested that the women should just pay their domestic workers and yard men higher salaries, thus implying that the women's concerns over low-wage workers were hypocritical, at best.[48] The women, accustomed to the privileges of southern white womanhood, were stunned by the council's failure to treat them with respect. "[W]e were so naïve," said one. Talking to the council was "like talking to a brick wall." The next day, Councilman Jerrod Blanchard described the treatment of the women as "utterly incredible" and accused the council of being racist.[49]

After a flurry of telephoning, more than two hundred women flooded the council chambers the following day. Jocelyn Wurzburg read a more forceful statement to the full City Council reminding the councilmen of the many ways these women had worked for the city, including campaigning for some of them. She again offered the women's considerable experience to "attack poverty." The council made no response at all to the women's statement and went directly into their regular business session. Furious at having been ignored *again*, the women regrouped in the hall; one of them mounted some steps and cried, "They didn't even thank us. Be assured—we are going to stay on the case!"

Thus did a band composed principally of white elite women adopt the confrontational strategies of their African American mentors and organize a new coalition of women for civic change. They called themselves the Concerned Women of Memphis and Shelby County (CWMSC), and they recruited members from all the organizations, neighborhoods, and churches in which they had contacts. They especially sought out the African American women with whom they had worked on other biracial projects. As one member noted, they brought together a "lot of women who cared deeply about what was going on and had no way to express their feelings."[50] Their willingness to act outside the constraints of idealized southern womanhood was joined with their experiences as volunteers in the schools, their friendships grounded in Rearing Children of Good Will Workshops or Faculty Women and Wives projects, their desegregation lunches on Saturdays, and their heightened sensitivity to prejudice and discrimination stimulated by the Panel of American Women. By their own later admission, they really believed they could "end hunger, poverty, and racism" in Memphis.[51]

CWMSC issued an eleven-point call to action to the city of Memphis and then organized task forces to study and recommend to the City Council programs that would support each of their eleven points, including: improve housing, health, and vocational training for the poor; establish free-lunch programs in *all* city schools; secure minority representation on the school board by calling for the creation of districts rather than having all at-large seats; and promote a minimum wage for domestic workers. Criticizing Memphis's reluctance to participate in President Johnson's War on Poverty, they recommended that the city hire someone to coordinate federal grant applications and urged a state constitutional amendment to allow a city payroll tax, necessary to finance their proposed social services. The CWMSC also sent telegrams to Mayor Loeb, City Council chair Bob James, and union negotiator Epps stating that they would hold *all* of them "equally responsible" if the wage impasse with sanitation workers was not settled before the July 1 deadline.[52] A reporter for the *Commercial Appeal* thought the CWMSC represented "a formidable foe...."

Many of them have money. All of them have affluent friends." City officials denied that the CWMSC had any influence on their decision making; however, the city did negotiate on all the union's demands, averting a threatened second sanitation workers' strike.[53]

Many members of CWMSC found that their public stance for racial and economic justice had landed them in trouble. The letters to the editor in the daily papers were highly critical of their "meddling" in city affairs, the writers suggesting that the poor had only themselves to blame for their problems. Some men insisted that their wives quit Concerned Women before their businesses suffered. Some women received harassing telephone calls and threats to their children's safety. One woman returned home from a committee meeting to find a load of sand dumped in her front lawn and received a telephone call suggesting that "something other than sand" would have been even better. She was also told by one councilman, "If you women were happy at home, you wouldn't be down here [at City Hall]."[54] The persistent paternalism these women experienced certainly sharpened their identification with African Americans, who had been routinely denied access to city planning, decision making, and authority.

The CWMSC task forces took on lives of their own, particularly when they joined with existing organizations working on similar issues. For example, some members of CWMSC, recognizing their own complicity in the exploitation of black women domestic workers, worked with the YWCA to design a training program for household employees and to solicit employers who would agree to pay a minimum wage to women who had completed the program. Another task force allied with the Fund for Needy School Children to bring the free-lunch and -breakfast programs into junior and senior high schools. Others joined a local poverty program, MAP-South, headed by the Reverend James Lawson, which brought in federal funds for recreational and job-training programs located in poor neighborhoods.[55]

White women, energized by a decade of volunteerism on behalf of racial justice and antipoverty, had believed that their social standing (as wives of prominent businessmen), their moral authority (as pillars of their religious communities), and their organizational skills would influence Memphis to redress poverty and racial discrimination in the city. Instead, they had experienced the kind of paternalism and exclusion that African Americans had long experienced. They discovered that confronting the privilege and status of the white male elite required more than good intentions. The underlying premise of early biracial efforts—that is, that friendship and common cause would eliminate racism and segregation—was flawed. For some, this knowledge produced a notable call to social action, which then included a more honest understanding of the dynamics of race and gender.

Several members of the CWMSC were instrumental in the founding of the Metropolitan Interfaith Association (MIFA), which grew out of a 1969 effort to coordinate the outreach services of several downtown churches while involving church members more in meeting the needs of the poor. The initial organizing progressed hesitantly. Many white clergy and congregations remained frightened of biracial cooperatives, especially in light of the emerging Black Power movement nationwide, while many black clergy despaired of any significant cooperation with whites. MIFA's board of directors was not only biracial but also included several of the white women who had been active in the Fund for Needy School Children and CWMSC. Julia Allen, an active laywoman and CWU member, was one of two paid staff and played a significant role in bringing women into the volunteer corps of MIFA. In 1970, MIFA applied for federally funded outreach personnel under the Volunteers in Service to America (VISTA) program. The first workers assigned were college-age students who required "a lot of supervision" and just "didn't know their way around." The following year, MIFA recruited local VISTA workers, black and white women who already knew the city and had contacts with church leaders, businessmen, and nonprofit organizations. These women, many of them housewives and mothers, became the backbone of MIFA's social service program, generating studies of Memphis's poverty and then implementing social programs to address the problems they uncovered.[56] Observing the success MIFA had in the 1970s in bringing white churches into greater social activism, one local minister commented, "Socialites are now servant ministers, and *that* changes attitudes. It has legitimized urban ministry in Memphis."[57]

Conclusion

Women's biracial cooperation in Memphis in the 1960s grew from the roots of century-old female municipal housekeeping. It was nurtured by the interracial organizing of the YWCA and Church Women United; it drew strength from the successes of the Saturday Luncheon Club and the Fund for Needy School Children. It expanded its vision through the Panel of American Women, and it flourished as a task-specific organization, the Concerned Women of Memphis and Shelby County. These activists valued the friendships made across the black-white divide of Memphis in the 1960s and believed that they could create a race-blind community on the basis of friendship and goodwill. Many white women failed to comprehend the growing separatism in the African

American community or to understand how deeply racism was imbedded in Memphis's institutional life—educational, political, business, and religious. Their biracial activism was made possible by the patient mentoring of middle-class black women whose participation in biracial groups often took them away from other community activities, but which they believed was worth their best efforts.

Although the white activists profiled here remained politically and socially active, their efforts eventually splintered into a host of political, feminist, and educational endeavors. Many transformed their volunteer experience into paid employment with social service agencies; others took additional college degrees and then joined an increasingly female workforce. As career opportunities and all-male service organizations opened to women in the 1980s, many women left gender-segregated volunteerism; but many remained civic gadflies, continuing to challenge racial, gender, and economic injustice. None lost her commitment to human rights and dignity or regretted the efforts expended to knock down barriers between white and African American Memphians. Their voices echo hauntingly through a city that remains highly segregated even today.

Notes

1. *Commercial Appeal,* June 19, 1969, 4.

2. No comprehensive study of civil rights activism in Memphis exists. For some aspects of that struggle, see David M. Tucker, *Memphis since Crump: Bossism, Blacks and Civic Reformers, 1948–1968* (Knoxville: University of Tennessee Press, 1980), and *Black Pastors and Leaders: Memphis, 1819–1972* (Memphis: Memphis State University Press, 1975); Michael Honey, *Southern Labor and the Civil Rights Movement: Organizing Memphis Workers* (Urbana: University of Illinois Press, 1993); Ann Trotter, "The Memphis Business Community and Integration," in *Southern Businessmen and Desegregation,* ed. Elizabeth Jacoway and David R. Colburn (Baton Rouge: University of Louisiana Press, 1982), 282–300; Laurie Beth Green, "Battling the Plantation Mentality: Consciousness, Culture, and the Politics of Race, Class and Gender in Memphis, 1940–1968" (Ph.D. diss., University of Chicago, 1999); Willie W. Herenton, "A Historical Study of School Desegregation in the Memphis City Schools, 1954–1970" (Ph.D. diss., Southern Illinois University, 1971); Deborah Brown Carter, "The Impact of the Civil Rights Movement on the Unionization of African-American Women: Local 282–Furniture Division–IUE, 1960–1988," in *Black Women in America,* ed. Kim Marie Vaz (Thousand Oaks, Calif.: Sage Publications, 1995).

3. *Memphis Press Scimitar*, April 23, 1953, November 27, 1953. The first president of the YWCA was Mrs. Charles Burch. Several prominent Memphis women had created an organization named the Women's and Young Women's Christian Association in 1875 "to improve the moral and social conditions among women & children." They incorporated in 1883 and ran a "Rescue Home and Orphanage" and later built a rooming house that would accommodate two hundred young working women. This group was *not* affiliated with the national YWCA (*Commercial Appeal*, August 17, 1934).

4. *Commercial Appeal*, February 27, 1942, June 22, 1942, October 4, 1944; Nancy Marie Robertson, "'Deeper Even Than Race?' White Women and the Politics of Christian Sisterhood in the Young Women's Christian Association, 1906–1946" (Ph.D. diss., New York University, 1997), 395–96. The African American branch was known as the Vance Avenue Branch due its location. Camp director Althea Price was the wife of Dr. Hollis Price, president of the historically black LeMoyne College founded by the American Missionary Society of the Congregational Church in 1862; Julia Allen, interview with the author, August 12, 1999.

5. Georgina Ensminger, interview with the author, September 23, 1999; Julia Allen, telephone interview with the author, August 1, 2001. The UCCW changed its name to United Church Women in 1950, then to Church Women United; see Charisse Jones's essay in this volume for more information.

6. Beverly Nicholson, interview with the author, August 14, 2001; Church Women United, *CWU Social Policies: 1941–1991* (n.p., 1992), 165–73.

7. Julia Allen interview, August 12, 1999.

8. Mary Frederickson, "'Each One Is Dependent on the Other': Southern Churchwomen, Racial Reform, and the Process of Transformation, 1880–1940," in *Visible Women*, ed. Nancy Hewitt and Suzanne Lebsock (Urbana: University of Illinois Press, 1993), 297.

9. Trotter, "The Memphis Business Community and Integration," 286; Selma Lewis, "Social Religion and the Memphis Sanitation Strike" (Ph.D. diss., University of Memphis, 1976), 71.

10. Selma Lewis, *Diversification and Unity: MIFA, 1968–1988* (Memphis: MIFA, 1988), 9. Rev. James Lawson, Vasco Smith (NAACP), Dr. Hollis Price (LeMoyne College), Rev. Blair Hunt, and lawyer A. W. Willis were some of the outspoken black members.

11. Tucker, *Memphis since Crump*, 119–20; O. Z. Evers interview, Oral History Collection, Mississippi Valley Special Collection, University of Memphis [hereinafter MVSC]; Green, "Battling the Plantation Mentality," 334–41. Evers claimed that when he first defied a bus driver's command to "move to the back of the bus," no Memphis lawyer, not even those active in the NAACP, would take his case against the city.

12. Green, "Battling the Plantation Mentality," 372–73; Tucker, *Memphis since Crump*, 120–21, 133–34. According to Tucker, MCCR used information from other cities where picketing had resulted in restaurants going out of business to convince local businesses to comply with desegregation (134).

13. Ann Shafer, interview with the author, August 17, 1999; Art Gilliam, "Saturday Luncheon Group Serves Purpose," *Commercial Appeal,* April 1, 1970; Diana Crump, interview with the author, August 7, 2001; James and Marjorie Cherry interview, February 8, 1969, "Search for Meaning," MVSC, C20, F38–39.

14. Carol Lynn Yellin, speaking of her own experience in the club as she was conducting an oral history interview with Peggy Jemison and Linda Allen, February 24, 1969, "Search for Meaning," MVSC, C20, F5.

15. Gilliam, "Saturday Luncheon Group"; Shafer interview, August 17, 1999; quote from Mattie Sengstacke, interview with the author, October 20, 1999.

16. Margaret Valiant interview (speaking about a friend), September 12, 1968, "Search for Meaning," MVSC, C24, F241.

17. Annabelle Whittemore, interview with the author, November 19, 1999.

18. Anne Whalen Shafer, *History of the Memphis City Beautiful Commission and Its Impact on Our Lives* (Memphis: n.p., 1996), 15–17, 20, 25–26.

19. Shafer interview, August 17, 1999; Shafer, "History," 33–35, 39. The black women appointed to the MCBC were Ophelia Byas, Margaret Rivers, and Calverta Ishmael.

20. Shafer interview, August 17, 1999. Shafer attributes her racial consciousness not only to the depressing realities of discrimination that she witnessed on family visits to Mississippi but also to a mystical vision she had while attending a Catholic mass in California.

21. Shafer interview, January 5, 2000. See Laurie Green, "Battling the Plantation Mentality," especially 290–97, for discussion of the political importance of the African American men's civic clubs and ward organizations.

22. Jed Dreifus, interview with the author, July 25, 2001; Selma Lewis, interview with the author, July 29, 1999.

23. Myra Dreifus interview, October 30, 1968, "Search for Meaning," MVSC, C21, F61.

24. Lewis interview, July 29, 1999; Jed Dreifus interview, July 25, 2001; William Thomas, "The Children's Crusader," *Commercial Appeal Mid-South Magazine,* March 8, 1970, 27.

25. Linda Allen and Peggy Jemison interview, "Search for Meaning," MVSC, C20, F5.

26. Lewis interview with author, July 29, 1999. Dreifus's style was more businesslike. Before an important City Council meeting, she counseled Lewis, "Now don't you go down there and just smile at all those men," suggesting that some hard-nosed lobbying was in order (Jed Dreifus interview, July 25, 2001).

27. Allen and Jemison interview, "Search for Meaning," MVSC, C20, F5.

28. When planning field trips, one organizer wanted to place five children with each volunteer, thus filling each automobile. Another volunteer responded, "All their lives these children stand in line for everything, and I want each child to have a hand to hold today." Thus two-to-one assignments became the norm (Lewis interview, July 29, 1999).

29. Selma Lewis and Myra Dreifus interview by Carol Lynn Yellin, January 16, 1969, "Search for Meaning," MVSC, C21, F62; *Tri-State Defender,* August 30, 1969, 1; Lewis interview, July 29, 1999.

30. Lewis interview, July 29, 1999; Nicki Elrod, "National Honor," *Commercial Appeal,* November 17, 1971.

31. Myra Dreifus Papers, MVSC.

32. Marie Wingfield, "The Memphis Round Table of the N.C.C.J., Part 2," *West Tennessee Historical Papers* 23 (1969): 67; "Rearing Children of Good Will," in "Search for Meaning" Collection, MVSC, C5, F2; Joan Turner Beifuss, *At the River I Stand: Memphis, the 1968 Strike, and Martin Luther King* (1985; reprint, Memphis: St. Luke's Press, 1990); *Tri-State Defender,* February 17, 1968, 3.

33. Beifuss, *At the River I Stand,* 178–79.

34. For details of the Memphis Sanitation Workers' strike and the King assassination, see Beifuss, *At the River I Stand*; Honey, *Southern Labor and the Civil Rights Movement*; Lewis, "Social Religion and the Memphis Sanitation Strike"; Earl Green Jr., "Labor in the South: A Case Study of Memphis—the 1968 Sanitation Strike and Its Effect on an Urban Community" (Ph.D. diss., New York University, 1980); Michael Honey, "Martin Luther King, Jr., the Crisis of the Black Working Class, and the Memphis Sanitation Strike," in *Southern Labor in Transition 1940–1995,* ed. Robert H. Zieger (Knoxville: University of Tennessee Press, 1997); Michael Honey, *Black Workers Remember: An Oral History of Segregation, Unionism, and the Freedom Struggle* (Berkeley: University of California Press, 1999); F. Ray Marshall and Arvil Van Adams, "The Memphis Public Employees Strike," in *Racial Conflict and Negotiation,* ed. W. E. Charlmers and G. Cormick (Ann Arbor: University of Michigan Press, 1971), 73–107.

35. Julia Allen interview, August 12, 1999; Papers of the Catholic Human Relations Council, Memphis Room, Memphis–Shelby County Library; Braxton Bryant interview, 1968, "Search for Meaning," MVSC, C20, F28; Beifuss, *At the River I Stand,* 179; Sengstacke interview with the author, October 20, 1999. Co-chairs of SOC were Memphis native Patricia Gilliom and Rev. Darrell Doughty, a Presbyterian minister; thirty-three individuals signed the newspaper ad, found in "Search for Meaning" collection, C5, F4.

36. Peggy Jemison Bodine, telephone interview with the author, July 9, 2001.

37. Wurzburg interview, August 24, 1999; Whittemore interview, November 19, 1999; Crump interview, August 7, 2001; Bodine interview, July 9, 2001. For more information on the Memphis Cares rally, see Beifuss, *At the River I Stand,* 331–36.

38. Sara Alderman Murphy, *Breaking the Silence: Little Rock's Women's Emergency Committee to Open Our Schools, 1958–1963* (Fayetteville: University of Arkansas Press, 1997), 236–38. For additional information on the Panel of American Women, see Laura Miller, "Challenging the Segregationist Power Structure in Little Rock," in this volume.

39. Dorothy "Happy" Jones, interview with the author, August 5, 1999.

40. Modeane Thompson, interview with the author, August 17, 1999.

41. Jocelyn Wurzburg, interview with the author, August 24, 1999; Shafer interview, August 17, 1999; Thompson interview, August 17, 1999.

42. Wurzburg interview, August 24, 1999; Shafer interview, August 17, 1999; Jones interview, August 5, 1999.

43. Joyce Morrison, interview with the author, October 5, 1999; personal papers of Joyce Morrison in her possession. The Fund for Needy School Children volunteers lobbied city and county governments for funds for summer programs in African American neighborhoods in 1968. They could not persuade Mayor Loeb to participate, but with fifty thousand dollars from the county and other private money they ran a summer program through the city Parks and Recreation Department (Dreifus interview, October 30, 1968, "Search for Meaning," F61).

44. Beifus, *At the River I Stand,* 347–49.

45. Wurzburg interview, August 24, 1999; *Commercial Appeal,* June 15, 1969. One participant noted that some of the women were employed as domestics in white homes, "so being gracious to visitors was something they automatically knew how to do" (Mary Collier Lawson, interview with the author, August 29, 1999). The women who organized the tour were interviewed by the Associated Press, *Time* magazine, and national TV networks. Photos and stories appeared in publications across the country. Concerned Women *Scrapbook,* Jocelyn Dan Wurzburg Collection, MVSC.

46. Taylor Rogers, interview with the author, July 30, 1998.

47. *Commercial Appeal,* June 15, 1969, June 17, 1969. Members of the steering committee were Diana Crump, Sister Adrian Marie Hofstetter, Anne Shafer, and Jocelyn Wurzburg.

48. *Commercial Appeal,* June 15, 1969. Although the women made no response to the councilman's charge, they did include a call for domestic workers to receive minimum wage when they formally organized into the Concerned Women of Memphis and Shelby County.

49. The woman was Carol Blackburn. She and Councilman Blanchard were attending a public forum sponsored by the Tennessee Council of Human Relations, as quoted in the *Press Scimitar,* June 18, 1969, 1.

50. Wurzburg interview, August 24, 1999; Whittemore, interview November 19, 1999.

51. Jones interview, August 5, 1999.

52. Concerned Women *Scrapbook; Commercial Appeal,* June 19, 969, 13. The one agenda item that the city did do on its own, without further agitation by the women, was to hire a federal grants coordinator.

53. Concerned Women *Scrapbook;* William Street, "Ladies' Place in Political Marketplace Awaits Outcome," *Commercial Appeal,* June 19, 1969, 41. In the settlement, city employees got an immediate eighteen-cent-an-hour increase, with the two-dollar minimum wage that the union wanted promised in one year. Workers also made gains in hazard and overtime pay, as well as in work-related medical care benefits; Marshall and Adams, "The Memphis Public Employees Strike," 104–5.

54. Wurzburg interview, August 24, 1999; Shafer interview, August 17, 1999.

55. *Commercial Appeal,* June 29, 1969, II, 7; Minutes from YWCA Public Affairs Committee, Wurzburg Collection, box 2, folder 5; Lewis and Dreifus interview, January 16, 1969, "Search for Meaning," MVSC, C21, F62; Lewis interview, July 25, 1999; Morrison interview, October 5, 1999. The reformers' motives were self-serving as well as altruistic. They worried that the abundant pool of domestic workers in Memphis would disappear, and their own privilege would be disrupted, if maids did not receive better pay and some benefits.

56. Suzanne Benson Darnell, "A Case Study of the Metropolitan Inter-faith Association" (master's thesis, University of Memphis, 1970), 47–48; Lewis interview, July 25, 1999; Allen interview, August 12, 1999. Other early MIFA activities included urging the creation of a municipal commission on police-community relations after an African American teen was killed by a policeman, organizing neighborhood organizations to combat white flight and to stabilize neighborhood development, matching church volunteers with public schools needing assistants, starting a food bank, and coordinating meal delivery to the elderly.

57. Lewis, "Diversification and Unity: MIFA," 28; Lewis interview, July 25, 1999.

Selected Bibliography

Alexander, Henry. *The Little Rock Recall Election.* New York: McGraw-Hill, 1960.

Alpern, Sara, Joyce Antler, Elisabeth Israels Perry, and Ingrid Winther Scobie. *The Challenge of Feminist Biography: Writing the Lives of Modern American Women.* Urbana: University of Illinois Press, 1992.

Ashmore, Harry. *Civil Rights and Wrongs: A Memoir of Race and Politics, 1944–1994.* New York: Pantheon, 1994.

Barnard, Hollinger F., ed. *Outside the Magic Circle: The Autobiography of Virginia Foster Durr.* Tuscaloosa: University of Alabama Press, 1985.

Bartley, Numan V. *The New South, 1945–1980.* Baton Rouge: Louisiana State University Press, 1995.

———. *The Rise of Massive Resistance: Race and Politics in the South during the 1950s.* Baton Rouge: Louisiana State University Press, 1969.

Bates, Daisy. *The Long Shadow of Little Rock.* New York: David McKay, 1962.

Beals, Melba Pattillo. *Warriors Don't Cry: A Searing Memoir of the Battle to Integrate Little Rock's Central High School.* New York: Pocket Books, 1994.

Beifuss, Joan Turner. *At the River I Stand: Memphis, the 1968 Strike, and Martin Luther King.* 1985. Reprint. Memphis: St. Luke's Press, 1990.

Berman, William C. *The Politics of Civil Rights in the Truman Administration.* Columbus: Ohio State University Press, 1970.

Blee, Kathleen. *No Middle Ground: Women and Radical Protest.* New York: New York University Press, 1998.

Blossom, Virgil. *It HAS Happened Here.* New York: Harper Brothers, 1959.

Blumberg, Rhoda Lois. "White Mothers as Civil Rights Activists." In *Women and Social Protest,* ed. Guida West and Rhoda Lois Blumberg. New York: Oxford University Press, 1990.

Boyle, Sarah Patton. *The Desegregated Heart: A Virginian's Stand in Time of Transition.* New York: Morrow, 1962. Reissued with Introduction and Letters, ed. Jennifer Ritterhouse. Charlottesville: University of Virginia Press, 2001.

Braden, Anne. *Free Thomas Wansley: A Letter to White Southern Women.* Louisville: Southern Conference Educational Fund Publications, 1972.

———. *The Wall Between.* 1958. Reprint. Knoxville: University of Tennessee Press, 1999.

Brewer, Vivion. *The Embattled Ladies of Little Rock, 1958–1963: The Struggle to Save Public Education at Central High.* Fort Bragg, Colo.: Lost Coast Press, 1998.

Bryan, Mary L. *Proud Heritage: A History of the League of Women Voters of South Carolina 1920–1976.* [Columbia, S.C.:] League of Women Voters of South Carolina, [1977].

Carson, Clayborne. *In Struggle: SNCC and the Black Awakening of the 1960s.* Cambridge: Harvard University Press, 1981.

Caute, David. *The Great Fear: The Anti-communist Purge under Truman and Eisenhower.* New York: Simon and Schuster, 1978.

Chappell, David L. *Inside Agitators: White Southerners in the Civil Rights Movement.* Baltimore: Johns Hopkins University Press, 1994.

Chepesiuk, Ronald J., Ann Y. Evans, and Thomas S. Morgan, eds. *Women Leaders in South Carolina: An Oral History.* Rock Hill, S.C.: Winthrop College Archives and Special Collections, 1984.

Church Women United. *CWU Social Policies: 1941–1991.* N.p., 1992.

Clark, Septima Poinsette. *Echo in My Soul.* New York: Dutton, 1962.

Cope, Graeme. "'Honest White People of the Middle and Lower Classes'? A Profile of the Capital Citizens' Council during the Little Rock Crisis of 1957." *Arkansas Historical Quarterly* 61 (spring 2002): 37–58.

———. "'A Thorn in the Side'? The Mother's League of Central High School and the Little Rock Desegregation Crisis of 1957." *Arkansas Historical Quarterly* 57 (summer 1998): 160–204.

Crawford, Vicki L., Jacqueline Anne Rouse, and Barbara Woods, eds. *Women in the Civil Rights Movement: Trailblazers and Torchbearers, 1941–1965.* Bloomington: Indiana University Press, 1990.

Curry, Constance, et al. *Deep in Our Hearts: Nine White Women in the Freedom Movement.* Athens: University of Georgia Press, 2000.

Dittmer, John. *Local People: The Struggle for Civil Rights in Mississippi.* Blacks in the New World series. Chicago: University of Illinois Press, 1994.

Donovan, Josephine. *Feminist Theory: The Intellectual Traditions of American Feminism.* New York: Frederick Ungar, 1992.

Duke, Lois Lovelace. "Virginia Foster Durr: An Analysis of One Woman's Contributions to the Civil Rights Movement in the South." In *Women in Politics: Outsiders or Insiders? A Collection of Readings,* ed. Lois Lovelace Duke. Englewood Cliffs, N.J.: Prentice-Hall, 1993.

Dunbar, Anthony. *Against the Grain: Southern Radicals and Prophets, 1929–1959.* Charlottesville: University of Virginia Press, 1981.

Eagles, Charles W. "Toward New Histories of the Civil Rights Era." *Journal of Southern History* 66 (November 2000): 815–48.

Egerton, John. *Speak Now against the Day: The Generation before the Civil Rights Movement in the South.* New York: Knopf, 1994.

Evans, Sara. *Personal Politics: The Roots of Women's Liberation in the Civil Rights Movement and the New Left.* New York: Vintage Books, 1980.

Fairclough, Adam. *Race and Democracy: The Civil Rights Struggle in Louisiana, 1915–1972.* Athens: University of Georgia Press, 1995.

Fleming, Cynthia Griggs. *Soon We Will Not Cry: The Liberation of Ruby Doris Smith Robinson.* Lanham, Md.: Rowman and Littlefield, 1998.

Fosl, Catherine. *Subversive Southerner: Anne Braden and the Struggle for Racial Justice in the Cold War South.* New York: Palgrave Macmillan, 2002.

———. "'There Was No Middle Ground': Anne Braden and the Southern Social Justice Movement." *National Women's Studies Association Journal* 11 (fall 1999): 24–48.

Fowlkes, Diane. *White Political Women: Paths from Privilege to Empowerment.* Knoxville: University of Tennessee Press, 1992.

Frankenberg, Ruth. *The Social Construction of Whiteness: White Women, Race Matters.* Minneapolis: University of Minnesota Press, 1993.

Frederickson, Kari. *The Dixiecrat Revolt and the End of the Solid South: 1932–1968.* Chapel Hill: University of North Carolina Press, 2001.

Frederickson, Mary. "'Each One Is Dependent on the Other': Southern Churchwomen, Racial Reform, and the Process of Transformation, 1880–1940." In *Visible Women,* ed. Nancy Hewitt and Suzanne Lebsock. Urbana: University of Illinois Press, 1993.

Freyer, Tony Allen. *The Little Rock Crisis: A Constitutional Interpretation.* Westport, Conn.: Greenwood Press, 1984.

———. "Politics and the Law in the Little Rock Crisis, 1954–1957." *Arkansas Historical Quarterly* 40 (autumn 1981): 195–219.

Frystak, Shannon L. "With All Deliberate Speed: The Integration of the New Orleans League of Women Voters, 1953–1963." In *Searching for Their Places: Southern Women across Four Centuries,* ed. Thomas H. Appleton Jr. and Angela Boswell, 261–83. Columbia: University of Missouri Press, 2003.

Gates, Lorraine. "Power from the Pedestal: The Women's Emergency Committee and the Little Rock School Crisis." *Arkansas Historical Quarterly* 55 (spring 1996): 26–57.

Giele, Janet Zollinger. *Two Paths to Women's Equality: Temperance, Suffrage, and the Origins of Modern Feminism.* New York: Twayne, 1995.

Gilmore, Glenda E. "Gender and *Origins of the New South.*" *Journal of Southern History* 67 (November 2001): 769–88.

Gladney, Margaret Rose, ed. *How Am I to Be Heard? Letters of Lillian Smith.* Chapel Hill: University of North Carolina Press, 1993.

Goldfield, David R. *Black, White, and Southern: Race Relations and Southern Culture, 1940 to the Present.* Baton Rouge: Louisiana State University Press, 1990.

Graham, Sarah Hunter. "The Suffrage Renaissance: A New Image for a New Century,

1896–1910." In *One Woman, One Vote: Rediscovering the Woman Suffrage Movement,* ed. Marjorie Spruill Wheeler. Troutdale, Ore.: New Sage Press, 1995.

Grant, Joanne. *Ella Baker: Freedom Bound.* New York: John Wiley and Sons, 1998.

Green, Christina. "'In the Best Interest of the Total Community'? Women-in-Action and the Problems of Building Interracial Cross-Class Alliances in Durham, North Carolina, 1968–1975." *Frontiers: Journal of Women's Studies* (spring 1996): 190–217.

———. "Our Separate Ways: Women and the Black Freedom Movement in Durham, North Carolina, 1940s–1970s." Ph.D. dissertation, Duke University, 1996.

———. "'We'll Take Our Stand': Race, Class, and Gender in the Southern Student Organizing Committee, 1964–1969." In *Hidden Histories of Women in the New South,* ed. Virginia Bernhard et al. Columbia: University of Missouri Press, 1994.

Green, Laurie Beth. "Battling the Plantation Mentality: Consciousness, Culture, and the Politics of Race, Class and Gender in Memphis, 1940–1968." Ph.D. dissertation, University of Chicago, 1999.

Greenberg, Cheryl Lynn. *A Circle of Trust: Remembering SNCC.* New Brunswick: Rutgers University Press, 1998.

Hall, Jacquelyn Dowd. *Revolt against Chivalry: Jessie Daniel Ames and the Women's Campaign against Lynching.* 1979. Reprint. New York: Columbia University Press, 1993.

Hartmann, Susan. *The Home Front and Beyond: American Women in the 1940s.* Boston: Twayne, 1982.

Heilbrun, Carolyn G. *Writing a Woman's Life.* New York: Norton, 1988.

Hewitt, Nancy, and Suzanne Lebsock, eds. *Visible Women: New Essays on American Activism.* Urbana: University of Illinois Press, 1993.

Higginbotham, Evelyn Brooks. "African-American Women's History and the Metalanguage of Race." *Signs* 17 (winter 1992): 251–74.

Hobson, Fred. *But Now I See: The White Southern Racial Conversion Narrative.* Baton Rouge: Louisiana State University Press, 1999.

Honey, Michael. "Industrial Unionism and Racial Justice in Memphis." In *Organized Labor in the Twentieth-Century South,* ed. Robert Zieger, 146–75. Knoxville: University of Tennessee Press, 1991.

———. *Southern Labor and the Civil Rights Movement: Organizing Memphis Workers.* Urbana: University of Illinois Press, 1993.

Horne, Gerald. *Communist Front? The Civil Rights Congress, 1946–1956.* Rutherford, N.J.: Fairleigh Dickinson University Press, 1988.

Horowitz, Daniel. *Betty Friedan and the Making of the Feminine Mystique: The American Left, the Cold War, and Modern Feminism.* Amherst: University of Massachusetts Press, 1998.

Inger, Morton. "The New Orleans School Crisis of 1960." In *Southern Businessmen and School Desegregation,* ed. Elizabeth Jacoway and David R. Colburn, 82–97. Baton Rouge: Louisiana State University Press, 1982.

Jacoway, Elizabeth, and David R. Colburn, eds. *Southern Businessmen and Desegregation*. Baton Rouge: Louisiana State University Press, 1982.

Jacoway, Elizabeth, and C. Fred Williams, eds. *Understanding the Little Rock Crisis: An Exercise in Remembrance and Reconciliation*. Fayetteville: University of Arkansas Press, 1999.

Johnson, Joan Marie. "'Drill into Us . . . the Rebel Tradition': The Contest over Southern Identity in Black and White Women's Clubs, South Carolina 1898–1930." *Journal of Southern History* 66 (2000): 525–62.

Jones, Jacqueline. "The Political Implications of Black and White Women's Work in the South, 1890–1965." In *Women, Politics, and Change*, ed. Louise A. Tilly and Patricia Gurin. New York: Russell Sage Foundation, 1990.

King, Mary. *Freedom Song: A Personal Story of the 1960s Civil Rights Movement*. New York: William Morrow, 1987.

Klarman, Michael. "How *Brown* Changed Race Relations: The Backlash Thesis." *Journal of American History* 81 (June 1994): 81–118.

Klibaner, Irwin. *Conscience of a Troubled South: The Southern Conference Education Fund, 1946–1966*. Brooklyn, N.Y.: Carlson, 1989.

Kolchin, Peter. "Whiteness Studies: The New History of Race in America." *Journal of American History* 89 (June 2002): 154–73.

Lawson, Steven F. "Freedom Then, Freedom Now: The Historiography of the Civil Rights Movement." *American Historical Review* 96 (April 1991): 456–71.

Lewis, John, and Michael D'Orso. *Walking with the Wind: A Memoir of the Movement*. San Diego: Harcourt Brace, 1999.

Lewis, Selma. "Social Religion and the Memphis Sanitation Strike." Ph.D, dissertation, University of Chicago, 1988.

Lindley, Susan Hill. *"You Have Stept out of Your Place": A History of Women and Religion in America*. Louisville: Westminster John Knox Press, 1996.

Loveland, Anne C. *Lillian Smith: A Southerner Confronting the South*. Baton Rouge: Louisiana State University Press, 1986.

Lynn, Susan. "Gender and Progressive Politics: A Bridge to Social Activism of the 1960s." In *Not June Cleaver: Women and Gender in Postwar America, 1945–1960*, ed. Joanne Meyerowitz. Philadelphia: Temple University Press, 1994.

———. *Progressive Women in Conservative Times: Racial Justice, Peace, and Feminism, 1945 to the 1960s*. New York: Oxford University Press, 1991.

McMillen, Neil R. "The White Citizens Council and Resistance to School Desegregation in Arkansas." *Arkansas Historical Quarterly* 30 (summer 1971): 95–122.

Mars, Florence. *Witness in Philadelphia*. Baton Rouge: Louisiana State University Press, 1977.

Matthews, Glenna. *The Rise of Public Woman: Women's Power and Women's Place in the United States, 1630–1970*. New York: Oxford University Press, 1992.

Meyerowitz, Joanne, ed. *Not June Cleaver: Women and Gender in Postwar America, 1945–1960*. Philadelphia: Temple University Press, 1994.

Moraga, Cherrie, and Gloria Anzaldúa, eds. *This Bridge Called My Back: Writings by Radical Women of Color.* Watertown, Mass.: Persephone Press, 1981.

Murphy, Sara. *Breaking the Silence: Little Rock's Women's Emergency Committee to Open Our Schools, 1958–1963.* Edited by Patrick C. Murphy II. Fayetteville: University of Arkansas Press, 1997.

Nasstrom, Kathryn L. "Beginnings and Endings: Life Stories and the Periodization of the Civil Rights Movement." *Journal of American History* 86 (June 1999): 700–711.

———. "Down to Now: Memory, Narrative, and Women's Leadership in the Civil Rights Movement in Atlanta, Georgia." *Gender and History* 11 (April 1999): 113–43.

———. *Everybody's Grandmother and Nobody's Fool: Frances Freeborn Pauley and the Struggle for Social Justice.* Ithaca: Cornell University Press, 2000.

Nelson, Susan McGrath. "Association of Southern Women for the Prevention of Lynching and the Fellowship of the Concerned and Racial Politics." Master's thesis, Emory University, 1982.

Norrell, Robert J. "One Thing We Did Right: Reflections on the Movement." In *New Directions in Civil Rights Studies,* ed. Armstead L. Robinson and Patricia Sullivan, 65–80. Charlottesville: University Press of Virginia, 1991.

———. *Reaping the Whirlwind: The Civil Rights Movement in Tuskegee.* New York: Random House, 1985.

O'Brien, Gail Williams. *The Color of the Law: Race, Violence, and Justice in the Post–World War II South.* Chapel Hill: University of North Carolina Press, 1999.

Omi, Michael, and Howard Winant. *Racial Formation in the United States: From the 1960s to the 1980s.* New York: Routledge and Kegan Paul, 1986.

Ostrander, Susan. *Women of the Upper Class.* Philadelphia: Temple University Press, 1984.

Parsons, Sara Mitchell. *From Southern Wrongs to Civil Rights: The Memoir of a White Civil Rights Activist.* Tuscaloosa: University of Alabama Press, 2000.

Payne, Charles. *I've Got the Light of Freedom: The Organizing Tradition and the Mississippi Freedom Struggle.* Berkeley: University of California Press, 1996.

———. "Men Led, but Women Organized: Movement Participation of Women in the Mississippi Delta." In *Women in the Civil Rights Movement: Trailblazers and Torchbearers, 1941–1965,* ed. Vicki Crawford, Jacqueline Anne Rouse, and Barbara Woods. Brooklyn, N.Y.: Carlson, 1990.

Piliavin, Jane Allyn, and Hong-Wen Charg. "Altruism: A Review of Recent Theory and Research." *Annual Review of Sociology* 16 (1990): 27–65.

Quint, Howard H. *Profile in Black and White: A Frank Portrait of South Carolina.* Washington, D.C.: Public Affairs Press, 1958.

Reed, Linda. *Simple Decency and Common Sense: The Southern Conference Movement, 1938–1963.* Bloomington: Indiana University Press, 1991.

Reed, Roy. *Faubus: The Life and Times of an American Prodigal.* Fayetteville: University of Arkansas Press, 1997.

Robertson, Nancy Marie. "'Deeper Even Than Race'? White Women and the Politics of Christian Sisterhood in the Young Women's Christian Association, 1906–1946." Ph.D. dissertation, New York University, 1997.

Robinson, Armstead L., and Patricia Sullivan. *New Directions in Civil Rights Studies.* Charlottesville: University Press of Virginia, 1991.

Robnett, Belinda. *How Long? How Long? African-American Women in the Struggle for Civil Rights.* New York: Oxford University Press, 1997.

Rosen, Ruth. *The World Split Open: How The Modern Women's Movement Changed America.* New York: Penguin, 2000.

Schultz, Debra. *Going South: Jewish Women in the Civil Rights Movement.* New York: New York University Press, 2001.

Seifer, Nancy. *Nobody Speaks for Me! Self-Portraits of American Working-Class Women.* New York: Simon and Schuster, 1976.

Shadron, Virginia. "Out of Our Homes: The Women's Rights Movement in the Methodist Episcopal Church, South, 1890–1918." Master's thesis, Emory University, 1976.

Shankman, Arnold. "Dorothy Tilly and the Fellowship of the Concerned." In *From the Old South to the New: Essays on the Transitional South,* ed. Walter Fraser Jr. and Winfred B. Moore Jr. Westport, Conn.: Greenwood Press, 1981.

Shannon, Margaret. *Just Because: The Story of the National Movement of Church Women United in the U.S.A., 1941–1977.* Corte Madera, Calif.: Omega Books, 1977.

Sosna, Morton. *In Search of the Silent South: Southern Liberals and the Race Issue.* New York: Columbia University Press, 1977.

South Carolinians Speak: A Moderate Approach to Race Relations. Compiled by Revs. Ralph E. Cousins, Joseph R. Horn III, Larry A. Jackson, John S. Lyles, and John B. Morris. Dillon, S.C., 1957.

Spritzer, Lorraine Nelson, and Jean B. Bergmark. *Grace Towns Hamilton and the Politics of Southern Change.* Athens: University of Georgia Press, 1997.

Sterne, Emma Gelders. *They Took Their Stand.* New York: Crowell Collier Press, 1968.

Sullivan, Patricia. *Days of Hope: Race and Democracy in the New Deal Era.* Chapel Hill: University of North Carolina Press, 1996.

Thompson, Becky. *A Promise and a Way of Life: White Antiracist Activism.* Minneapolis: University of Minnesota, 2001.

Trotter, Ann. "The Memphis Business Community and Integration." In *Southern Businessmen and School Desegregation,* ed. Elizabeth Jacoway and David R. Colburn, 282–300. Baton Rouge: Louisiana State University Press, 1982.

Tyson, Timothy. "Dynamite and 'The Silent South': A Story from the Second Reconstruction in South Carolina." In *Jumpin' Jim Crow,* ed. Jane Dailey, Glenda Gilmore, and Bryant Simon. Princeton: Princeton University Press, 2000.

Wagner-Martin, Linda. *Telling Women's Lives: The New Biography.* New Brunswick: Rutgers University Press, 1994.

Ware, Vron. *Beyond the Pale: White Women, Racism, and History.* London: Verso, 1993, 1996.

Wilkerson-Freeman, Sarah. "The Creation of a Subversive Feminist Dominion: Interracialist Social Workers and the Georgia New Deal." *Journal of Women's History* 13 (winter 2002): 132–54.

Wyatt-Brown, Anne M., and Janice Rossen, eds. *Aging and Gender in Literature: Studies in Creativity.* Charlottesville: University Press of Virginia, 1993.

Yancey, Dorothy Cowser. "Dorothy Bolden, Organizer of Domestic Workers: She Was Born Poor but She Would Not Bow Down." *Sage* 3 (spring 1986): 53–55.

Yarbrough, Tinsley E. *A Passion for Justice: J. Waties Waring and Civil Rights.* New York: Oxford University Press, 1987.

Contributors

Catherine Fosl (formerly Foster) is a historian who holds a joint appointment in communication and women's and gender studies at the University of Louisville. She is the author of two works of history.

Shannon Frystak is a Ph.D. candidate at the University of New Hampshire, where she is completing her dissertation titled "'Woke Up This Morning with My Mind on Freedom': Women and the Black Struggle for Equality in Louisiana." She is a visiting scholar at Newcomb College Center for Research on Women in New Orleans and recently published "With All Deliberate Speed: The Integration of the League of Women Voters of New Orleans, 1953–1963," in *Searching for Their Places: Southern Women across Four Centuries,* ed. Thomas Appleton Jr. and Angela Boswell (2003).

Cherisse R. Jones is currently assistant professor of history at Arkansas State University in Jonesboro. Her research interests are women's history and African American history.

Laura A. Miller currently serves as a historian with the National Park Service at Little Rock Central High School National Historic Site. Her thesis, *Fearless: Irene Gaston Samuel and the Life of a Southern Liberal,* a biography of one of the leaders of the Women's Emergency Committee, was published in 2002.

Gail S. Murray is associate professor of history at Rhodes College, where she teaches courses in southern women's history, the history of childhood, and the history of poverty in America. She is the author of *American Children's Literature and the Construction of Childhood* (1998).

Kathryn Nasstrom is associate professor of history at the University of San Francisco. Her research interests focus on women's history, civil rights history, and oral history. In addition to publishing several articles, she is the author of

Everybody's Grandmother and Nobody's Fool: Frances Freeborn Pauley and the Struggle for Social Justice (2000). She is currently working on a project about autobiographies of the civil rights movement.

Edith Holbrook Riehm is currently a Ph.D. candidate in history at Georgia State University in Atlanta and a graduate teaching assistant for the United States and world history surveys. Her chapter in this anthology is her first publication.

Marcia G. Synnott is professor of history at the University of South Carolina, where she teaches courses in women's history and historic site interpretation. Her research interests include affirmative action and higher education as well as civil rights. She is completing a full-length biography of Alice Norwood Spearman Wright.

Index

Page numbers in italics refer to illustrations.

Jewish women, 18, 63, 134
Johns Island (S.C.), 144, 145
Johnson, Carrie Parks, 1, 19n.1
Johnston, Ann, 208
Johnston, Olin D., 65
Joint Legislative Committee to Maintain Segregation, 186
Jones, Cherisse, 18
Jones, Dorothy "Happy," 220
Jones, Jacqueline, 183
Josie, Alice Waltena, 147, 148
Juvenile delinquency, programs to combat, 135–36

Keller, Rosa Freeman, 13, 15, 18–19, *181*; in Community Relations Council, 196; early life of, 184; in LWV, 187; in Save Our Schools, 186–87, 189, 192–93; in Urban League, 184; in YWCA, 184
Kennedy, Grace T., 140
Kennedy, John F., 23, 36–37
Killers of the Dream (Smith), 10
King, Coretta Scott, 33, 120
King, Marion, 87
King, Dr. Martin Luther, Jr., 84, 94; assassination of, 5, 11, 215; effect of assassination, 205, 209, 216–17, 218; and striking sanitation workers, 215, 219; and women, 92, 120
King, Mary, 8, 92
Kolchin, Peter, 105
Ku Klux Klan, 39, 56, 60, 61
Kurault, Charles, 192

Lake Junaluska, 27
Lamb, Ted, 162
Lambright, Katherine, 172
Langford, L. L., 164
Laurel, Miss., 111
Law, W. W., 84
Lawrence, David, 115
Lawson, Rev. James, 222
League of Women Voters: Charleston County, S.C., 59; Columbia, S.C., 65; Little Rock, 164, 165, 166; New Orleans,

185, 186, 187, 192; providing experience for women activists, 80–81, 91, 155, 208
Ledbetter, Browie, 171
Ledeen, Elizabeth Cowan, 64, 66, 68, 143
"Left feminism," 112
Lemley, Judge Harry, 160
LeMoyne College, 206
Leppert, Alice, 145
Lessing, Doris, 87, 97
Letter to White Southern Women (Braden), 120
Lewis, Selma, 213
Little Rock high schools: closed by Faubus, 154, 159, 160; reopened, 167
"Little Rock Nine," 158, 165
Little Rock Panel, Inc., 173
"Little Rock Report," 168
Little Rock School Board: members recalled, 159–60, 165–67; renewal of teacher contracts, 165; special election for, 160–63
Littleton, Helen, 172
Loeb, Mayor Henry, 210, 215, 216, 221
Lopez, Ian Haney, 122
Lorde, Audre, 101, 120, 122
Louisiana Citizens' Council, 185
Louisville, Ky., 107, 114–15
Louisville Defender, 107, 113
Louisville Times, 107, 108
Loveland, Anne, 7
Lynn, Susan, 2

MacDonald, Lois, 52, 53, 68
Malakoff, Grace, 168
MAP-South (Memphis), 222
Mars, Florence, 7
Marshall, Thurgood, 59
Martin, James, 83
Marx, Gary, 197, 198
Mason, Lucy Randolph, 115
Maternalism, 12, 34, 53, 55, 67
Maybank, Gov. Burnet R., 56
Mays, Sadie, 84
McCarthyism. *See* Cold War
McCarty, Anita, 106
McCarty, Gambrell, 106